THE POET'S VOICE IN THE MAKING OF MIND

How did the human mind evolve and how does it emerge, again and again, in individual lives?

In *The Poet's Voice in the Making of Mind*, Russell Meares presents a fascinating inquiry into the origin of mind. He proposes that the way in which mind, or self, evolved, may resemble the way it emerges in childhood play and that a poetic, analogical style of thought is a biological necessity, essential to bringing to fruition the achievement of the human mind. Taking a fresh look at the language used in psychotherapy, he shows how language, and conversation in particular, is central to the development and maintenance of self. His theory incorporates the ideas from William James, Hughlings Jackson, Janet Hobson, Gerald Edelman, Wolf Singer, Vygotsky and others. It is illuminated by extracts from literary artists such as Wallace Stevens, W. S. Merwin, Virginia Woolf, Joseph Conrad and Shakespeare.

Encompassing psychotherapy, psychoanalysis, evolution, child development, literary criticism, philosophy, studies of mind and consciousness, *The Poet's Voice in the Making of Mind* is an engaging, ground-breaking and thought-provoking work that will appeal to psychotherapists and psychoanalysts, as well as anyone interested in the emergence of mind and self.

Russell Meares is Emeritus Professor of Psychiatry at the University of Sydney. He trained in psychiatry at the Royal Bethlem and Maudsley Hospitals where he formed an enduring friendship with the late Robert Hobson, with whom he collaborated to develop the Conversational Model of psychotherapy, devised to treat people who could not be treated by other means and who would now be called 'borderline'. His most recent books for Routledge are *Intimacy and Alienation* (2000) and *The Metaphor of Play* (revised and enlarged edition) (2005).

'*The Poet's Voice in the Making of Mind* is a truly monumental work, the product of Meares' lifetime exploration of the development of symbolization, language, and the self. It is a beautifully written book in which Meares speaks with the unassuming intelligence of the finest of teachers. Meares brings to life, in a highly thought-provoking way, aspects of the work of William James, Edelman, Geertz, Cassirer, Trevarthan, Vygotsky, Hughlings Jackson, Hobson and other major contributors to the study of human development. But the triumph of this book lies in Meares' ability to encompass their ideas and the voices of poets, as well as his own original contributions, and to go on to offer a unifying conception of the development of symbolization, language, self, and culture – a unifying view that the reader will find nowhere else. This is one of the finest books I have read on the subject of what is uniquely human.' – Thomas Ogden

'This beautifully written book is rich in information for psychotherapists, psychologists, neuroscientists, as well as philosophers and physicists, on the poetry of life. Russell Meares' humanism transcends disciplinary boundaries, offering a picture of the developing personal self as made for discovery of joy in intimate and responsive company; for sharing the symbolic "make believe" of culture. The emotional foundations of metaphor he finds in the melody of mothers' conversations with infants gives hope for those who have suffered extreme misfortune in living and sharing life, a way to help them recover self-confidence and a feeling for the common sense of life.' – Colwyn Trevarthen, Emeritus Professor of Child Psychology and Psychobiology, Department of Psychology, The University of Edinburgh, Scotland, UK

'In this remarkable feat of scholarship, Russell Meares offers a large body of evidence from science, including very recent neuroscience, physics, cognitive science, developmental psychology and anthropology, in order to more deeply elucidate the central questions about the human condition long addressed by poetry, literature, and philosophy. Utilizing an interpersonal neurobiological perspective, he offers a compelling central thesis, that right brain-to-right brain affective communications between mother and infant in early proto-conversations play an essential role in the development and expression of not only all later emotional functions, but also higher cognitive functions, including symbolization, metaphor, music, poetry, higher forms of consciousness, and indeed the self and culture. This groundbreaking integrative work represents a creative interdisciplinary bridge between the sciences and humanities.' – Allan N. Schore, Ph.D., Department of Psychiatry and Biobehavioral Sciences, University of California at Los Angeles David Geffen School of Medicine

THE POET'S VOICE IN THE MAKING OF MIND

Russell Meares

Routledge
Taylor & Francis Group
LONDON AND NEW YORK

First published 2016
by Routledge
2 Park Square, Milton Park, Abingdon, Oxon OX14 4RN

and by Routledge
711 Third Avenue, New York, NY 10017

Routledge is an imprint of the Taylor & Francis Group, an informa business

British Library Cataloguing in Publication Data
A catalogue record for this book is available from the British Library

Library of Congress Cataloging in Publication Data
Names: Meares, Russell, author.
Title: The poet's voice in the making of mind / Russell Meares.
Description: First Edition. | New York : Routledge, 2016.
Identifiers: LCCN 2015037537 | ISBN 9780415572330 (978-0-415-57234-7)
Subjects: LCSH: Thought and thinking. | Consciousness. | Developmental psychology.
Classification: LCC BF442 .M43 2016 | DDC 150—dc23
LC record available at http://lccn.loc.gov/2015037537

ISBN: 978-0-415-57233-0 (hbk)
ISBN: 978-0-415-57234-7 (pbk)
ISBN: 978-1-315-67063-8 (ebk)

Typeset in Times New Roman
by Florence Production Ltd, Stoodleigh, Devon, UK

With thanks to

Robert Hobson (1920–1999) for our friendship,
his generosity, and our creative conversation

and
Michelle Phillips whose skills and tireless efforts
made this book possible

and
to Susanne

CONTENTS

ACKNOWLEDGEMENTS

We would like to thank the following for granting permission to use the following material in this book:

Edelman, G. (2006). *Second Nature: Brain Science and Human Knowledge*. Yale, CT: Yale University Press, p. 57 is reprinted by kind permission of Yale University Press, New Haven & London.

Johnson, D. (2000). The Pleiades in Australian Aboriginal and Torres Strait Islander Astronomies. In S. Kleinert and M. Neale (eds), *Oxford Companion to Aboriginal Art and Culture* (pp. 24–28). Oxford: Oxford University Press.

Reprinted with kind permission.

Merwin, W. S. (1988). *Utterance from Rain in the Trees*. New York: Alfred A. Knopf. Reprinted with kind permission of Penguin Random House.

Tolkien, J. R. R. (1950). *Beowulf and the Finnesburg Fragment*, A Translation into Modern English Prose by John R. Clark Hall, with Prefatory Remarks by J. R. R. Tolkien (revised edn). London: George Allen and Unwin Ltd. Reprinted by kind permission of Harper Collins Publishers.

Heaney, S. (1999). *Beowulf*. London: Faber & Faber. Reprinted by kind permission.

Morphy, H. and Morphy, F. (2006). Tasting the Waters: Discriminating Identities in the Waters of Blue Mud Bay. *Journal of Material Culture*, *11*(1–2). Copyright © 2006. Reprinted by kind permission of Sage Publications.

Auden, W. H. (1966) *Collected Shorter Poems*, 'Taller Today' p. 20 and 'Anthem for St Cecilia's Day' p. 173. Reprinted by kind permission of Faber & Faber Ltd.

'Anthem for St. Cecilia's Day,' copyright © 1945 by W. H. Auden and renewed 1973 by The Estate of W. H. Auden; and 'Taller To-day,' copyright © 1934 and renewed 1962 by W. H. Auden; from *W. H. Auden Collected Poems* by W. H. Auden. Used by permission of Random House, an imprint and division of Penguin Random House LLC. All rights reserved.

1

INTRODUCTION

Conversational play and the evolution of self

One January morning in 1798, the 19-year-old William Hazlitt rose 'before daylight, to walk 10 miles in the mud' [1] to hear the sermon of the new minister of Shrewsbury, Samuel Taylor Coleridge. Hazlitt was a contemplative young man, full of ideas taken from readings in philosophy, but as yet, he had no clear idea of the direction that his life might take. The beginning of such an idea was formed by his experience that morning. The voice of the poet, not only his words but also their sound, helped shape what Hazlitt was to become. His experience is touched upon further in Chapter 5.

The shaping effect of the sound of another's voice begins very early in life, when the mother[2] sets up a game with her baby in which she plays at having a conversation with her. The main theme of this book is that this game is necessary not only to the development of mind but also to its evolution. Within this game can be seen the origin of the symbol, the basis of the peculiarly human mind and of culture.

Mind is a word that is used in various ways. I am using it in a particular way, which is suggested by common usage. People say such things as, 'he must have been out of his mind' and refer to certain activities as 'mindless'. They imply that mind is a state which we do not always occupy. It can come and go, disappearing when personal existing is troubled or disrupted, and put on hold in the performance of automatic behaviour. In this book, 'mind' refers not to all forms of consciousness but to a specific consciousness, which is believed to be peculiar to the human primate. It is a relatively fragile state that is lately evolved and not achieved by all human beings. William James called it self. How it develops and evolves is the subject of the book. This opening chapter gives a sketch of the main proposal, together with an outline of the argument as it will unfold in the following chapters. The focus of the early chapters is upon the emergence of self and symbol in childhood, and how early generative patterns of relating are carried into adult life. The main theme in later chapters is the emergence of culture from these early beginnings and the relation of this story to that of the evolution of humanity.

The mystery of our origins is a subject of universal fascination. In recent years a more particular evolutionary focus has developed, upon the way in which human consciousness has evolved. The proposals come from widely differing disciplines

– comparative anatomy, neurophysiology, computer science, mathematics, biology, anthropology, linguistics, philosophy, psychology, information theory, ethology and so forth. Each writer's viewpoint is determined, in part, by a particular background, both professional and personal. Some of these proposals are unsatisfactory in that they treat consciousness as a global issue, without addressing the idea that consciousness has a number of forms, most of which we share with other creatures. A suitable theory of the human mind must offer an explanation for the appearance of the special form of consciousness, which is unique to *Homo sapiens*. Its nature is discussed in Chapter 2. Its outstanding characteristic is doubleness. William James called it the 'duplex self'.[3] Its bipolarity is not to be confused with Cartesian dualism which posits a distinction between material and immaterial aspects of mental life, between *res extensa* and *res cogitans*.

The duality of human consciousness is an emergent phenomenon, which develops from birth and grows through several larval stages before it can be clearly demonstrated between the ages of 3½ and 5½. Indices of this achievement are, at the same time, markers of the appearance of self.

One index of the experience of doubleness is the child's awareness of the concept of secrecy.[4] When children understand this idea, they realize that they exist simultaneously in two worlds, one public and the other private, the latter known only to oneself. Along with this realization comes another; that other minds may harbour feelings, ideas, motivations and imaginings, which differ from one's own. The capacity for empathy now emerges.

A second index tests for 'false belief'. A number of versions exist but all resemble the original version of Wimmer and Perner.[5] An example might be as follows. The subject is asked to watch a scene in which a little girl enters a room carrying a box of chocolates. She puts it in the top drawer of a chest of drawers and then leaves. A wicked witch enters. She finds the chocolates and puts them in the bottom drawer. She then exits. The little girl re-enters and pauses. The subject is then asked where the girl will look for her chocolates. A child of 5 will say the top drawer but a 3-year-old will choose the bottom. She acts as if what is known to her is known to everybody. Her world is not made up of two co-ordinated zones, inner and outer. Rather, it is one world, which is 'personal'.[6] The 5-year-old, on the other hand, can hold in mind two versions of reality, one's own and someone else's.

James discerned a basic doubleness in the ordinary and unified feeling of personal existing. An abstract distinction can be made between an 'I' who is observing or knowing inner events – a 'stream' of images, ideas, memories, imaginings and so forth – and those events themselves. This state describes the process of introspection, which to many authorities is the identifying feature of 'self', although not self itself.

These authorities include the legendary English neurologist, Hughlings Jackson, who believed himself to be the first to use the word 'self' in the medical literature.[7] He was certainly the first to build a plausible model of its neural origins. Considered by his close colleagues as a near genius, Jackson's ideas were ahead of their time and not fully comprehended. The relevance of his ideas to modern neuroscience and to the understanding of traumatically induced mental illness is increasingly acknowledged.[8] Jackson's evolutionary approach to the emergence of self forms an essential background to the book.

The book is written from a viewpoint of a psychiatrist who, for many years, has striven to understand and to develop a mode of treatment for a group of people suffering a seemingly intractable condition that is protean in its manifestations, some of which are life-threating, including suicidal ideation and behaviour.[9] The condition is currently given the name 'borderline', which means in essence, puzzling. The original observers could not fit this illness into a known category. At times it verges on the severity of psychosis but at others, resembles normality. A body of evidence now suggests that the so-called 'borderline' state is an outcome of an early life marked by repetitive interpersonal, or 'relational', traumata. The symptoms form two categories, one related to the disruption of the development of self and the other to the recurrent intrusion of conscious and unconscious traumatic memories.[10] Most treatments approach the latter system. There is, however, no generally accepted theory or method for the regeneration of self, which, it can be argued, is the primary deficit.

My search for such a theory and method began with the idea that the experience of self will emerge in therapy in the same way that it emerges in child development. The assumption depends upon a resemblance of principles governing two different though analogous situations. Resemblance is not a replication, in the same way that an analogue is not a copy, a topic discussed in Chapter 3. Therapy is not re-mothering.

The fundamental assumption that the same developmental principles underlie both the emergence of self in childhood and its appearance in therapy lead to the question: what brings into being the doubleness of consciousness, identified by both Jackson and James as central to the structure of self. The answer given here is play.

Play

There are many different forms of play.[11] Some are mere frolic; others are rule-based; still others seem designed as a rehearsal for adult roles.[12] None of these is the play that leads to the duplex self. It is 'make-believe' play that has the generative potential. The 'make-believe' is autotelic. It has no purpose beyond the enjoyment of the activity itself. It has no apparently 'adaptive' function, for example, of rehearsal.

'Make-believe' is double in that it makes an object, person, or situation both real and unreal. The thing is what it is and also something else that it is not. This is the essence of the symbol (Chapter 3). The capacity to use symbols, rather than merely signals, has given the human primate its enormous evolutionary advantage through the creation of culture, a view put forward for example by Ernst Cassirer, who conceived myth as the core of culture[13] (Chapter 15). The thesis, then, is that a particular kind of 'make-believe' leads to the use of symbols, which is the enabling factor in the formation of culture.

Culture is understood here as a system of symbolically mediated behaviours shared by a particular society and transmitted intergenerationally by symbolic means. Cultural transmission is distinguished from behaviours learnt by simple mimesis, which chimpanzees can achieve.[14] Societies are seen as a 'total network of relations' between the members of a group.[15] Chimpanzees live in culture-less societies.

The 'make-believe' begins at birth, with the game of conversational play. A mother seeing her new-born for the first time speaks to her baby, as if her infant could understand. Her voice is particular. It is a sound that is rather high and melodious, made with a rising inflection. She compounds her fiction by replying on behalf of the baby in an answer to herself.[16] Nobody has told her to act like this. It comes to her naturally, as if part of her phylogenetically given make-up.

By the age of 2–3 months, the baby has become a participant in the conversational game. The mother and baby jointly engage in a reciprocal interplay, the patternings of which resemble mature conversation. Colwyn Trevarthen,[17] borrowing the term from Mary Bateson,[18] has called it a 'proto-conversation'. The mother's contributions are determined by the baby's state rather than some agenda of her own. Her responses are finely attuned to what the baby presents in facial expression, vocalization and body movement. Characteristically, these responses show, in her face and the melodic contours of her voice, the 'shape' of her infant's immediate reality, to which they are in 'fit.' This state of 'fit', or connection, evokes a feeling of pleasure[19], which typically increases with each iteration of the to-and-fro exchange.

The sound of the mother's voice has a representing value, giving 'meaning' in the same way that a poet creates non-verbal meaning through the choice and arrangement of words. Her series of expressions, together with the vocalizations of the baby, have the quality of music that Robert Frost has compared with birdsong. In a garden imagined to be the original garden of mankind, 'the daylong voice of Eve' has transformational effect such that 'Never again would birds' song be the same.'[20] This effect is beautifully intimated by Thomas Ogden[21] in an exploration of the Frost poem.

The early music of the proto-conversation becomes the later 'music of what happens,' the inner rhythms of what James called the 'stream of consciousness.'[22] This is the thesis underlying the concept of 'Communicative Musicality' developed by Stephen Malloch and Colwyn Trevarthen.[23]

Poetry, as Eliot pointed out, is a kind of music. 'It may appear strange, that when I profess to be talking about the "music" of poetry, I put such emphasis upon conversation.'[24] Although Hazlitt believed the first poet's voice he had heard was that of Coleridge, there was another voice that resembled a poet's, which he would have heard 19 years before, during proto-conversation with his mother.[25] The mother's voice resembles a poet's not only in the effect of its sound but also in its 'shaping' function, making whole an otherwise diffuse and amorphous experience. Hers is a creative, rather than mimetic act, analogous to the larger creation of the poet, dependent, as Coleridge put it, on 'the shaping spirit of imagination'[26] (Chapter 5). She gives a re-representation of the baby's presentation. Her re-representation is an analogue of the baby's feeling state at that moment, an analogue being a thing that resembles another thing in its proportion and shape (Chapter 3). This primary analogue becomes the starting point in the development of symbolization.

Duality of human consciousness

Analogical relatedness is the beginning of the duality of consciousness. Two elements can be distinguished in the baby's personal reality. One is a feeling state that is without the 'meaning' given to it by a name. The other is a portrayal of that state, which makes 'real' the experience. It has an effect similar to that of naming.

The mother's face and voice, however, is more than a name. It is a picturing. The later development of selfhood will require a means of depiction beyond the capacities of voice and face (Chapter 6). A certain kind of language is required. It is not the language of facts, or single names, but a form of expression that once again, is double. It uses aspects of the world to portray a state that is embryonically 'inner'. These expressions are metaphors, or have a structure similar to metaphor. Metaphor, of course, is central to poetic creativity. Robert Hobson called such portrayals 'forms of feeling.' [27] He conceived them as necessary, both in ordinary living and in the therapeutic situation, to the ongoing 'becoming' of the experience of self. Their creation, he remarked, resembles that of an artist or a poet.[28]

Metaphor is the outcome of the capacity we all have of recognizing patterns and shapes. Its usage emerges, I am suggesting, after the initial experience of analogical representation in the proto-conversation. The analogue, as Edelman remarks, is 'pre-metaphorical'.[29]

The idea being developed here is that symbol, self and culture are all part of a single theme. The theme begins with the proto-conversation in which the duality of human consciousness first appears, not as an inner state, but outside, between two people. Those primates, the chimpanzees, to which we are most closely related cannot develop a symbolic theme since they only have a language of signs, dependent upon gesture and an unmodified vocal tract not capable of the musical expressiveness of the human voice. Mother and infant pairs do not engage in proto-conversation. Not having a language of depiction, by which the second element of duality is created, chimpanzees can generate neither self nor culture. Although they share with us the capacity to recognize patterns they cannot re-represent them.

Culture is identified by the use of symbol. Its evolution at least 75,000 years ago is marked by such discoveries as those in the Blombos Cave in South Africa, where multiple perforated tick shells were found. They had once been coloured red and blue, and presumably used as beads. These beads were aspects of 'symbolically mediated behaviour'.[30] They were symbols in that they were two things at the same time – shells and also something else, about which we can merely speculate.

The idea that the proto-conversation is an essential element in the development of the human capacity for symbolization seems, at first sight, surprising. After all, it is only a game, conducted without any purpose other than enjoyment. It seems to have no adaptive value just as music and poetry appear to some authorities to be merely diversionary activities, not central to the story of human evolution. Nevertheless, studies of children relatively deprived of the proto-conversation provide evidence in favour of the idea. Babies born blind or deaf, so lacking their mother's 'picturing' of their feeling states in one sensory modality, show deficits in their capacities for symbolization and pretend play (Chapter 12). Some of the children in those studies were so impaired that they fulfilled the diagnostic criteria for autism. Autism is a disorder in which the subject lives largely without the sense of a personal self. Most sufferers respond to the 'false belief' situation in the manner of a 3-year-old,[31] suggesting they have not developed the doubleness of consciousness, which Jackson liked to call 'mental diplopia',[32] that is indicative of self. Sufferers from autism typically lack the capacity for pretend play.[33]

In order to illustrate how an individual without a self may live in an apparently normal way, a fictional portrait is given in Chapter 12 of a woman who has the indices of Asperger syndrome, an autism spectrum disorder. She has interpersonal difficulties that are the result of a profound failure in empathy. She has no capacity of identifying with another person as a means of knowing this person's experience. Empathy, as remarked earlier, can be seen as an outcome of the emergence of the duality of consciousness demonstrated in the 5-year-olds' response to the false belief situation. Saga, the subject of Chapter 12's portrait, shows various failures in the achievement of a 'duplex self'. She cannot, for example, understand figurative language, that is, the use of a symbol.

Although without a self, Saga has an identity as a senior police officer. Within the rules expected of this identify, she performs well.

Emergence of a proto-symbolic story

The proto-conversation continues beyond infancy. During this time, the child begins to appropriate to himself its essential features – its make-believe, its analogical nature and expressive use of words. During the second year of life a new game develops which is predicted by the behaviour of conversational play.[34] It is a game the child plays alone. Piaget called it symbolic play.[35] It is better called analogical or proto-symbolic play. There is pleasure in this pasttime or the little boy or girl would not go on with it. The game consists of a miniature story, told as if to the child himself or herself but also to someone else, who is not there, except as a feeling of presence.

The telling of this story is analogical. The child uses objects in the environment that have shapes resembling the elements of the tale.

The story itself is imaginative, an elaboration of simple 'make-believe'. Like a dream, it seems to be a representation of some aspect of the child's experience. The representation of itself to itself, formerly the role of the mother or other caregivers, is now taken over by the child. This story is the prototype of myth, which is at the core of culture (Chapters 9 and 14).

The idea that the human primate can describe itself to itself is of crucial significance. It suggests a system in which, through a process of self-organization, self creates itself. Wolfgang Pauli, the Nobel prize winning physicist, gave this process the name of 'automorphosis' – self shaping. Pauli's intuition arose out of a relationship with Carl Gustav Jung and certain of his ideas (Chapter 16).

The principal outcome of Pauli's complex explorations, going hand in hand with his theorizing in the field of quantum physics, was the view that self 'reveals itself'[36] in a kind of conversation between the experiences given to us by the world through the senses, leading to phenomenal awareness and another system or registration of reality which, as he said, is a 'second meaning'. This system is the world of symbols that Pauli found in dream life but which is an essential feature of poetical expression.

The emergence of self through a self-organizational process may help explain the mystery pondered by the neuropsychologist, Endel Tulving,[37] who introduced the concept of episodic memory into the psychological lexicon. In considering the 5–6 million years of the evolution of the creatures who became *Homo sapiens* he noted

> that for long stretches of this very long time, human culture changed exceedingly slowly. It was only in the last few tens of thousands of years[38] that the curve of cultural evolution began inching upward on its relentless march towards its present explosive acceleration.[39]

What, he wondered, had 'driven' this dramatic acceleration? The answer has two parts. First, since culture is created by minds, the 'drive' towards the experience of culture was, and is, determined by the evolution of self. Second, this emergence can be explained by a process of self-organization, in which the evolution of a certain kind of language affords the means of analogical/metaphoric representations of presentational states, of showing self to itself, not as in a mirror but in a different mode. Reverberations within such a system resemble mathematical models, such as that of Mandelbrot,[40] out of which develop new, enlarged and unexpected patterns.

This idea suggests that the evolution of analogic/symbolic language must be closely linked to the creation of culture. Evidence from Philip Lieberman supports the possibility that this kind of language and culture evolved together. Lieberman is a main authority on the anatomy of the human vocal tract and its difference from that of chimpanzees and Neanderthals.[41] He and his colleagues found that supralaryngeal evolution of the human tract has given to *Homo sapiens* a vocal capacity which is beyond that of chimpanzees. The use of vowels is facilitated.[42] They have also shown that we are not born with this modification of the vocal tract. The larynx does not descend in human development until about the age of 3 or 4, the age when the markers of self first appear. In a curious parallelism with the emergence of mind, fossil evidence of the first appearance of the properly human voice tract is not found until the period during which culture is believed to have emerged, about 100,000 years ago.[43]

These observations suggest that language, self, and culture grew hand in hand, synergistically, each contributing to the others while being recreated in return. Such a system of reverberating patterns and re-patternings leads to a view resembling that of Lévi-Strauss. Lévi-Strauss believed, using anthropological evidence, that language, self, and culture share similar structures (Chapter 15).

A 'superorganic' aspect of human consciousness

A further inference from the relationships between self and culture is that the development of self may have no particular evolutionary significance. Its principal contribution to survival of the species may be its potentiation of a social group who share in the creation of a culture, the fabric of which is made of a network of stories (Chapters 9, 14 and 15). These stories, exemplified by the Australian Aboriginal Dreaming, created for the group who 'possess' these stories an immense evolutionary advantage. The stories are the bearers of a vast body of information, which operates as an extracorporeal memory bank – like an oral encyclopaedia.

This system not only provides knowledge necessary to survival, such as sources of food, but also ways in which to conduct tribal activity that creates cohesion, co-operative endeavour being essential to the emergence of *Homo sapiens* domination of the planet. In addition, the stories are about people who resemble the members of the social group. They are re-presentations of their own lives.

The eminent anthropologist Alfred Kroeber called the function of culture within the human system, superorganic.[44] It operates in a society, he believed, in a way that is analogous to a mind, or self, in an individual person. He contemplated the theoretical possibility of mindless societies. The cultural system is as much part of us as, say, the capacity to walk upright. William James, preceding Kroeber, said something similar. Speaking of the increased complexity of human consciousness relative to other animals, he wrote: 'It seems an organ, superadded to other organs which maintain the animal in the struggle for existence; and the presumption of course is that it helps him in some way in the struggle, just as they do.'[45]

We are not born as cultural animals. The propensity to create symbols, as a system of pattern recognition and portrayal, must be brought into being, in each individual life, by a special provision of the social environment, a form of relatedness I call 'analogical relatedness'.

Many theories of the evolution of human consciousness fail to consider that man emerged from adaptions not only to the inhuman environment but also in relation to a cultural environment that *Homo sapiens* had himself created, in the circular manner of self-organization. It is out of the interplay with this later evolved social environment that we achieve both culture and the higher order consciousness of self. Clifford Geertz describes the nature of this paradoxical process. Geertz sees culture and cultural patterns 'as organized systems of significant symbols', which are 'an essential condition'[46] for human existence. He wrote:

> By submitting himself to governance by symbolically mediated programs for producing artefacts, organizing social life, expressing emotions, man determined, if unwittingly, the culminating stages of his own biological destiny. Quite literally, though quite inadvertently, he created himself. . . . We are, in sum, incomplete or unfinished animals who complete or finish ourselves through culture.[47]

Two kinds of language

The kind of story at the core of culture is myth, as Ernst Cassirer has influentially argued.[48] Its proto-type, as remarked earlier, is the story told by the child engaged in analogical play. Much of the language used by the child in playing this game is asyntactical. It is unsuitable for communicative purposes. In order to become the shared property of a group it must be translated into another language having a syntactical structure. This is a public language, directed towards outer events. The language of analogical play, on the other hand, is directed towards inner events. Vygotsky called it 'inner speech'.[49]

The creation of myth as a tribal property becomes possible when the two languages are co-ordinated together, after the age of about 4 or 5. Following this landmark, ordinary conversation can be conceived as a unification not only of two languages but two modes of thought, one manifest syntactically and the other symbolically, the former being the vehicle of the latter.

The two modes of thought have different developmental pathways and different neurophysiological bases. Their different developments can be traced through the behaviours of 'pointing and depicting' (Chapter 8). These are the forerunners of language forms that have been called 'diachronic' (syntactical) and 'synchronic' (symbolic, analogical). The former derives from left hemisphere function and the latter from the right.

Self has a brain basis. Its nature is considered (Chapter 4), using proposals from Vygotsky, Wolf Singer and Gerald Edelman. Their ideas, taken together, suggest that higher order consciousness arises in a social context in which the form of the 'interactions among brains'[50] resembles the interaction in a single brain necessary in earlier forms of consciousness. This might lead to the realization of self 'by a reflexive interactions of self-similar cortical processes'.[51] (The proto-conversation seems likely to be a necessary and enabling social context, since it also involves an iteration of self-similar representations).

The suggestion is made, based on a growing body of evidence, that the human brain is as if set up for the proto-conversation (Chapter 4).

In Chapter 14 an evolutionary hypothesis is outlined, in which the emergence of *Homo sapiens*, as identified by the use of symbols in the creation of culture, is seen as an almost accidental event, consequent upon the extra maternal care necessary to the survival of late hominid babies, born prematurely because of their big brains. The impetus for the extra maternal care was provided by the evolution of a game the mother could play with her baby, which gave her pleasure, so rewarding her behaviour. The game, although this was not its purpose, was the origin of symbols. The book concludes with a return to the therapeutic situation. A session near the end of a successful therapy illustrates the idea that, like evolution, the emergence of myth is a culminating event. A personal myth is told half-consciously, as a series of images implicit to and underlying the interplay of words.

Notes

1 Hazlitt, W. (1991, p. 212).
2 I am using the word mother in this book to refer to any caregiver, in addition to the actual mother, who has a maternal role.
3 James, W. (1892, p. 176).
4 Meares and Orlay (1988).
5 Wimmer and Perner (1983).
6 Winnicott, D. W. (1974) uses this term to refer to the child's experience before 'inner' and 'outer' zones are clearly conceived.
7 Jackson, J. H. (1958, II, p. 96).
8 Meares, R. (1999).
9 Meares, R. (1993, 2000, 2004, 2005, 2012, Meares *et al.*, 2012).
10 Meares, R. (2012a).
11 Meares and Lichtenberg (1995).
12 Groos, K. (1898, 1901).
13 Cassirer, E. (1944, 1953–1957).
14 McGrew, W. (1992).
15 Toynbee, A. (1972).
16 Kaye, K. (1982).
17 Trevarthen, C. (1974).
18 Bateson, M.C. (1979).
19 Meares, R. (2012a, pp. 313–315).
20 Frost, R. (1955).
21 Ogden, T. H. (1998).
22 Vendler, H. (1988) uses Heaney's words from his poem 'Song' as the title for her exploration of the craft of the poet.
23 Malloch and Trevarthen (2009).
24 Eliot, T. S. (1957).
25 Stephen Malloch and his colleagues (2012) supposed that hospitalized newborn infants, relatively deprived of such 'conversation', might benefit from hearing a singing voice. Their study demonstrated that his kind of music 'can facilitate the neurobehavioural development of the medically fragile newborn infant' (p. 394).
26 Coleridge, S. T. (1802).
27 Hobson, R. F. (1985).
28 Hobson, R. F. (1985, p. 91).
29 Edelman, G. (2004).
30 Henshilwood *et al.* (2004, p. 404).
31 Baron-Cohen *et al.* (1985).

32 Jackson, J. H. (1958, II, p. 359).
33 Hobson, R. P. (2004).
34 Bornstein and Tamis Le Monda (1997).
35 Piaget, J. (1951).
36 Enz, C. P. (2002, p. 503).
37 Tulving, E. (2002).
38 Eldredge and Tattersall (1992).
39 Tulving, E. (2002).
40 Mandelbrot, B. (1983).
41 Lieberman, Crelin and Klatt (1972).
42 Lieberman, Klatt and Wilson (1969).
43 Lieberman, P. H. (2006, 2007).
44 Kroeber, A. (1948).
45 James, W. (1890, vol. 1, p. 138).
46 Geertz, C. (1973, p. 46).
47 Geertz, C. (1973, pp. 48–49).
48 Cassirer, E. (1944).
49 Vygotsky, L. S. (1962).
50 Singer, W. (2001).
51 Singer, W. (2001, p. 124).

2

JAMES

What we mean by personal selves

The quest for how mind, or self, comes into being must begin with some definition of what self is. Such a definition, if it is to be useful, and by this I mean clinically useful, must derive from experience. This criterion makes William James pre-eminent among those who have sought to grasp the nature of '*what we mean* by personal selves'.[1] Like his brother Henry, the novelist, his professional life was spent in trying to capture in words the essence of the shifting, evanescent phenomenon that is at the heart of human existing. What he discovers is something 'incomplete'.

Incompleteness

James contended against those who maintained that 'what we mean' by self is found through reason and the practice of logical argument. A definition of self can never be proved, never deemed correct. The unprovability of much of ordinary life is behind William James' philosophy of pragmatism. As a simple example he uses the proposition 'All crows are black'.[2] This statement is not proved by finding numerous black crows. It can only be disproved, and by a single instance, of finding one white crow, e.g. *Corvus albus* in tropical Africa.

The realization that such statements as 'all crows are black' refer only to probability and not to absolute truth does not make them valueless. They have a pragmatic value, i.e. they are useful. James did not follow up his idea about falsifiability and truth, which is more complicated than it seems at first sight. The idea, however, was further developed in the twentieth century by Karl Popper and by certain of the positivist school, of which a core element was the famed Vienna Circle. A mathematician, Kurt Gödel, attended weekly meetings of the Circle from 1926 to 1928. He made perhaps the most intriguing contribution to the issue of unprovability in 1931, while privately disagreeing with central tenets of positivism.[3] He showed that in any relatively complex mathematical system there are some statements that cannot be proved. His 'incompleteness' theorems have profound philosophical implications. As Goldstein puts it in her fascinating account of 'incompleteness': 'The necessary incompleteness of even our formal systems of thought demonstrates that there is no non-shifting foundation on which any system rests.'[4]

In a work that appeared before Gödel's, Wittgenstein approached the subject of unprovability in a somewhat poetic and, even mystical, way. Towards the end of his Tractatus (1922), he wrote:

> We feel that even if *all possible* scientific questions be answered, the problems of life have still not been touched at all. Of course there is then no question left, and just this is the answer.[5]

His famous last line, 'whereof one cannot speak, thereof one must be silent', suggests that there is a zone of reality that cannot be encompassed by logical propositions, which were the principal theme of his thesis. This is a zone for which there seems to be no language, at least of a philosophical kind. Philosophy, therefore, can provide only an incomplete picture of reality.

Following the idea that a definition of self can never be proved 'correct', James has this to say:

> A philosophy is the expression of a man's intimate character, and all definitions of the universe are but the deliberately adopted reactions of human characters upon it . . .
>
> If we take the whole history of philosophy, the systems reduce themselves to a few main types, which, under all the technical verbiage in which the ingenious intellect of man envelops them, are just so many visions, modes of feeling the whole push, and seeing the whole drift of life, forced on one by one's total character and experience, and on the whole *preferred* – there is no other truthful word – as one's best working attitude.[6]

James' preferred vision of 'the whole drift of life', an expression that echoes his famous metaphor 'the stream of thought', is humanistic. Indeed, he chose, in the end, to call his approach one of humanism rather than pragmatism. The freshness and verve of his writing style conveys, in an implicit way, what was his principal purpose. He was trying to describe the nature of reality as we live it in the moment of existing.

Essential to his description is the notion that our world is incomplete, in a state of constant becoming. Anything complete is finished, without life. Despite what he called the 'orderly conceptions of philosophers',[7] 'incompletely unified appearance is the only form that reality may yet have achieved',[8] compared to the rational and intellectual viewpoint he 'offers but a sorry appearance. It is a turbid, muddled, gothic sort of affair, without a sweeping outline and with little pictorial nobility'.[9]

In the Jamesian theory of incompleteness, there are no absolutes, no 'block universe'. James contrasts his view with an absolutist and monist concept of a totality, an 'all-form'. He is

> willing to believe that there may ultimately never be an all-form at all, that the substance of reality may never get totally collected, that some of it may remain outside of the largest combination of it ever made, and that a distributive form of reality, the *each-form* is logically as acceptable and empirically as probable as the all-form commonly acquiesced in as so obviously the self-evident thing.[10]

The 'radical empiricism' of James is not all-or-none. 'Some' is an essential word. 'Each part of the world is in some ways connected, and in some other ways not connected with its other parts'.[11]

What is true and real, for James, is what is felt to be true and real, that is, our immediate experience and the sense at any instant of the passage of this experience as a continuous stream-like phenomenon in which there is the 'feeling of myself'. This has been described, somewhat earlier than James, by the poet Gerard Manley Hopkins.

> I consider my selfbeing, my consciousness and feeling of myself, that taste of myself, of *I* and *me* above and in all things, which is more distinctive than the taste of ale or alum . . . and is incommunicable by any means to another man. . . . Nothing else in nature comes near this unspeakable stress of pitch, distinctiveness and selving, this selfbeing of my own. . . . And even those things with which I in some sort identify myself, as my country or family and those things which I own and call mine, as my clothes and so on, all presupposes the stricter sense of self and me and mine and are from that derivative.[12]

Hopkins' change of the noun 'self' to a verb highlights the dynamic nature of the experience in which there is the feeling of liveliness,[13] vitality and a sense of movement. It is not static, not an entity or a thing. It is a process, analogous to an activity.

The selving described by Hopkins would be called by James 'acquaintance-knowledge'[14] since it is directly experienced, only fully known by the subject and able to be conveyed to others in only a partial and incomplete way. This is the bedrock of reality. It is to be distinguished from 'knowledge-about', which is an aspect of a fuller sense of human reality, gained through the process of reflection. It is secondary to the more fundamental 'feeling' aspect of reality, as Damasio and his colleagues have demonstrated in a series of publications.[15]

Intimacy and foreignness

The Jamesian self is incomplete in a way beyond what has already been intimated. It cannot be contained, or conceived, as within a single person. The 'stream of consciousness'[16] is not made up solely of inner experiences such as ideas, memories, imaginings and so forth. Sensation can never be excluded from consciousness, as Descartes found in his attempt at observing what is 'inner':

> I shall now close my eyes, stop up my ears, turn away all my senses, even efface from my thought all images of corporeal things, or at least, since this can hardly be done, I shall consider them vain and false.[17]

Descartes chose to consider that sensation, the feelings in the body and the sensing of what we see, hear, touch and smell, 'vain and false', as alien to self and separate from it. James' view was the opposite. We are part of the world and the sensory experience it gives to us. Self is a state that includes the world around.

James saw that there were two ways of approaching the problem of self, two kinds of philosophies:

> In the former case the philosopher means by the universe everything *except* what his own presence brings; in the latter case his philosophy is itself an intimate part of the universe, and maybe a significant part momentous enough to give a different turn to what the other parts signify.[18]

These two attitudes are contrasted: 'living against a background of foreignness and one of intimacy means the difference between the general habit of wariness and one of trust'.[19] In the end, however, James believes all philosophies are struggling against estrangement. For example, he quotes Hegel in saying: 'The aim of knowledge is to divest the objective world of its strangeness and to make us more at home in it.' [20]

James remarks 'whether we be empiricists or rationalists, we are, ourselves, parts of the universe and share the same one deep concern in its destinies'. [21]

James' distinction between two ways of understanding, and so, experiencing, the world has important implications. His proposal resembles those of Bohr and Heisenberg in the field of quantum physics. Heisenberg's uncertainty principle tells us that the act of measuring, i.e. observing aspects of a system, alters the system so that other aspects change. Put more specifically, measurement of the position of a particle cannot be done without altering its momentum and vice versa. James' conception of the relationship of the philosopher with the universe is analogous. He was saying that the way in which the philosopher makes this relationship, to a tiny degree, affects the universe: 'His philosophy is an intimate part of the universe, and may be a part momentous enough to give a different turn to what the other parts signify'. [22]

The Jamesian conception, however, is an intersubjective, to and fro, reciprocal arrangement. In this way he goes beyond the Uncertainty Principle. He suggests that the way we observe the world influences who we become, that a way of seeing is a way of being. In his example, we become a person who is either wary or trustful. A way of being is also a form of relationship.

James does not develop this idea, but in these conceptions he is edging towards a conception of a relationship with the world that is a dynamic interplay and which, most importantly, is the world of other people. The way we set up this relationship engenders a mood, a state of mind. This has a further effect, of influencing what we perceive. This is implied by Wallace Stevens' poem 'Idea of Order at Key West', which tells of a walk by the sea at night, where he hears a woman singing.[3] The song created a particular feeling, a mood, out of which came a way of seeing the world, an experiencing of its shapes that were the forms of that feeling. In a reciprocal relation, the forms create the mood.

The Jamesian depiction of the philosopher in relationship to the universe is a model for similar relationships. They include that between the therapist and the world of the other; the literary critic and the text; the historian and a bygone era; and the archaeologist and the ruins of an ancient city. In each case, the 'meaning' derived depends upon the form of relatedness between an individual subject and a creative life as object.

Bohr's Complementarity Principle provides a further analogy in James' argument concerning the philosopher's inferences about nature of reality. Bohr's principle, enunciated in 1928, arose out of de Broglie's revolutionary idea that an electron, which had been experimentally observed as a particle, could, under certain circumstances, behave like a wave. Bohr's integrating proposal stated that whether it were a particle or a wave depended upon the way the electron was 'observed', or measured. The information gained was not right in one case and wrong in the other. Rather, both situations provide 'complementary' information about the nature of the system.

I.A. Richards has pointed out that Bohr himself believed that the Complementarity Principle is applicable to psychology and even to psychologists – and perhaps even philosophers.[24] Bohr insisted that what he claimed was not mere analogy. Even in a more complex system such as psychology, the outcome of an inquiry is determined by the method of inquiry.[25] Psychic events are changed when attention is fixed upon them.[26] We cannot distinguish between mental phenomena themselves and the fact of perception.[27]

James' ideas about the foreignness or 'intimacy' of a form of relatedness have important therapeutic implications.

Some cardinal features of self

James combined a scientific purpose with the sensibility of a poet. His principal purpose was to say 'what we mean' by self. His words – 'what we mean' – are addressed to those who want to define the sense of existing in a way which is 'deeper' than what we actually experience. Of this, he remarks, 'we have no positive conception, and we have no right to discredit our actual experience by talking in such a way'.[28] Since they built a philosophy upon the basic data of human experience, James found himself, to this extent, in the tradition of British empirical philosophers, particularly as epitomized by John Locke. Locke described a cardinal feature of selfhood. He wrote: 'In every act of sensation, reasoning, or thinking, we are conscious to ourselves of our own being; and in this matter come not short of the highest degree of certainty.'[29] There is a doubleness in this conception, a distinction between consciousness and 'ourselves'. This abstractly conceived duality is necessary to the experience of self. In considering what is meant by 'personal identity', Locke wrote that:

> We must consider what *person* stands for; which, I think, is a thinking intelligent being, that has reason and reflection, and can consider itself as itself, the same thinking thing, in different times and places; which it does only by that consciousness which is inseparable from thinking, and, as it seems to me, essential to it: it being impossible for any one to perceive without *perceiving* that he does perceive. When we see, hear, smell, taste, feel, meditate, or will anything, we know that we do so. Thus it is always as to our present sensations and perceptions: and by this every one is to himself that which he calls *self.*[30]

The Lockean idea is very like the duplex self of James, which is fundamental to his system.

> Whatever I may be thinking of, I am always at the same time more or less aware of *myself*, of my *personal existence.* At the same time, it is I who am aware; so that the total self of me, being as it were duplex, partly known and partly knower, partly object and partly subject, must have two aspects discriminated in it, of which for shortness we may call one the *Me* and the other the *I.*[31]

The abstractly conceived duality of self, the reflective awareness of inner events, is a commonly accepted criterion of the activity of that kind of consciousness that is called 'self' in this book.[32] This activity, exhibited in autobiographical memory and in imaginative processes that create scenes 'in the mind' that have never been witnessed before, was used as the identifying feature of self by Hughlings Jackson,[33] whose hierarchial conception of mind and self was cited by James[34] but not developed. Nevertheless, I am taking the Jacksonian hierarchy, organized by the history of evolution, as implicit in the Jamesian system.

Jackson's hierarchy allows us to understand shifts in states of consciousness, not all of which are those of self. There are times, for example, when one is 'out of one's mind' or 'beside oneself'.

James went beyond Locke and the empiricists. He was critical of their tendency to break personal experience into bits. His attempt was to grasp it in its fullness. Like Henri Bergson, who was working independently of James, he believed that the task of the philosopher is 'to give the purest possible description of the way we actually experience the world'.[35] In this way he was able to sense, and to describe, aspects of existing that might seem obvious to the lay person but which were neglected by philosophers. For example, he ascribed a sense of 'ownership' to our thoughts, an idea that seemed outlandish to some philosophic critics.

He wrote: 'It seems as if the elementary psychic fact were not *thought* or *this thought* or *that thought*, but *my thought, every thought* being *owned*.'[36]

Another overlooked feature of self is feeling. James, in several ways, indicates that at the heart of healthy existing is a feeling of positivity, of pleasure. The style of his writing implicitly conveys his viewpoint since it gives pleasure to the reader. He seemed to enjoy his debate with those who believed that, in excluding feeling from their concepts of self and building them on reason and logic alone, they were creating 'scientific' constructs. For example, he concluded an address to the Aristotelian Society in 1884, on 'The Function of Cognition', in the following way:

> Beautiful is the flight of conceptual reason through the upper air of truth. No wonder philosophers are dazzled by it still, and no wonder they look with some disdain at the low earth of feeling from which the goddess launched herself aloft. But woe to her if she return not home to its acquaintance. . . . Every crazy wind will take her, and like a fire-balloon at night, she will go out among the stars.[37]

James called the positive feeling at the core of self 'warmth and intimacy'. Such a designation has been often overlooked as if it were sentimentality. Yet it is apposite. Like the sense of 'ownership', positive feelings fade or are lost in traumatic states. So also is the feeling of an 'intimate' relationship with the world around, of which James spoke. Rather the relationship is one of alienation, of estrangement.

The identifying feature of selfhood, an awareness of the movements of inner life, has within it a number of other cardinal features. They include the notion of 'agency' – the sense that we have control over these various movements. As James puts it: 'Each personal consciousness . . . is *interested* in some parts of its object to the exclusion of others, and welcomes or rejects – *chooses* from among them, in a word – all the while.'[38] The important element in this experience is the individual's consciousness of the part he or she plays in the evolution of the stream. There is also a very large element of selective attention and inattention that is unconscious.

Although self is identified as a consciousness that is conscious of itself, this consciousness is not self itself. There is one fundamental characteristic of self, overarching all of its other features, containing them and indeed creating them. It is the quality of continuity and coherence: 'Consciousness, then, does not appear to itself chopped up in bits. Such words as "chain" or "train" do not describe it fitly as it presents itself in the first instance. It is nothing jointed; it flows.'[39]

Although, once again, James does not make this explicit, the continuity of mental life reflects an underlying process of unification out of which the capacity for introspection emerges. This idea comes from Hughlings Jackson who postulated that higher order consciousness is a consequence of a co-ordination of the basic elements of brain-mind function that is more complete than that of young children and of other primates. This enhanced co-ordination leads to a larger state of mind in which we may roam around among old memories and new imagined worlds, such as the future. These introspective activities, then, are conceived not as an independent faculty of reflection, appearing at about 4 years of age, but as an outcome of a prior process of integration.

Change and the paradox of self

A cardinal feature of the Jamesian self is change. 'What I wish to lay stress on is this, that *no state once gone can recur and be identical with what it was before.*'[40] He argues his case from a number of viewpoints, including the most fundamental, the effect of a simple stimulus: 'Every sensation corresponds to some cerebral action. For an identical sensation to recur it would have to occur the second time *in an unmodified brain.* But as this, strictly speaking, is a physiological impossibility' (illustrated, we might add, by the phenomenon of habituation) 'so is an unmodified feeling an impossibility'.[41]

A paradox seems to be created by the experience of change. How is it that my self, which I experience day after day as the same self, is also one that is changing? Hume asked himself this very question. In contemplating the nature of his mind, or self, he observed its evanescent, shifting, quality and wrote of it in the following way: 'The mind is a kind of theatre, where several perceptions successively make their appearance, pass, re-pass, glide away, and mingle in an infinite variety of postures and situations.'[42] The definition of the word 'self' includes the characteristic of sameness. Hume's observations contradicted the definition. 'Consequently' he included, 'there is no such idea'.[43]

Hume's conclusion was based on the idea that existence is rational and can be conceived in a logical way. Since self cannot be conceived in terms of logic, it does not exist and the concept is irrational. This kind of argument caused James to reject philosophies built on the practice of logic of this kind.

Change is a quality of life. The tree outside the window is changing, imperceptibly, from moment to moment yet it is always the same tree although the colour of the leaves may alter and blossoms appear from time to time. The world is in constant change as if depicted in a Van Gogh painting where trees are writhing upwards and stars whirl in the sky.

The co-existence of sameness and change in self and in the world, contains a second paradox – that of unity and multiplicity. The state of existing is sensed as coherent, as a relative one-ness, yet it is made up of multiple states. Perhaps it might be said that paradox is a quintessential feature of *what we mean* by self.

The 'cash value' of the Jamesian self

The pragmatic philosophy of James stated that a concept that is true is useful. It has, in his words, a 'cash value'. His description of self, particularly as given in his famous 'Stream of Thought' chapter,[44] has a pragmatic value in that it is helpful in the clinical sphere. From it can be derived the main features of self, which can be operationally defined in linguistic terms. The usefulness of the Jamesian self is exemplified by the experiences of survivors of a traumatic environment, in which, day after day, the individual has inflicted upon him or her repetitive insults, which may be physical, social, or emotional, or a combination of these. In order to understand the resultant psychopathology it is necessary to know how trauma works and what it does.

It is hard to think about trauma without thinking about self. Psychotherapists and psychologists, however, tended to do so in the latter part of the twentieth century, treating traumatic memories as isolated phenomena to be detoxified or modified in some way so as to diminish their malignant effects. This approach did some good, particularly in cases where the trauma was a single event. However, when the traumata were multiple and cumulative, these methods are inappropriate, ineffective, or worse.

Trauma means damage, an injury. In order to properly treat the consequences of trauma it is necessary to know what this injury might be. If the Jamesian concept of self is to have a 'cash value' it should be useful in predicting the outcome of what D. W. Winnicott called an 'impingement'. Since continuity and cohesion are cardinal features of self, the theory predicts that they will be lost. Virginia Woolf describes such an outcome.

> The past only comes back when the present runs so smoothly that it is like the sliding surface of a deep river. Then one sees through the surface to the depths. In those moments I find one of my greatest satisfactions, not that I am thinking of the past; but that it is then that I am living most fully in the present. For the present when backed by the past is a thousand times deeper than the present when it presses so close that you can feel nothing else, when the film on the camera reaches only the eye. But to feel the present sliding over the depths of the past, peace is necessary. The present must be smooth, habitual. For this reason – that it destroys the fullness of life – any break – like that of house moving – causes me extreme distress; it breaks; it shallows; it turns the depth into hard thin splinters. As I say to L[eonard]: 'What's there real about this? Shall we ever live a real life again?[45]

For Woolf: 'Life is not a series of gig lamps symmetrically arranged; life is a luminous halo surrounding us from the beginning of consciousness to the end.'[46] Where 'impingements' persist so also does a relative fragmentation. It is as if a 'luminous halo' no longer envelops the traumatized individual and only the gig lamps remain, disconnected from each other. Pierre Janet, who remains a principal theorist in the sphere of psychological trauma, considered that its main effect was a failure of 'personal synthesis'.

In cases of severe abuse, such a repetitive sexual abuse, the splintering becomes pronounced, as in Dissociative Identity Disorder in which James' 'community of selves' is no longer a community. The paradoxical nature of self, in its diversity in unity, is lost. Those suffering this condition have an incidence of a background repetitive sexual abuse that is higher than any other clinical group.

The James theory also predicts loss of the other main features of self, in addition to the sense of continuity. As the effect of the trauma increases, the sense of personal reality and what was once 'my thought, my experience', fades. As 'ownership' becomes tenuous, so also does the sense of agency, particularly of an inner kind. The freedom to choose where one roams in one's mind gives way to thoughts that are automatic or that seem to be forced upon one. Reflective activity lessens, the feeling of change wanes and is succeeded by states of mind that are repetitive. Most importantly the positive feeling at the centre of self is replaced by a chronic 'dysphoria', which Mary Zanarini has likened to 'psychic pain'.[47]

Analogical basis of coherence

With his statement that 'thoughts connected as we feel them to be connected are *what we mean* by personal selves',[48] William James identifies the central feature of selfhood – the sense of connectedness, or cohesion. Since this experience is impaired in those whose personality development has been impeded, often by 'relational traumata', the question of personal cohesion and how it may develop, is of major practical importance. A fundamental therapeutic approach, beyond concern with the intrusion of conscious and unconscious traumatic memory, must be to foster the sense of wholeness and feeling a coherence. At present, there is no accepted idea of how it might be done. This book describes what James might call a theory of 'how things hang together'.

James grappled with what he called 'the nature of the synthetic unity of consciousness',[49] throughout his career. Without ever coming to a complete formulation, he pondered the problem of 'how, on the supposition that the manyness of things precedes their unity, does any unity come into being at all?'[50] This is a problem of paramount importance in his philosophical and psychological explorations. His musings on the mystery of continuity and coherence, scattered throughout his writing, provide the starting point in the development of a thesis about its origins.

One of James' more extended considerations of the nature of cohesion is found in an essay titled 'The Knowing of Things Together', where he remarks that 'the experience', that is, the present sense of existing, 'can be referred to either of the two great associative systems, that of the experiencer's mental history or that of the experienced facts of the world'.[51] He uses a diagram to illustrate his idea. A horizontal line represents public history. Vertical lines, 'the experienced facts of the world', cross it, representing 'the experiencer's mental history'. These axes resemble, but are not the same as, those found by Saussure in his study of language. Saussure found that a text is usually constructed according to two axes. One is of succession, concerning one thing after another. It can be visualized as horizontal. He called it 'diachronic'. The other is concerned with simultaneities and what he called 'value'. This axis is the 'synchronic'. It is absent, or relatively so, in scientific and legal texts. Saussure's *Course of General Linguistics* was not published until 1916. James and Saussure had come across the two axes independently. In essence, the axes reflect two different realities, the public and private, the outer and the inner.

The Jamesian moment, the 'experience', arises at the point of intersection of these two axes of personal reality, creating a third domain of personal existence, which we call self. The experience is constantly being made, reconstituted at every moment, while retaining a paradoxical feeling of sameness[52] and continuity.

In considering the problem of coherence in terms of these two systems, James found it easier to understand in the zone of public reality. It is made by what he referred to as the Law of Contiguity. The facts of the world are arranged as they appear in the world. As James put it, 'Seen things and heard things cohere with each other, and with odours and tastes, in representation, in the same order in which they cohered as impressions in the outer world.'[53]

The linkages of the internal aspect of the system of reality are of a different kind and made, James believed, according to the Law of Similarity. Among the examples he gave of what he meant by similarity was a friend's remark 'that stories in passing from mouth to mouth make a great deal of lee-way in proportion to their headway'.[54] The shape of one is similar to the other. Put another way, the path of a yacht is an analogue of the digressions of gossip.

Elaborating from James, we can say that the matrix of inner life hangs together, though not entirely, but at least in part, and characteristically, through analogical connectedness. In this book, the idea is put forward that the first analogues in life are the mother's face and voice and that they are part of a connectedness, which is later internalized. Before embarking upon this proposal, it is necessary to consider the nature of analogy.

Notes

1 James, W. (1892, pp. 152–153).
2 Richardson, R. D. (2007, p. 261).
3 Goldstein, R. (2005, p. 75).
4 Goldstein, R. (2005, p. 25).
5 Wittgenstein, L. (1922, 6.52).
6 James, W. (1909a, pp. 20–21).
7 James, W. (1909a, p. 45).
8 James, W. (1909a, p. 44).
9 James, W. (1909a, p. 45).
10 James, W. (1909a, p. 34).
11 James, W. (1909a, p. 79).
12 Cited by White, N. (1995, p. 7).
13 Korner, A. (2000).
14 James, W. (1890, p. 221).
15 Damasio, A. R. (1996, 1999). Damasio remarks that he has 'come to favor the writings of William James as an anchor for my own thinking' (2012, p. 7).
16 James, W. (1892, pp. 151–175).

17 Descartes, R. (1637–1641, p. 113).
18 James, W. (1909a, pp. 35–36).
19 James, W. (1909a, p. 31).
20 James, W. (1909a, p. 11).
21 James, W. (1909a, p. 12).
22 James, W. (1909a, pp. 35–36).
23 Stevens, W. (1954, pp. 129–130).
24 Richards, I. A. (1976, pp. 110–111).
25 Richards, I. A. (1976, pp. 111–112).
26 Bohr, N. (1958, p. 11).
27 Bohr, N. (1958, p. 21).
28 James, W. (1909b, p. 107).
29 Locke, J. (1690, vol. I, p. 305).
30 Locke, J. (1690, vol. I, pp. 448–449).
31 James, W. (1892, p. 176).
32 E.g. Armstrong, D. (1981, p. 67).
33 Jackson, J. H. (1958, vol. II, pp. 92–102).
34 James, W. (1890, vol. I, p. 64, vol. II, pp. 125–126).
35 Matthews, E. (1999, p. 119).
36 James, W. (1892, p. 153).
37 James, W. (1909b, p. 41).
38 James, W. (1892, p. 152).
39 James, W. (1892, p. 159).
40 James, W. (1892, p. 154).
41 James, W. (1892, p. 156).
42 Hume, D. (1739–1740, p. 253).
43 Hume, D. (1739–1740, p. 252).
44 James, W. (1890, vol. I, pp. 224–290).
45 Woolf, V. (1978, p. 114).
46 Woolf, V. (1925, p. 189).
47 Zanarini *et al.* (1998).
48 James, W. (1892, pp. 163–164).
49 James, W. (1895, p. 152).
50 Cited by Richardson (2007, p. 446).
51 James, W. (1895, p. 15, 7n).
52 Damasio, A. R. (1994, p. 240).
53 James. W. (1890, vol. I, p. 555).
54 James. W. (1890, vol. I, p. 582).

3

ANALOGY AND TRUTH

Caroline Spurgeon, in exploring Shakespeare's imagery, spoke of analogy in the following way: 'I incline to believe that analogy – likeness between dissimilar things – which is the fact underlying the possibility and reality of metaphor, holds within it the secret of the universe.'[1] This is a remarkable and important intuition. She was implying that the universe, by which she presumably meant her universe, the experiential zone in which life goes on, is found and created through analogy. She was putting forward, in another way, the main argument of this book, which is that self grows in a relationship in which the other represents the essence of our experience by means of a 'picturing' capacity, which is usually verbal but may be visual or auditory. 'Other' is used here in a broad way to refer to the environment as a whole, including cultural expressions, such as those of poets and storytellers, and also oneself, in inner conversation.

Analogy defined

Spurgeon did not define analogy in a formal way but suggested its defining characteristic in remarking that it was the gift of the poet: 'He is a poet largely by nature of the power he has, greater than other men, of perceiving hidden likenesses.'[2]

The concept of analogy comes from the Greek. It refers to a thing that has a proportion or shape similar to another thing. The term is made up of the prefix 'ana', which has meanings of 'back, again, anew',[3] and 'logos' meaning 'word, statement'. Taken literally, these roots together make analogy a statement of something anew, a restatement. This bald definition, however, does not capture the essence of analogy, which is suggested by larger meaning of logos. Dent writes of it from the philosophical point of view:

> A Greek word, of great breadth of meaning, primarily signifying in the context of philosophical discussion the rational, intelligible principle, structure, or order which pervades something, or the source of that order, or giving an account of that order.[4]

This passage highlights the centrality of structure and order in the concept of logos. It contributes the notion of 'shape' to the concept of the analogue. The creation of an analogue shows an awareness of resemblance between two objects, or, more complexly, scenes, events and even stories based on their form. In a paper entitled 'Analogy as the core of cognition', Douglas Hofstadter gives a good example of analogue as 'shape'.[5] On an aeroplane trip he had been reading a book that included, as a small part of the book, an account of a boat crossing the Atlantic from east to west. As it neared the American coast, it was in danger of running into a hurricane which was travelling from south to north up the coast. The boat diverged south, behind the course of the hurricane and then headed north again to resume its previous trajectory. Later, as he walked along the corridor in the airport a woman began to cross the corridor in front of him, moving with a suitcase in a path at right angles to his. Since he was in danger of bumping into her, he diverged so as to walk behind her before resuming the original direction of his walk. His path was an analogue of the course of the boat.

He gave as a second example of analogy, a 'rain shadow' created by a range of mountains that block clouds and beyond which no rain falls, in the same way as a wall creates a shadow by blocking out light.

Certain analogues, more than others, evoke a feeling that is positive and hard to describe. I call it 'fit'.[6] It is the kind of analogue I believe to be generative of self. It has something of the quality of music in that it is felt as harmonious and since it arouses a positive emotional response. Caroline Spurgeon seems to give an example of such an analogy:

> The bare fact that germinating seeds or falling leaves are actually another expression of the processes we see at work in human life and death, thrills me, as it must thrill others, with a sense of being here in the presence of a great mystery, which, could we only understand it, would explain life and death itself.[7]

Structure mapping, analogy and the hippocampus

Dedre Gentner is a major figure in the study of analogy. Her main argument about the nature of analogy depends upon the fundamental issue of 'shape'. She has put forward a 'structure mapping' theoretical framework for analogy.

> The central idea is that an analogy is a mapping of knowledge from one domain (the base) into another (the target) such that a system of relations that holds among the base objects also hold among the target objects.[8]

The idea that analogy may involve a 'mapping' function, as suggested by Gentner, is intriguing because it links the analogical process to a known neurological function, that of hippocampal remapping.

The early spatial processing system provided by the otoliths of the vestibular apparatus, is linked up, in mammals, to a more complex system – the hippocampus. The hippocampus operates like a 'cognitive map'.[9] In 1971, O'Keefe and Dostrovsky showed that it has a multitude of so-called 'place-cells', which fire successively as the animal moves around.[10] A specific cell is activated in a particular location. If, say, the animal is in the south-west corner of a cage, a certain cell fires. If it goes to the north-east corner, another cell fires. When it returns to the south-west corner, the specific cell for this location fires again.

If the animal moves cages, the 'place-cells' change their firing pattern. As the space changes a 're-mapping' occurs. If the hippocampus is damaged, the rat loses its capacity for navigation.

Recently, place-cells have been identified in primates, including the human. In humans, as in other animals, they are involved in navigation, our movement from space to space as we live. In an interesting study, London taxi-drivers were asked to imagine traveling particular routes through the city while they were in a PET scanner. As they did so, their hippocampi lit up.[11] This was not so in the case of landmarks. It seems, then, that the place-cells are mapping a particular kind of space, created by the position of the body. Bodily experience is with us all the time. With every thought there is some bodily activity, however minor or imperceptible. When landmarks are used in navigation, the parahippocampal gyrus is involved.[12] They seem to be aspects of another kind of space, created by the eyes. We live within different kinds of personal space, which are co-ordinated to create a unified experience.

A recent finding enlarges the complexity of the spatial mapping system in the brain. In 2005, Moser and his colleagues described what they call 'grid cells' in the entorhinal cortex, which neighbours the hippocampus. These cells fire in a regular geometric pattern: 'In moving animals, the multiple firing fields of an individual grid cell form a triangular pattern tiling the entire space available to the animal.'[13] Grid cells function together with the place cells in the formation of a virtual map.

The system of spatial mapping is fundamental to our ordinary sense of existing. It is necessary to episodic and autobiographical memory, since an event or episode goes on within a space. Each kind of event will have a particular circuitry unique to that event. This pattern of neuronal activity is mapped onto the hippocampus. Memory depends upon recognition of these patterns.

John O'Keefe, Mai Britt Moser and Edvard Moser won the 2014 Nobel Prize in Physiology in Medicine.

Analogy versus homology

Although the structure-mapping idea of analogue is consistent with the notion of 'shape' that is at the core of the concept, it leads to a negation of the concept if used literally. Precise structure mapping produces homology not analogy. A homologue is something having a structure the same as another thing. An example of a homologue is the resemblance between a small triangle and a large triangle. An example of analogue is similarity in the shape of a triangle and the delta of a river such as the Nile. A perfect homologue is a replica. The map is the same as the terrain and, therefore, useless.

Homology is a dead-end. It can lead to no expansion, no series of iterations out of which comes a much larger complex of ideas, feelings, imaginings and so forth, larger than the original image. Analogy, on the other hand, as Hofstadter points out, creates conceptual expansion. The effect of homology resembles 'mirroring' in developmental and therapeutic settings. Precise duplication of the subject's expression by the other, the caregiver or therapist, creates a cage of mirrors, which was where Narcissus found himself. His lover could no longer respond to him adequately, that is, not analogically but only homologically. In searching for a replacement and vitalizing responsiveness, he found only the ultimate homologue, a reflected image of himself. The consequence was withering and death.[14]

Analogy and a shared element

The representation that creates an analogy cannot always operate on the simple basis of the shape of the two entities that are being compared. Gentner, in an influential article, gives the example of a reservoir as an analogue of a battery.[15] They do not have a shape in common, but they both have the capacity for storage. This shared function might evoke an image of a bowl or a tank. Such an image provides a third element, which enables the resemblance between the 'base' and the 'target' to be figuratively visualized. This example leads to a definition of analogy, which is an extension of the fundamental criterion of shape. It is a 'correspondence between two things because of a third element they are considered to share'.[16]

Différance

An essential feature of analogy is that it is both the same as, and different from, that which it represents. The difference may be very slight. The words one has spoken may be repeated, in part, by the other with a somewhat different tone or emphasis. This kind of response is not one of mimicry. The concept of sameness and difference is reflected in Derrida's concept of 'différance'. The misspelling is emblematic of his concept. The word sounds the same as 'difference' but is written differently. He considered that no single word or expression can ever say what it means. It needs expansion by other words or expressions, which both contain but go beyond the original expression. This response, which can be called analogical, is not an end-point, a culmination in the quest for this particular meaning. There is always another step to be taken, another analogue to be found. In this way, ultimate meaning is 'deferred'. The word 'defer' is implied in the condensation of meaning implicit in 'différance'. The notion of 'différance' has a generative value.

The generative potential of différance and of analogy can be illustrated arithmetically by making a comparison with Gentner's structure mapping. She asks us to consider the arithmetical statement, 3:6::2:4 'as an example of the selectiveness of analogical mapping'.[17] A similar example would be, 3:2::6:4. The second ratio replicates the first. It is a homologue not an analogue. It leads to a series of

$$\frac{3}{2},\frac{6}{4},\frac{9}{6},\frac{12}{8},$$

etc. in which there is no development, no change. In the following series, there is both sameness and difference. The numerator and denominator in one ratio are added to make a new denominator for the following ratio and a new numerator is created by the new denominator being added to the previous numerator:

$$\frac{3}{2},\frac{8}{5},\frac{21}{13},\frac{55}{34}.$$

This sequence is created from the Fibonacci numbers. It moves towards the Golden Ratio described by Euclid. This ratio is formed when a line is cut at the point where the ratio of the whole length of the line over the larger part of the two parts made by the cut equals the ratio of the larger over the smaller part. Like the idea and experience of self, the Golden Ratio can never be fully reached. An approximate value is 1.618. The Fibonacci based series is associated with the generation of many of the fundamental patterns found in the natural world such as seashells, flowers, pine cones and pineapples.[18]

The generative potential of the series depends upon the curious paradox of co-existing sameness and difference. The same numbers are used in the progression from one figure to the next but they are used in a different way e.g.

$$\frac{8}{5} \rightarrow \frac{8+5+8}{8+5} \rightarrow \frac{8+5+8+8+5}{8+5+8}$$

and so on. This series provides a metaphor for the seamless progression of mental life. Before, however, considering this matter it is necessary to approach the distinction between metaphor and analogy.

Analogy and metaphor

Caroline Spurgeon implied both a relation and difference between analogy and metaphor when she spoke of 'analogy – likeness between dissimilar things' as 'the fact underlying the possibility and reality of metaphor'. Her statement suggests that analogy is something prior to metaphor, a precursor.

Whereas a metaphor is a symbol, analogue is not. Darwin's use of analogical thought illustrates this difference. He observed the 'framework of the bones being the same in the hand of man, the wing of a bat, the fin of a porpoise, the leg of a horse'.[19] A hand is not a symbol of a bat's wing. It is a likeness, similarity, or correspondence. An awareness of such correspondences has a creative value, as it had for Darwin. In this example, both the 'target' and the 'base', to use Gentner's language, have a material existence and are both to be found in the outer world. The metaphor retains the formal structure of analogy but typically involves a more abstract form of likeness, in which it is used to represent something that cannot otherwise be represented, like the 'flow' of thought. It then becomes a symbol. An analogue can be conceived as a proto-symbol, the primordium, or first form of the symbolic function.

Although analogy and metaphor can be distinguished, particularly in terms of inner and outer worlds, they can also work together, representing both inner and outer at the same time. For example, Cleopatra, in speaking of her dead husband Antony, says: 'His delights were dolphin-like; they showed his back above the element they lived in.'[20] The shape of the dolphin's movement represents a feeling of joy (inner, metaphoric) and also its bodily expression (outer, analogic).

Symbols and signs

Symbols are distinguished from signs. They have different functions. Signs 'point to' something in the present, nearby, or imminent. A placard showing two legs walking indicates an adjacent pedestrian crossing. Cloud is sign of rain. The former is an example of an invented or conventional sign; the latter is a natural sign.

Some conventional signs may show a resemblance to that which they indicate. A placard on the roadside showing the outline of a wombat is a sign that wombats are around. Other conventional signs show no or little resemblance to the thing of which they are indicators. Such signs are arbitrary and must be learnt. They include, for example, the logo for the underground railway and a bus conductor's badge.

Words are conventional signs. Saussure stated that the 'linguistic sign is arbitrary'.[21] A word, i.e. the signifier, is a sound image which is not linked by any inner relationships to that which it signifies. 'The linguistic sign', he points out 'unites not a thing and a name, but a concept and a sound image'.[22] This formulation suggests that the written word is a third element that mediates between the sound-image, which may be unspoken, but held in memory, and the signified.

In ordinary conversation, signs for things and concepts are often parts of those things and concepts. For example, the highest echelon of the administration of the United States is referred to as the White House. Where, one part of the system is used as a sign of the whole, the figure of speech is metonymic. Lakoff and Johnson give a colourful example of metonymy. A person in a restaurant has ordered a ham sandwich, and another person, presumably a waiter, says, 'The ham sandwich is waiting for his check'. The sandwich is the most salient signifying feature among a range of other features, which might have been used to point to this particular individual.[23] 'Don't put your daughter on the stage' is another metonymic expression, where the word 'stage' is a short hand for the whole world of acting.

Synecdoche is a figure of speech very like metonymy. A 'whole is used for part' and vice versa.[24] I am taking, however, metonymy to be the principal figure in the system of signs.

The same image can function either as a sign or symbol, metonym or metaphor. For example, 'crown' is metonymic when referring to a system of monarchial administration, as in 'crown land'. It may also be a symbol of glory, as in 'crowning achievement'. Words have a double function. As signs they are used not only as signs but as a part of the symbolic process. In poetic language the situation may become more complex when the same words are used as metonyms and metaphors/analogues at the same time. An example is Shakespeare's famous 'bare ruined choirs', to which we shall come later. The use of signs differs from the use of symbols, of which metaphor is the basic figure, in the same way that two basic modes of human thinking differ from each other. The differences in thought are reflected in language although the distinction between modes is not absolute in ordinary conversation since, in usual circumstances, they are co-ordinated. The thought mode associated with signs deals with discrete events, having a single meaning, which are arranged in an orderly progression towards a goal. The second mode has no goal. Its elements are not clearly defined, as representing units. They are characterized by multiplicity – the feature of symbols. Their arrangement is non-linear.

Saussure used the sense of time to give names to the linguistic manifestations of the two kinds of thinking. The first – the linear, logical and syntactical form – he called diachronic; the other, non-linear – which I call analogical – he termed synchronic. These concepts will be discussed further in later chapters.

Conventional symbols

This chapter, so far, is an attempt to say as clearly as possible what is meant by the terms sign and symbol used in this book. The brevity of the account obscures the complexity of this issue. No major formulation of these concepts agrees with any other. C. S. Peirce and Saussure are, perhaps, the main authorities on the subject yet their proposals are dissimilar. For example, Saussure's conception can be seen as binary while Peirce's is triadic. Peirce's brilliant and difficult proposals include three distinctions in language, which he called 'index', 'icon' and 'symbol'. An 'index' belongs to the system of signs. Smoke from a fire, for example, is an index. It points to something. An icon is an image, essentially an analogue. As such, it is part of the system of symbolization. The 'symbol' in Peirce differs from the usage in this book. It is a sign which is conventionally linked to that which signifies.

Despite the disparities, between Peirce and Saussure, Piaget was able to draw on the work of these men to create a limited schema distinguishing between symbol and sign that is broadly consistent with my own, particularly with regard to his notion of symbol, 'which exhibits some analogical correspondence with the signified'.[25]

In aiming to achieve a coherent view of sign and symbol and the distinctions between them, certain difficulties arising from formulations of other contributors to the conception of sign and symbol have been avoided in this brief account. One of these difficulties, however, cannot be overlooked since it is put forward by the eminent figure of W. V. Quine. In an authoritative essay entitled 'Symbols' he begins with the sentence: 'A symbol, broadly speaking, is something that stands for something else.'[26] This is not what a symbol is, at least in my view. There is however, a way of reaching a limited agreement with this statement. It concerns the notion of a conventional symbol.

Just as there are conventional signs there may be conventional symbols. A conventional sign has a single meaning, a terminus. The sign of an X on a country road means only that a level crossing lies ahead. A Christian cross, on the other hand, has many connotations, associations and meanings, relating to a whole body of theological thought and practice, a story, notions of suffering and love and so forth. There is no end point. Within this large system there are created a multitude of small conventional symbols. This was manifest in the Christianity of Europe during the Middle Ages.

In his beautiful book *The Autumn of the Middle Ages*, Johan Huizinga wrote of this time as one dominated by 'that noble and lofty idea of the world as a great symbolic nexus – a cathedral of ideas, the highest rhythmic polyphonic expression of all that can be thought'.[27] He said of those living at this time:

> They never forgot that everything would be absurd if it exhausted its meaning in its immediate function and form of manifestation, and that all things extend in an important way into the world beyond. That insight is still familiar to us as an inarticulate feeling in those moments when the sound of rain on leaves or the light of a lamp on a table penetrates momentarily into a deeper level of perception than that serving practical thought and action.[28]

This consciousness, in which the universe provides the means to represent aspects of our reality that cannot otherwise be expressed, faded with the 'dying spirit of the Middle Ages'.[29] Analogic and metaphoric linkages with the natural world, which are created by imagination and feeling, now became conventional, without the life given to them by their imaginative and poetic origins. They continued to be called symbols even though they more closely resembled signs.

The outcome for this 'worn-out apparatus of medieval expression',[30] as Huizinga called it, was the situation described by Émile Mâle in his classic work *The Gothic Image*:

> The Middle Ages had a passion for order. They organized art as they had organized dogma, secular learning and society. The artistic representation

> of sacred subjects was a science governed by fixed laws, which could not be broken at the dictates of individual imagination. It cannot be questioned that this theology of art, if one may so put it, was soon reduced to a body of doctrine, for from very early times the craftsmen are seen submitting to it from one end of Europe to the other.[31]

These craftsmen had to learn a vast range of conventional symbols in order to form in their sculptures, the icons of a sacred writing. The ordinary people of the time also knew these links between the universal and personal worlds, originally created by analogical and symbolic thought. Now these links were fixed. Huizinga observed that in the choosing of colours for clothing 'blue and green held symbolic significance and these meanings were so specific that they nearly rendered both colours unsuitable for regular clothing. Both were the colours of love: green symbolized the state of being in love, blue faithfulness'.[32] This is a kind of symbolism in which one thing 'stands for' another.

Van Eyck's 'Arnolfini Portrait' (1434) provides an example of this kind of conventional symbolism. The bride wears green, which stands for being in love; the groom is in blue, which stands for faithfulness. The whiteness of her cap stands for purity. Erwin Panofsky, a prime authority in the field of medieval iconography supplies us with the meaning of more of these 'symbols'. Between the couple's feet is a small dog – an image indicating loyalty. The mirror may refer to money. The oranges on the window sill may be emblems of purity and innocence before the Fall of Man in the Garden of Eden.[33]

These various aspects of the image are signs of entities. They are indicators rather than symbols. Quine, it seems, had a view of symbolization and the metaphor that was constructed in a way that was like the medieval, which led to a conceptualization of symbol as more nearly resembling a sign.

Quine talked of signs as if they were symbols. He uses the word 'horse' to exemplify a symbol[34] whereas for Saussure it is a sign. This conception of symbol as sign implies a fixity, a singular meaning towards which the symbol/sign 'points'. It is emblematic of a world view in which freedom of thought is curtailed and meaning is pre-ordained. The creation of symbol, on the other hand, is a manifestation of freedom. Whereas 'horse' as a sign has only one meaning, we can use the word as a symbol in any way we like – as an image of strength, for example, or a particular kind of play, in 'horsing around'.

As Aristotle pointed out, metaphor, at the highest level, is not learnt but created anew.

> But the greatest thing by far is to be a master of metaphor. It is the one thing that cannot be learnt from others; and it is also a sign of genius, since a good metaphor implies an intuitive perception of the similarity in dissimilars.[35]

Quine's approach is odd. He is credited with having one of the finest philosophical minds of the twentieth century, yet it seems constrained as if held within limiting boundaries. This constriction differs from that imposed by the doctrines of the Middle Ages. Instead, it seems, it was the doctrines of logical positivism (of which Quine was an important proponent) that imposed the shackles. In this system of thought, 'truth' is to be discovered within narrow confines, dictated by the criterion of 'verifiability'.[36] Such phenomena as feeling and imagination, which cannot be observed and verified were discarded as 'nonsense'. The influence of positivism upon the academic world during the twentieth century was such that the subject of metaphor was largely excluded from philosophical discourse.[37]

Quine used metaphor and he used it well. Yet however sympathetic he might have been to its appearance in 'ordinary' speech, he found himself in the ambivalent situation of Plato, as he expressed himself in 'The Republic'. Plato was antipathetic to poetry, of which, as Northrop Frye points out, metaphor is the basis.[38] Nevertheless, at an important symposium on the subject of metaphor, Quine spoke as if released from positivist bondage. He was now 70 years of age. To start with, he noted the significance of metaphor in scientific invention.[39] Many famous examples exist. They have a strong analogical structure. They include Harvey's comparison between the heart and a pump; Rutherford's between an atom and the solar system; Kekule's between the formula of benzene and a ring of snakes; and recently Edelman's view of the immune system as an analogue of brain-mind function. Notable among the great scientists who explicitly acknowledge imagery of an analogical kind in the origin of their theories are James Clerk Maxwell and Michael Faraday. Maxwell wrote that metaphors are not only 'legitimate products of science, but capable of generating science in return'.[40]

Quine concluded that the 'crux of metaphor is creative extension through analogy' and that it 'governs both the growth of language and our acquisition of it'. His final sentence, however, displays his ambivalence: 'The neatly worked inner stretches of science are an open space in the tropical jungle, created by clearing tropes away'.[41] The remark is ambiguous. Is he saying that the basic reality is the analogical 'jungle' and that 'the neatly worked inner stretches of science' is a secondary ability, neat, narrow and lacking the fullness of life? Or, on the other hand, is he arguing that a higher form of consciousness, of which science is emblematic, is a state towards humanity strives by overthrowing – 'clearing away,' – more 'primitive' forms of psychic life?

Quine does not extend the role of analogy/metaphor in human affairs to include what I argue is its most important function, that is, to 'picture' that which cannot be seen and so to say what otherwise cannot be said. It is the 'visibility of discourse', making possible the representation of states of feeling and imagination. In this way, 'shape' and substance are given to an otherwise amorphous and fleeting 'reality'. This kind of 'reality' is at the heart of those relationships that are unique to the human primate and are, in my view, central to the creation of culture. The functions of culture, which the anthropologist Alfred Kroeber called 'super-organic',[42] gave mankind its evolutionary advantage and is its unique and identifying feature.

Cross-modal matching

The notion of 'shape' in the creation of analogy gives emphasis to the role of visualization, suggesting that analogy is a figure confined to one sensory modality. But this is not so. Expressions coming from different forms of sensory input, notably sound, can also be conceived as having a shape. Saussure, as remarked in the previous section, considered a 'sound-image' the fundamental communicative unit. Implicit in this viewpoint is the concept of cross-modal matching, which is an essential element of the analogical process.

Roman Jakobson (1896–1982), the Russian linguist, was influenced by Saussure and became particularly interested in the sound of the voice as a communicative vehicle. He tells a story about the use of what he calls 'sound shape' to convey feeling.

An actor of the Moscow Theatre auditioning before the famous director Stanislavski, was instructed to make forty different messages of the words 'this evening' (in Russian) by 'diversifying its expressive tint'.[43] A list of forty emotional situations was created and then the actor devised a particular way of speaking these words that would communicate the nature of the situation. The audience had to recognize the situation 'only from the sound shape of the same two words'. Jacobson, who had fled to America from the Nazis in 1941, asked the actor to repeat the experiment in their new situation in the United States. Some 50 emotional situations were described and 50 different ways the actor said 'this evening' were recorded on tape. Jakobson said that most of the messages could be correctly linked by the audience to an emotional situation.

Jakobson found that different 'sound-shapes' were analogues of particular emotional states. In this account of analogy, I am taking all sensory imprints on the brain that produce conscious awareness as having a particular 'shape', whatever their origin. This idea resembles Damasio's remarks that:

> A spectacular consequence of the brain's incessant and dynamic mapping is the mind. The mapped patterns constitute what we, conscious creatures, have come to know as sights, sounds, touches, smells, tastes, pains, pleasures, and the like – in brief images.[44]

A similarity between the electrical patterns, or maps, evoked in neural circuits leads, it would seem, to 'cross-modal matching', in which a correspondence is found between experiences in different senses. Using the criterion of shape, these correspondences are analogical. William James pointed out that:

> All sorts of analogues obtain between the spheres of sensibility. Why are 'sweet' and 'soft' used so synonymously in most languages? And why are both these adjectives applied to objects of so many sensible kinds. Rough sounds, heavy smells, hard lights, cold colours, are other examples.[45]

The basis of such analogies, as James implies, are mysterious. They presumably depend upon the forms of patterning evoked in neural tissue by the various stimuli. He does, however, imply a solution. He suggests sounds, such as the sound of a word, have, as their counterpart in the brain, notional shapes into which they fit like a mould. He wrote:

> Suppose we try to recall a forgotten name. The state of our consciousness is peculiar. There is a gap therein; but no mere gap. It is a gap that is intensely active. . . . If wrong names are proposed to us, this singularly definite gap acts immediately to negate them. They do not fit its mould. And the gap of one word does not feel like the gap of another.[46]
>
> . . . The rhythm of a lost word may be there without a sound to clothe with it.[47]

The Jamesian image of 'mould' can be translated into the modern idiom by exchanging it for 'network' or 'pattern'. A stimulus evokes a particular network of neurocircuitry, which is manifest in patterns of electrical activity. All stimuli, whatever their sensory origins, are transmuted into this common language in the brain. As such, these patterns can be matched. Matching involves a comparison between patterns, or maps, of the present event with records of maps of previous events, a process for which the hippocampus is necessary. Memory, as noted earlier in the chapter, is pattern recognition.

The concept of pattern recognition is central to Gerald Edelman's theory of the origins of mind, which, most importantly, involves the centrality of metaphor. The way he supposes it works is, in a sense, analogical, that is, it is not on or off, binary, as in a digital system. He writes:

> This process is *not* precise, as is logic and mathematics. Instead, it trades off specificity and precision, if necessary, to increase its range. It is likely, for example, that early human thought proceeded by metaphor, which, even with the late acquisition of precise means such as logic and mathematical thought, continues to be a major source of imagination and creativity in adult life.[48]

The feeling that comes with analogical matching is characteristically one of pleasure. At times this can be intense, as in the legendary effect on Archimedes upon discovering the principle of flotation. This realization is said to have come to him while having a bath, causing him to cry 'Eureka' and, forgetting his clothes, to run naked and excitedly through the streets of Syracuse.

A more usual effect of analogical matching is like that of harmony in which different notes combine to create a pleasing chord. In a speculative way, we may conceive the way in which analogical matching 'works' in terms of the ways in which the different electrical patterns in the brain, which are evoked by different tones, combine, as both similar and dissimilar, to produce the feeling of pleasure.

Analogical comparisons come easily to children. For example, in one of our studies, children were asked why people whisper. One little girl aged 3 said it was to sound like the grass rustling.[49] Cross-modal matching is evident almost as soon as the child begins to talk.

Cross-modal matching and synaesthesia

It needs to be said that cross-modal matching is not synaesthesia, in which images from one sensory modality inter-penetrate a perception in another sensory modality. For example, if a little boy says that certain men have 'dirty voices' he does not see dirt, feel dirt on his skin, or taste it. He is talking analogically. In an entertaining book on metaphor, James Geary cites the account of Daniel Tammet, who is both a synaesthete and a savant and who 'experiences individual numbers up to 10,000 as having specific colours, shapes, movements and even emotional tones'.[50]

Ramachandran and his colleagues point out that

> the cortical colour area in the brain and the area representing the visual appearance of Hindu/Arabic numbers and letters (graphemes) happen to be right next to each other in the fusiform gyrus. Given that grapheme-colour synaesthesia is the commonest form, we suggested that the phenomenon is caused by an abnormal cross activation between these two areas.[51]

This may come about by a gene mutation or by acquisition. It is sometimes a feature of temporal lobe epilepsy, perhaps by disturbance of the 'hippocampal comparator' and produced by drugs such as LSD and occasionally by high doses of marijuana.

In the early part of the twentieth century the concept of an almost synaesthetic equivalence between elements of music and those of the visual world became something of a vogue. Wassily Kandinski (1866–1944) was most prominent in this quest, aiming to create paintings which would evoke the experience of music. He may have been a true synaesthete.[52] On listening to Wagner, he said: 'I saw all my colours in spirit, before my eyes. Wild almost crazy lines, were sketched in front of me.'[53] Roy de Maistre explored the opposite equivalence, 'translating' a Haydn trio into coloured patterning represented in a large scroll.[54]

Shakespeare: the fluidity and multiplicity of analogue/metaphor

Whereas in the logical system the meaning is fixed and discrete, in analogical processing it is the opposite. Logic follows the mode of succession, in which the elements of language have specific meanings that appear one after the other. Metaphor involves a system in which a word may have several meanings at the same time. Consider, for example the opening lines of Shakespeare's Sonnet 86.

Was it the proud full sail of his great verse
Bound for the prize of all too precious you . . .

Using the grandeur and grace of a ship in full sail, Shakespeare intimates an essential quality of a rival's verse, the sounds of which presumably had a shape, a melodic 'contour', resembling the sight of a great vessel, say a galleon, asway on the high seas. Ben Jonson's famous remark about Christopher Marlowe's 'mighty line' seems to be resonant with Shakespeare's image.

Marlowe and Shakespeare were the same age, but at the time of his death, by stabbing at the age of 29, Marlowe was already regarded as a great dramatist and poet, while Shakespeare's reputation was merely on the rise. Jonathan Bate [55] believes that an artistic competition with Marlowe drove Shakespeare to greater heights. A. L. Rowse, a noted and combative Shakespearean scholar, in a 1963 publication, claimed to have discovered that Marlowe was indeed the mysterious Rival Poet.[56] However, more recent opinion tends to favour George Chapman, of Chapman's Homer fame, whose case as the Rival Poet had been argued a century ago by Arthur Acheson.[57]

The image of the ship, however, has not a single meaning. The 'proud full sail' evokes the image of a privateer, like Sir Francis Drake, intent upon a 'prize' to be looted from a foreign ship.

Beyond such specific 'meanings', the image may convey notions of power, dominance, even arrogance. The symbol contains multiple 'meanings', all expressed at the same time.

Shakespeare was a master in using language in this way. At times he develops a multiplicity of meaning not only in the use of a single image, but through the creation of a series of metaphors, each of which has the potential for multiplicity and each of which is a metaphor of the others. In this way, the poem forms a coherent whole, a unity of feeling, becoming itself a symbol, larger than its constituent elements and having a fluid form capable of expansion in terms of meaning. An example is Sonnet 73.

This poem was probably written in the late 1590s[58] although dating is debated.[59] The 154 Sonnets appear to be arranged chronologically but there is no evidence about their actual chronology. Shakespeare seems to have had no hand in their ordering. It was presumably made by the publisher after Shakespeare's death. Nevertheless, this series is grouped in a way that gives the collection a sense of coherence. Their story is essentially one of a love triangle, between Shakespeare, a beautiful boy and the Dark Lady. The first poems display the poet's entrancement by the boy's beauty and his love for him, which may not have been physical. The relationship with the Dark Lady is of a different kind, involving the expression of a passionate sexuality. After a while it becomes evident that she has also established a sexual liaison with the youth. Shakespeare senses himself as displaced and betrayed, an outcome resonant with the main theme of the Rival Poet sonnet. By the late 1590s Shakespeare's relationship with the Dark Lady seems to be in deep trouble.

The background to Sonnet 73, also includes a catastrophic event in Shakespeare's life. His only son Hamnet died in 1596. He was 11 years old. This tragedy, Michael Wood believes brought about a change in Shakespeare's writing. The style and imagery darkened and became more profound.[60] Sonnet 73 conveys a mood of melancholy and of the sense of the transience of life.

> That time of year thou mayst in me behold
> When yellow leaves, or none, or few, do hang
> Upon those boughs which shake against the cold,
> Bare ruin'd choirs, where late the sweet birds sang.
> In me thou see'st the twilight of such day
> As after sunset fadeth in the west;
>
> Which by and by black night doth take away,
> Death's second self, that seals up all in rest.
> In me thou see'st the glowing of such fire
> That on the ashes of his youth doth lie,
> As the death-bed whereon it must expire,
> Consum'd with that which it was nourish'd by.
> This thou perceiv'st, which makes thy love more strong
> To love that well which though must leave ere long

Although it is sometimes supposed that the poem is addressed to the beautiful youth, it does not seem necessary to suppose that all the sonnets have a specific addressee. Some may have been analogous to an inner conversation, in which the 'you' is an aspect of oneself, addressed as the other. This mode of expression is a feature of the Shakespearean voice. In the soliloquies, 'To be, or not to be . . .' for example, the tone is not declamatory, addressed to the audience alone. It is also addressed to himself, both inner and outer at the same time. Barbara Everett is struck by this characteristic: 'None of his predecessors speak as Shakespeare does, like a voice in the next room – even a voice of the reader's mind – an "inward voice".'[61]

The poem illustrates the way in which specific analogues and discrete metaphors can be orchestrated so as to create a larger analogue/metaphor and a more extensive picture of a certain reality.

Each of the three quatrains depicts an image of the imminence of death – autumn, evening, embers. Each of these is a metaphor of the others. The second, curiously, is an image Aristotle used in his classic definition of metaphor, which, as he said, is created by a 'transference' that

> consists in giving the thing a name that belongs to something else. [Metaphor] from analogy is possible whenever there are four terms so related that the second (B) is to the first (A), as the fourth (D), to the third (C), for one may then metaphorically put D in lieu of B, and B in lieu of D . . . As old age (D) is to life (C), so is evening (B) to day (A).[62]

Most critical attention has focused on the first quatrain, in particular the 'bare ruined choirs', as an analogue of autumnal boughs. There are layers to this image, which brings to mind not only the wooden stalls of church choirs but also the desolate ruins of abbeys, monasteries and priories left abandoned in the English countryside after Henry VIII laid them waste.[63] And their gaunt outlines might resemble the face of ageing 'that thou mayst in me behold'. Furthermore, since 'choirs' are found in a holy place, the work evokes, at least faintly, a sense of the sacred.

Layering is increased by what follows 'the ruined choirs', 'where late the sweet birds sang'. The adjective 'sweet' suggests a particular song, perhaps a love song. The fusion of two ideas, of lovers and birds, implied in the image resembles the structure of dream in which such condensations occur. The depth and allusive layering of the quatrain is further enhanced by 'where late'. Does this refer to the loss of love?

In the two previous lines, a series of metaphors gather to convey not only a sense of ageing but also a mood. The leaves are yellow (enfeebled, losing life) and few (an image of solitude and loneliness). The boughs shake (infirm) against the cold, the desolation.

The whole sonnet now becomes, a connected network, of imagery, allusions, analogues and metaphors, creating a much larger metaphor used to convey the sense and feeling of a life coming to a close. In this way, it shows, in miniature form, the structure of culture as Lèvi-Strauss understood it. His studies led him to conceive culture, in its original form, as a unified organization made coherent by a 'vast system of correspondences'.[64] Reversing the equation, we can say that culture has the shape of a poem.

The unifying image is the face, pointed to in each quatrain, first with 'thou mayst in me behold'. The face in the poem is an analogue we can only imagine. It is painted for us by metaphors. In real life, however, the face functions as an actual analogue, showing the contours of a personal reality. This is the most fundamental of human expressions of 'meaning' and personal 'truth'.

Personal truth and meaning

'Truth' has three main meanings, according to the Oxford English Dictionary. Two are tautologies – 'the quality of being true' and 'something that is true'. The third involves a matching process. It is 'conformity with fact, agreement with reality'. A particular statement of event is matched against a pre-existing representation, the outcome of which is a verdict on truth. This third meaning implies a world in which 'truth' is already known, made up of a series of facts to which only replicas of these facts can be considered 'true'. It is a constricted and limited world somewhat like Mâle's description of medieval thought.

What would be the outcome where no pre-existing representation is available? No 'reality' can be given to a particular experience, statement, or event. This is the situation of an infant who comes into the world with no facts and no known reality. In this case, 'meaning' is supplied by a resemblance.

The baby looks into her mother's face, and finds there a 'meaning' for her feeling at that moment. This face and this voice are re-representations of the baby's experience. As D. W. Winnicott put it: 'The mother is looking at the baby and *what she looks like is related* to what she sees there.'[65] Her face is an analogue of the baby's state.

The infant might say, if she had the words: 'This is me I'm seeing, this is my "truth".'

The solution to the baby's dilemma, of finding oneself in a meaningless world, to speak of the baby in an adultomorphic way, is to discover in the surrounding world some 'shape' that resembles her immediate feeling, which pictures it and shows her what her experience is. The mother's face is the first analogue in the baby's life. I believe that the repeated experience of such analogical responsiveness is necessary to the facilitation and emergence of analogical thought, which leads to the symbolic capacity.

This concept of infantile truth is not dissimilar to scientific truth. The scientist is faced with a confusing mass of data. The scientific aim is to find a coherence in these disconnected observations that will make sense of them and give the whole field a 'meaning'. Coherence is found in the discovery of a pattern that unifies the data. This discovery has an aesthetic quality and is accompanied by pleasure, even excitement. Such a response is also the infant's in the game of the proto-conversation that the mother and infant play in the first weeks and months of life. In this face-to-face interplay the mother displays in her face and voice a pattern of responding that shows her baby a resemblance of who the baby is.

This idea, then, is that 'truth' or 'meaning' can be created through a resemblance, not to something that is previously known, but to the thing itself, which has no known meaning. This resemblance is not a replica but a shaping of the data in the form of a pattern. The shaping has the effect of a picture. This picture is not a truth in any absolute way. The pattern, hypothesis, or theory must be tested. If it cannot be disproved it becomes a reality, based on the criterion of probability.

The process of creating resemblances extends not only scientific knowledge but also personal reality. This idea has important implications for psychotherapeutic practice. The 'data' that the patient brings to the therapeutic conversation must be matched by resemblances that are derived from what is presented rather than a theoretical system, although the two may coincide. This resemblance, or analogical picture, is not 'correct' in terms of the theory but by 'what happens next'.[66] These observations lead to the idea that analogical representation can establish not only the 'truth' of a certain reality, but also extend a reality that currently exists.

Notes

1 Spurgeon, C. (1935, p. 6).
2 Spurgeon, C. (1935, p. 7).
3 *Oxford English Dictionary: Compact Edition* (1971).

4 Dent, N. J. H. (2005, p. 543).
5 Hofstadter, D. (2001).
6 Meares, R. (1977, 1993, 2005).
7 Spurgeon, C. (1935, p. 6).
8 Gentner and Jeziorski (1993, p. 449).
9 O'Keefe and Nadel (1978).
10 O'Keefe and Dostrovsky (1971).
11 Maguire *et al.* (1997).
12 Janzen and van Turennout (2004).
13 Giocomo, Moser and Moser (2011).
14 Meares (2000, pp. 141–145).
15 Gentner, D. (1983).
16 McArthur, T. (1992).
17 Gentner, D. (1983, p. 156).
18 Livio, M. (2002).
19 Darwin, C. (1859, p. 467).
20 *Antony and Cleopatra*, vii. 89–90. Arden edition.
21 Saussure, F. (1970, p. 45).
22 Saussure, F. (1970, p. 44).
23 Lakoff and Johnson (1980, p. 35).
24 Gruber and Vonèche (1977, p. 485).
25 *Oxford English Dictionary: Compact Edition* (1971).
26 Quine, W. V. (2004, p. 896).
27 Huizinga, J. (1996, pp. 235–236).
28 Huizinga, J. (1996, p. 235).
29 Huizinga, J. (1996, p. 382).
30 Huizinga, J. (1996, p. 382).
31 Mâle, E. (1961, p. 1).
32 Huizinga, J. (1996, p. 326).
33 Panofsky, 1953, pp. 202–203).
34 Quine, W. V. (2004, p. 896).
35 Aristotle (1941, p. 22).
36 Ayer, A. J. (1936).
37 Cohen, T. (1979).
38 Frye, N. (1971 p. 91).
39 Quine (1979, p. 159).
40 Maxwell (1890, p. 227, cited by Hoffman).
41 Quine, W. V. (1979, p. 160).
42 Kroeber, A. L. (1917).
43 Jakobson, R. (1960b, p. 354).
44 Damasio, A. R. (2012, p. 70).
45 James. W. (1890, vol. I, p. 209).
46 James. W. (1890, vol. II, p. 251).
47 James. W. (1890, vol. II, p. 252).
48 Edelman, G. (2006, p. 58).
49 Meares and Orlay (1988).
50 Geary, J. (2012, p. 79).
51 Ramachandran and Gregory (2004, p. 899).
52 Ione and Tyler (2003).
53 Kandinski, W. (1913).
54 Art Gallery of New South Wales.
55 Bate, J. (1998).
56 Rowse, A. L. (1963).

57 Acheson, A. (1903).
58 Wood, M. (2005, p. 191).
59 Rowse, A. L. (1963).
60 Wood, M. (2005, p. 180).
61 Everett, B. (2008).
62 Aristotle (1941, p. 21).
63 Empson, W. (1973, p. 21).
64 Lévi-Strauss, C. (1966, p. 40).
65 Winnicott, D. W. (1974, p. 131).
66 Meares, R. (2001).

4

BRAIN BASES OF SELF

The capacity to create analogues comes out of our ability, shared with other animals, to recognize patterns. We have, however, an ability beyond other creatures. Human beings can form 'pictures', which re-present those patterns. We can create a patterned form of interplay in which feeling-toned personal states are re-pictured in a certain kind of conversation. This form of interplay is seen in this book as the necessary forerunner to the experience of self.

Self must arise from the activity of the brain. This being so, a conversational pattern involving analogical representation of feeling states must activate, in some ways, brain systems essential to the experience of self. This chapter gives consideration to this idea.

The proto-conversation, as the first form in human life of this kind of interpersonal interplay, is an activity that presumably resembles the patterning of already existing systems neurocircuitry necessary to earlier forms of consciousness, as if they were in 'fit' with the characteristic operative forms of the circuitry. It is supposed that such resemblance allows these systems to be used in a new and extended way, in the manner of neuroplasticity. This suggests that self is a potential state. The brain has the capability to produce this kind of consciousness but only if the appropriate social environment is provided. This notion was been most famously espoused by Lev Vygotsky (1896–1934), the brilliant Russian psychologist who died very young from tuberculosis. He maintained that the higher mental functions – abstract thought, certain kinds of memory and attention, volition and so forth – have a social origin. A 'biogenetic' strand of development can only take these functions to a certain point. The interwoven theme of 'sociogenesis' is required to achieve their normal maturation. The brain, in this condition, is functioning in a way that shows greater connectedness and co-ordination between its elements than at the earlier level.

Vygotsky's theory depends upon the difficult and somewhat mysterious concept of 'internalization'. Drawing on the ideas of Pierre Janet,[1] he puts forward the view that the first form of a higher mental function is found in the outer world where it appears as an activity conducted between two people. He gives an example of the social roots of voluntary attention:

> In the early stages of development the complex psychological function was *shared between two persons*: the adult *triggered* the psychological process by naming the object or by pointing to it; the child *responded* to this signal and picked out the named object either by fixing it with his eye or by holding it with his hand. In the subsequent stages of development this socially organized process becomes reorganized. The child himself learns to speak. He can now name the object *himself*, and by naming the object himself he distinguished it from the rest of the environment, and thus directs his attention to it. The function which hitherto was shared between two people now becomes a method of *internal organization of the psychological process*. From an external, socially organized attention develops the *child's voluntary attention*, which in this stage is an internal, self-regulating process.[2]

A child's pointing becomes a mind 'pointing'. Vygotsky summarized the progression as follows:

> Any function in the child's cultural development appears twice, or on two planes. First it appears on the social plane, and then on the psychological plane. First it appears between people as an interpsychological category, and then within the child as an intrapsychological category. This is equally true with regard to voluntary attention, logical memory, the formation of concepts, and the development of volition.[3]

The activity on the 'social plane', he was saying, mirrors the form of the 'intrapsychological category'. Self is made of a coherence of such categories. I am suggesting that it has its social origins in a relationship of analogical connectedness, a state that is central to the integration of psychic life.

Vygotsky called the gap between the psychological level that can be reached by what is genetically given and the level attained with the aid of appropriate social facilitation the 'zone of proximal development (ZPD)'.[4] He defined level as the developmental age of a child as indicated by performance on a particular task or test. The zone of proximal development is the difference between the level the child achieves alone compared with level displayed when the task is carried out in collaboration with others. In the latter situation, for example, a child with a chronological age of 8 may have an advanced developmental age, say eleven.

The wording of Vygotsky's definition of the ZPD might suggest that the collaboration with others is instructional, dependent upon a unidirectional relationship with the collaborator. This is not what he meant. He thought that the relationship should be bi-directional, an asymmetric 'co-operation' with others.[5] Without this form of relatedness, he believed, the child's development has 'an extremely limited, compressed, and impoverished nature'.[6]

The kind of collaboration Vygotsky had in mind is illustrated by an experiment described by Vygotsky's colleague, Alexander Luria. The experiment was set up as a game. In this game

> a child who can hardly memorize five or six words of the series read out to him is asked to commit them to memory with the aid of pictures laid out on the table . . . Not one of the pictures actually reproduces the word in question, and the task can be performed only if the child connects in one structure the word in question with one of the pictures. It is obvious that for such an experiment it is essential somehow to evidence one's power of association in order to direct associative ideas every time in a definitely fixed direction. We note that such mastering of the ideas of association can be acquired, but by no means by all the children.[7]
>
> We had occasion to observe how a child in establishing and utilizing such connections could, by looking at the cards, reproduce 25–30 and more words after one reading, while his natural memory could fix five or six at the most. Moreover, the connecting links were established with extraordinary subtlety. Thus, in order to remember the word 'spade' the child chose a picture of chickens picking up grains 'because they picked it just as the spade digs the earth'; for the word 'theatre' the child chose the picture of a crab on the seashore 'because the crab looks at the pebbles in the sea, and they are just as pretty as a theatre', etc.[8]

This child used the images produced by the experimenter to make an association in a way that was analogical/metaphoric. The word and the image had a 'structural connection'.[9] By these means, the child moves to a higher level of memory function. The procedure resembles the 'art of memory' used by the ancients in their practice of rhetoric.

A history of 'The Art of Memory' is given by Frances Yates in her wonderful book with that title. In brief, someone wishing to deliver a speech without the benefit of notes is aided by a memorial process, in which the elements of the speech are likened to images. These images are found in a familiar house, room, street, or landscape, which can be easily recovered in memory. They are made to become analogues or metaphors of the elements of the speech. During the speech, the orator is at the same time making an imaginary tour of the place in which the various analogues appear in the order of the orator's argument. Yates quotes Cicero's description of the process:

> He inferred that persons desiring to train this faculty (of memory) must select places and form mental images of the things they wish to remember and store those images in the places, so that the order of the places will preserve the order of the things, and the images of the things will denote the things themselves, and we shall employ the places and images respectively as a wax writing-tablet and the letters written on it.[10]

The same scene – the house or whatever place is chosen – can be used for different speeches in which case the various features and objects of which the scene consists become analogues or metaphors of different speech elements.

The fact that a single object can serve as the basis of multiple representations illustrates the fluidity and complexity of symbolic representation. A sign, in contrast, is indicative only of something singular.

The ancients were enabled by their 'art of memory' to achieve prodigious memorial feats beyond the memory capacity that would normally be expected of the brain. Something extra was added, which Luria called 'cultural memorizing'. He found that

> The use of pictures and the 'cultural' memorizing when applied to schoolboys of 10 to 12 gives a 60 per cent increase in the productivity of their memory as compared to the ordinary memory of a 'natural' kind; the same method on mentally defective schoolboys produced no effect whatsoever in improving their memory.[11]

Luria's use of the term 'cultural memorizing' is intriguing. He implies that symbolism and culture are inextricably linked, an idea that will be developed in later chapters.

The zone of proximal development, doubling and symbolization

The child in Luria's experiment was using imagination to find analogues of the images that had been given to her. In the way that Vygotsky used this term, the child was playing. He wrote that in 'distinguishing a child's play from other forms of activity we conclude that in play a child creates an imaginary situation'.[12] 'Play', he remarked, 'creates a zone of proximal development. In play a child . . . always behaves above his average age. . . . The child moves forward essentially through play activity.'[13]

The collaboration with another person that creates the maturational shift is often understood as one in which the other provides a 'scaffolding' for the child's behaviour. This is sometimes interpreted as quasi-instructional. Vygotsky, while not discounting the effect of instruction, explained that his conception referred to something beyond and different to instruction. 'Though the play-development relationship can be compared to the instruction-development relationship, play provides a much wider background for changes in needs and consciousness.'[14]

The activity of play, as Vygotsky defined it, is central to the 'doubling', which he saw as the main characteristic of human consciousness. Its origin, he believed, is social, brought about by an interplay between the child and another person, which is internalized. He did not study mother-infant interaction at the level of the proto-conversation, but depended on observations of older children. Consequently he did not formulate the idea that the first form of the 'doubling' of consciousness is the proto-conversation. Instead, he exemplified the doubling phenomenon by referring to activities that occur later in development. They include imaginary play and imitation.

The imaginary play of the child of 3 illustrates a growth in the development of 'doubling' – 'a condition is reached in which the child begins to act independently of what he sees'.[15] This separation is evident in the scene of symbolic play. In this game, the child chooses an object and calls it something else. Vygotsky uses the example of a stick for a horse. Two things are now distinguished – the real object and the imaginary object. However, at this stage 'the child cannot as yet detach thought from object'.[16] The 3-year-old's behaviour is 'transitional'[17] using the term of D. W. Winnicott.[18] It is the first manifestation of freedom from situational constraints.

Vygotsky points out that the choice of object representing the real object cannot be entirely arbitrary – 'a postcard cannot be a horse for the child'.[19] He does not suggest a determining factor. It is the shape of the representing object. The imaginary object must share some qualities of that which it represents. It must have some analogical resemblance to it.

A hierarchy of consciousness

The implication of the remarks that opened this chapter is that the 'doubling' of the proto-conversational game and the symbolization that grows out it has its basis in brain systems used for the creation of earlier forms of consciousness. This idea leads a conception of mind, or self, composed of a notional hierarchy, in which the upper tiers are given to us only as tendencies towards, or propensities for, their emergence. Their realization depends upon a suitable environmental provision.

Hughlings Jackson described such a hierarchy, a system made of a co-ordinated series of layerings of different forms of consciousness decreed by evolutionary history.[20] This system is not a fixed entity but a process in which self is constantly created from moment to moment.[21] In this creation all the layers or tiers of older mental function are represented and woven together to produce an outcome experienced as a 'stream', to use the Jamesian image. The poet Seamus Heaney called it 'the music of what happens'.[22]

The notion of layering of consciousness is, of course, an abstraction since a state of mind is the product of various distinguishable sub-systems of the brain working together. Nevertheless, the abstraction gives us a way of thinking and talking about a complex subject. Jackson's concept is useful since it is derived from functional studies. It is complementary to Paul MacLean's notion of the 'triune brain'.[23] A consideration of the development of emotional life provides a more discriminated picture, of a seven tiered system, composed of states of increasing complexity and unification (see Chapter 6). However, the simplicity of the Jacksonian model makes it more suitable for heuristic purposes and for a consideration of higher order consciousness, the top level of the Jacksonian hierarchy.

Wolf Singer: self-similar iteration

Wolf Singer is one of the main neuroscientists whose quest is for the basis of human consciousness. He began with the idea that a cardinal characteristic of consciousness is coherence. His important contribution has been made against a growing background of data showing that every perception, which we sense as unified, is made by the binding together of the activity of multiple different processing streams in different parts of the brain. Every detail of the percept has a separate stream. Its colour, its depth, its edging, its movement and so forth, each contribute in a specific way. The problem neuroscience confronts is the mystery of how these disparate systems can be co-ordinated so as to produce a unified experience. It has been called the 'binding problem'.

The approach to the problem involves consideration of the issue at a number of scales and levels. At the most fundamental level, the neuronal, Wolf Singer has proposed, based on his own evidence, that a particular neuronal assembly is created among the billions that are possible, by a synchronous firing of those processing elements relevant to the stimulus. This synchronicity is associated with high frequency electrical pulsing in the gamma band (about 40 Hz). Only patterns reaching a certain level of organization, he suggested, reach consciousness.[24]

In a major paper, in which he summarizes the work of his scientific group, Singer points out that although his data provides an explanation for what he calls 'phenomenal awareness', it does not provide a basis sufficient to explain the origins of 'self', a state, as he remarked, that involves a sense 'immaterial entities'[25] working within us and the capacity for 'inner-eye function'.[26]

Singer contends that the forms of higher order consciousness 'cannot solely be accounted for by the performance of individual brains, but require for their development interaction among brains'.[27] This is an intuition of fundamental importance. Of the many different approaches to the problem of human consciousness, of which the most compelling are, perhaps, neurophysiological, very few consider the matter in a social context. Mind is seen as the product of a particular brain-state.

A brain-state is an abstraction. The living brain is not an isolated mechanism but part of a larger system involving a constant dynamic interplay between the brain and the environment. The form of the interplay determines the brain-state. This is the somewhat revolutionary proposal of Singer, who concludes the summary of his argument in the following way: 'It is concluded that phenomenal awareness is amenable to neurobiological reductionism; but it is also proposed that self-consciousness requires a different explanatory approach because it emerges from the "dialogue between different brains".'[28] A crucial question now arises: What is the nature of this dialogue? Singer writes: 'My proposal is that the concept of the 'self' with all its subjective mental attributes, emerges from . . . dialogues among human beings, above all from the early interactions between caregivers and babies.'[29]The character of this interaction might be inferred from his concluding remarks: 'Phenomenal awareness', which can be seen as a second tier in a three tiered model of consciousness, 'emerges from an iteration of self-similar cognitive operations'.[30]

Following the notion that biological patters tend to repeat themselves, an idea underpinning the work of such neuroscientists as C. S. Sherrington and Gerald

Edelman, it is not unreasonable to suppose that the third layer of consciousness arises in the same way as the second, by the iterations of self-similar representations, that is, by analogues of feeling-toned mental states as in the proto-conversation. In this case, at the highest level of development and of evolution, the iteration is at first extra-corporeal, as in the proto-conversation. It is internalized during maturation. This is consistent with the proposal that the precursor to the Jamesian duplex self has the double first appearing in the outer world.

Edelman and the role of re-entry

For many years, Gerald Edelman has been building an impressive and interesting theory of the emergence of consciousness, which parallels that of Singer. Although approaching the subject in a very different way, he arrives at a model that is not unlike Singer's in that re-entry and synchronization are key features in both conceptions.

Using the words of the French art historian Henri Focillon (1881–1948), Edelman presents the idea that is central to his theory.[31] Focillon wrote: 'The chief characteristic of mind is to be constantly describing itself.'[32] These descriptions, re-descriptions and re-re-descriptions are made, in the Edelman conception, by means of the reverberating neuronal loops underpinning the systems of re-entry. They pass back and forward between the thalamus and the cortex, and also, particularly later in evolution, between areas of the neocortex.

The reverberatory interplay of re-entry has a remarkable feature. The number of fibres returning from the cortex to the thalamus is greater than the number going to it. We infer that the re-presentation returns enlarged. What is being pictured in the higher order re-description is not a copy but an abstraction of essential features.[33]

Patterns are repeated, each repetition being an analogue of the previous pattern, a basic process Edelman calls 'selectionism' (or pattern recognition)[34]. It can be seen as a reverberating system of analogical depiction.

Edelman's focus is upon the shift between a percept and a concept. This leads him to an explanation for the emergence of primary consciousness, which is equivalent to Singer's phenomenal awareness. He does not venture, as he admits, beyond this stage to consider the emergence of the peculiarly human consciousness, which he calls higher order. He does, however, suggest that it emerges as a consequence of language.[35] The use of words provides a new way for the mind to describe itself, in this way creating an extracorporeal system of re-entry. Edelman tells us, implicitly, that the form of this language is analogical.

Re-entry, he believes, depends upon a process of 'selectionism' or 'pattern recognition'. He writes:

> There are two main modes of thought–logic and selectionism (or pattern recognition). Both are powerful, but it is pattern recognition that can lead to creation, for example, in the choice of axioms in mathematics. . . .

> Because the brain can function by pattern recognition even prior to language, brain activity can yield what might be called 'pre-metaphorical' capabilities. The power of such analogical abilities, particularly when ultimately translated into language, rests in the associativity that results from the degeneracy of neural networks.[36]

The proto-conversation might have an effect similar to that proposed by Vygotsky for the role of the facilitating other person who provides 'scaffolding' for the zone of proximal development.

Synchrony and timing

A crucial aspect of Singer's account of 'self-similar iteration' is timing. In his thesis, 'binding' comes about through synchrony, a state depending upon 'internal dynamic co-ordination of spike-timing'.

The way in which its investigators speak of the proto-conversation resembles the language the neuroscientists talking of intracerebral reciprocity. For example, a pioneer in observing the features of the proto-conversation was T. Berry Brazelton. In the accounts of his studies the words 'rhythm' and 'synchrony' recur. So also does 'reciprocity', the essential element of 're-entry'. [37] In one study, for example, he and his colleagues studied the second by second interplay between mothers and their 3- month and 5-month term babies over a 3-minute period.[38] The dynamic structure of such a small and apparently simple observation is exceedingly complex. Each second was coded for affective involvement of both mother and child. 'Spectral and cross-spectral techniques were used to quantify periodicities in each member of the dyad and to estimate the synchrony or coherence of interactional rhythms between each infant and mother.'[39] An increase in coherence was shown in the 5-month-old babies compared with the 3-month-old babies. A comparison was also made between preterm and term babies, the latter showing the greater coherence.

Observations of a similar sort and using similar words to describe the kind of relatedness between mother and child come from the group of researchers who, all about the same time began to study mother-infant interaction. A pioneer in using microanalysis in the study of early mother-infant interaction was Daniel Stern. He used terms like 'rhythmic coupling', 'matching' and 'bidirectional co-ordination' in his influential accounts of this face-to-face play.[40] Beatrice Beebe found 'timing' and 'congruence' to be essential elements of the interplay.[41]

Trevarthen and Malloch have likened this patterning to a dance and to music.[42]

A conversation between two right brains

The formulations of both Singer and Edelman give support to the idea that 'self' arises in the context of an interpersonal situation in which a reciprocal interplay of self-similar or analogical, representation reflects a specific form of 'interaction among brains'.[43] A growing body of evidence, gathered by Allan Schore,[44] suggests that this 'interaction is between two right brains, involving particularly the orbitofrontal cortex.[45] The right hemisphere functions as if designed for the proto-conversation. Recognition of faces,[46] and especially the emotions they represent,[47] is largely a right-hemispherical process. So also is the sensing of prosody, that is, of the sound of the voice, its inflections, intonations,[48]and rhythm.[49]

The baby's right brain is particularly responsive to the mother's face. For example, babies of 4–9 months move their eyes more quickly to the mother's face than a stranger's face when the stimuli are presented in the left visual field, i.e. to the right hemisphere. In contrast, simple geometric shapes are discriminated equally well in either field.[50]

The interplay of the proto-conversation involves neurophysiological activation of a similar kind in both partners. For example, the emotional tonings of the voice are not only 'heard' right hemispherically but also created as a consequence of right brain activation.[51] It is only partially figurative to say that the proto-conversation represents an interplay between two right brains.[52]

In this interplay, activation of the orbitofrontal cortex (OFC) is prominent, at least in the case of the mother. It occurs when mothers view pictures of their babies.[53]The OFC, the part of the brain overlying the eye socket, switches on when a mother views her baby smiling at her as she plays with her baby.[54] Viewing her infant's distress evokes a different neural response. The baby's smile is likely to enhance activation in the medial OFC beyond that evoked by the image of the baby alone.[55] An interesting recent study supports the possibility of a reciprocity of brain activation between mother and baby during face-to-face interplay. The OFC was activated in the brains of mothers and babies when shown a video of the other. In the mother's case, the activation was right-sided.[56] Such observations lead to the hypothesis that analogical matching behaviour of the mother during the proto-conversation might evoke a mirrored neurophysiology with her baby and tend to stimulate activation and maturation of right-sided neurocircuitry involving the OFC.

The OFC is an important reward centre.[57] The mother's behaviour and that of her baby, in creating the to-and-fro interplay seems likely to be 'driven' by the rewarding effect of OFC activation, leading to the pleasure of their game.

Allan Schore cites evidence regarding maturation of the right hemisphere showing that it may be particularly vulnerable during the first years of life.[58] The right hemisphere is in a growth spurt during the first two years of life, a period of right brain dominance. Right hemisphere resources are the first to develop.[59]

This growth is not totally encoded in the genome, but is indelibly shaped by experiences with the environment. The neurobiological maturation of the emotion processing right hemisphere in the early critical period of the first two years of life is thus 'experience-dependent'. It is specifically the affect communicating and analogically representing interplay between mother and child involving prosody, facial expressions and rhythm that impact the experience-dependent maturation of prefrontal cortical-limbic circuits of the early developing right cortical hemisphere.[60]

Data are now beginning to accrue suggesting that failure of the protoconversation to be adequately established may lead to disturbances of the maturation specific parts of the brain, namely the OFC and the neighbouring ventral medial prefrontal cortex, which Damasio[61] has associated with the development of self. For example, Lyons and colleagues demonstrate that varying maternal behaviours in infancy produce 'significant differences in right but not left adult prefrontal volumes, with experience-dependent asymmetric variation most clearly expressed in ventral medial prefrontal cortex measured in vivo by magnetic resonance imaging'.[62]

Conclusion

The main gist of this chapter is that the iteration of self-similar neural processes, which Wolf Singer contends are necessary to the emergence of primary, or phenomenal, consciousness[63] are also those necessary to the development of higher order consciousness, or self. The precursor to this development is the iteration of self-similar processes of an interpersonal kind, in the protoconversation and subsequent more complex exchanges having the same fundamental form, a maturational trajectory predicted by Vygotskian theory. Such processes, I am supposing, contribute to the developing connectedness of that network believed to be the neural basis of self. This system, called the default mode network,[64] is active when the mind is apparently at rest, when the 'stream of consciousness' becomes salient.

Notes

1 van der Veer and Valsiner (1988).
2 Cited by Luria, A. R. (1973, p. 262).
3 Vygotsky, L. S. (1978, p. 163).
4 Vygotsky, L. S. (1978, p. 86).
5 van der Veer and Valsiner (1991, p. 317).
6 van der Veer and Valsiner (1991, p. 318).
7 Luria, A. R. (1994, p. 53).
8 Luria, A. R. (1994, p. 54).
9 Luria, A. R. (1994, p. 53).
10 Yates, F. (1966, p. 2).
11 Luria, A. R. (1994, p. 54).
12 Vygotsky, L. S. (1978, p. 93).
13 Vygotsky, L. S. (1978, pp. 102–103).
14 Vygotsky, L. S. (1978, pp. 102–103).
15 Vygotsky, L. S. (1978, p. 97).
16 Vygotsky, L. S. (1978, p. 97).
17 Vygotsky, L. S. (1978, p. 97).
18 Winnicott, D. W. (1974, pp. 1–30).
19 Vygotsky, L. S. (1978, p. 98).
20 Jackson, J. H. (1958, pp. 3–120).
21 Damasio, A. R. (1996, p. 240).
22 From Seamus Heaney 'Song' cited by Vendler, H. (1988).

23 MacLean, P. D. (1990).
24 Singer, W. (1999).
25 Singer, W. (2001, p. 125).
26 Singer, W. (2001, p. 124).
27 Singer, W. (2001, p. 125).
28 Singer, W. (2001, p. 123).
29 Singer, W. (2001, p. 125).
30 Singer, W. (2001, p. 142).
31 Edelman, G. (1992).
32 Edelman, G. (2004, p. 147).
33 Focillon, H. (1942, p. 52)
34 Edelman, G. (1992, p. 124).
35 Edelman, G. (2004, p. 147).
36 Edelman, G. (2004, p. 101).
37 Singer, W. (2001, p. 131).
38 Lester, Hoffmann and Brazelton (1985).
39 Stern, D. (1985, 2001).
40 Stern, D. (1985, 2001).
41 Beebe *et al.* (1985; 1988).
42 Trevarthen (2004); Malloch and Trevarthen (2009).
43 Singer, W. (2001, p. 125).
44 Schore, A. (1994, 2003a, 2003b).
45 Meares, Schore and Melkonian (2011).
46 Kim *et al.* (1999)
47 Iidaka *et al.* (2003); Tamietto *et al.* (2006); Harciarek and Heilman (2009).
48 Buchanan *et al.* (2000).
49 Riecker *et al.* (2002).
50 Rapp and Bachevalier (2008, p. 1046).
51 Ross and Monnot (2008).
52 Meares, Schore and Melkonian (2011).
53 Nitschke *et al.* (2004).
54 Noriuchi *et al.* (2008).
55 O'Doherty *et al.* (2003).
56 Minagawa-Kawai *et al.* (2009).
57 Rolls, E. (2002).
58 Schore, A. (1994, 2003a, 2003b).
59 Chiron *et al.* (1997); Decety and Chaminade (2003).
60 Schore, A. (2005).
61 Damasio, A. R. (1996).
62 Lyons, *et al.* (2002, p. 51).
63 Singer, W. (2001, p. 124).
64 The network has two main nodes – the medial prefrontal cortex and the posterior cingulate cortex. Important connections include the medial temporal cortex and the angular gyrus. Its activity is associated with states of introspection and those functions associated with the achievement of selfhood. They include, for example, autobiographical memory (Gusnard *et al.*, 2001; Buckner and Carrol, 2007), 'metalizing' (Frith and Frith, 1999, 2003) and also certain tests of 'theory of mind', such as false belief, which are likely to reflect a developed sense of inner life (Gallagher and Frith 2003; Vogeley *et al.* 2001).

5

THE POET'S VOICE

William Hazlitt described the effect upon him that cold winter morning when, as a young man, he heard Coleridge deliver his inaugural sermon to a packed congregation in Shrewsbury. He wrote,

> when I got there the organ was playing the 100th psalm, and, when it was done, Mr Coleridge rose and gave out his text, 'And he went up into the mountain to pray, HIMSELF, ALONE'. As he gave out his text, his voice rose like a steam of rich distilled perfumes, and when he came to the two last words, which he pronounced loud, deep, and distinct, it seemed to me, who was then young, as if the sounds had echoed from the bottom of the human heart, and as if that prayer might have floated in solemn silence through the universe.[1]

Hazlitt gave an inkling of the 'shapes' of these sounds, of how they rose and fell, hovered and sank and of how they formed a kind of music: 'The preacher, then launched upon his subject, like an eagle dallying on the wind. . . . I could not have been more delighted if I had heard the music of the spheres.'[2]

This experience remained forever imprinted in his memory. Using a Rousseau quotation to express himself, he wrote: 'There are impressions which neither time nor circumstances can erase.'

At that time in his youth he was 'dumb, inarticulate, helpless'. He had no realization that he might be able to express to others the feelings stirred within him by the world around him by, for example, the tops of the Welsh mountains 'seen through wintry branches, or the red rustling leaves of the sturdy oak-trees by the road-side'.[3]

Hazlitt's use of the word 'helpless' to describe himself is significant. He felt himself as if in 'bondage', a state in which the self was a 'prison-house'. The inspiration of Coleridge set him free.

> Now, bursting from the deadly bands that bound them, my ideas float on winged words . . . that my understanding also did not remain dumb and brutish, or at length found a language to express itself, I owe to Coleridge.[4]

The compass of Hazlitt's life was now set. It was towards words and how they are used. He became one of the greatest English essayists. His freedom, however, was incomplete. He sensed that there was something beyond personal expression; that what words say needs a response, an answering 'picture', which may be merely the sound of a voice, which shows recognition of that expression and its feeling. Such responsiveness is found in a particular kind of interplay between people, in which what is felt as 'inner' can be safely exchanged. Hazlitt did not find such an answering voice. He said:

> My soul has indeed remained in its original bondage, dark, obscure, with longings infinite and unsatisfied; my heart, shut up in the prison-house of this rude clay, has never found, nor will it ever find, a heart to speak to.[5]

Hazlitt's experience that winter morning has as its template and original form in the voice of the caregiver, particularly in the proto-conversation, when the sounds she makes together with what the child sees in her face, give some 'meaning' to an ill-formed immediate experience. 'Meaning', here is a re-presentation. With the use of words later in the child's development, this re-presentation is enhanced, allowing possibilities of 'picturing' beyond the fundamentals of voice and face. These fundamentals, however, remain central in that kind of engagement that I am calling analogical, which involves feeling. Although the words 'himself alone' were important in what Hazlitt heard, it was the way these words were spoken that had their powerful effect, the way the speaker seemed like 'an eagle dallying with the wind'.[6]

Transformational conversation

This book is concerned with how self comes into being not only in therapy but also in human development and in evolution. It is supposed that these processes share a common feature, which is fundamental to the emergence of the experience in different settings.

In approaching the subject of self, we confront something elusive, a feeling of something happening within us that gives us a sense of being alive, a movement the great physicist Wolfgang Pauli called 'becoming'. We enter a world of feelings, of shades of feeling, of nuances and shift, a world in which reality is not an absolute but that is penetrated by illusion, fantasy and imagination. It is a state that cannot be grasped and apprehended by a language of facts, the discourse of science, in which the words say only one thing at a time. What is required is a different kind of expression, one that can capture both feeling and multiplicity. Its form is intimated by Hazlitt's description of his experience in listening to Coleridge that winter morning. What he heard was not poetry, but the voice of a person having a poetic sensibility.

Personal transformation of a kind akin to that described by Hazlitt comes about by means of a language having the combined structures of familiar conversation and the poetic. It can make analogical representations of inner states that create a feeling 'fit', for the listener, such as Hazlitt seems to have felt that morning. It left him exultant. This chapter attempts a brief outline of the nature of the poetic.

Antinomial structure of the poetic

The structure of the poetic is illustrated by an example, a short poem of Octavio Paz, which can be translated as follows:

> If man is dust,
> he is the one
> who travels the plains [7]

An image of the scene in which the words 'ashes to ashes, dust to dust' are being intoned is linked to another scene, of the dry inland where, in the far distance, men are moving, perhaps in a camel train, dust rising from it. The superposition of the two images has a 'meaning' that is greater than each image alone. The linking is created through a framework of subtle rhythms, a patterning of words that convey a feeling that is the essence of the poem.

The words of the poem are used in a symbolic way, having more than a single meaning. Dust is not merely the particles we see in the air. It is an emblem of death. The plains have the double reality of a geographical entity and a zone of experience few men encounter, a kind of frontier beyond the ordinary zone of habitation. Travel is not merely getting from one place to another. It is also the journey of life. The larger antinomy of the poem's structure, between death and life, is built on smaller dualisms, characteristic of the symbolic process.

The effect of a few simple words combined in a particular way is to evoke a sense of a reality that none of them possess alone. The nature of this reality is not precise, as in the digital mode. It is indefinite, characteristic of analogic representation. Does the poem 'mean' that though man is bounded by mortality, in another sense his reality is boundless? Or is it the purpose of the poet to remind us that in death there is life? Or is it both of these things and something more besides.

The title of the poem, 'Apparition', creates another antinomy, as if in a conversational interplay with the poem itself. It seems to say the reality evoked by the poem is unreal, a mere 'apparition'. Or is he saying that a real scene, which he has glimpsed with his own eyes, evokes images that, although unreal, when juxtaposed with the actuality, create the true reality of what is perceived?

An analogical representation of an antinomial kind is made at the beginning of the illustrative session described in Chapter 16. The linking between restriction and freedom, is done in a simple, conversational way.

The shaping sound of the voice

A poem creates a mood, as music does, which is hard to exactly pin down and to express in words. This effect is enhanced, in the manner of polyphonic music, by the sound of the words that accompany their lexical meaning. In the original Spanish of the 'Apparition' poem, for example, the vowel tones of 'polvo' and 'son hombres' create an expressive dimension beyond the English translation, giving the poem a larger or more profound 'meaning'.

An example of the shaping effect of sound in creating mood and giving this mood a representation, is provided by the following two translations of the Old English poem, *Beowulf*, the earliest European vernacular epic. In this passage, the young Swedish prince Beowulf sets sail for Denmark with a small band of warriors in a bid to kill a monster that is nightly ravaging the Danish king's mead hall and devouring his people. Beowulf's warriors are boarding the ship. Here is Tolkien's translation.[8]

> In her bows/mounted
> brave men/blithely. Breakers/turning
> spurned the/shingle. Splendid/armour
> they bore/aboard

And here is the translation by Seamus Heaney,[9]

> Men climbed eagerly up the gang plank,
> Sand churned in surf, warriors loaded
> A cargo of weapons.

Tolkien's language builds on affective tone. 'In her bows/mounted brave men/ blithely' conveys the sense of something grand and reckless, while the sound of the words has in it the elements of a dark music, a hard beating, like a drumbeat, or the beat of waves. In this form of expression, there is an intensity lacking in the Heaney lines: 'Men climbed eagerly up the gangplank' (as if they were a mob of tourists).

An affective tone, including the sense of aliveness that is at the core of going on being, is conveyed by intonation and also by rhythm. Tolkien's passage seems strange, bare, even awkward yet it is my view, the better poem.

Although, as Aristotle wrote of the art of poetry that 'the greatest thing by far is to be a master of metaphor'.[10] I will not touch upon the use of metaphor in this chapter since its subject is sound, the voice of the poet. Nevertheless, it is worth comparing the use of metaphor and analogy in these two translations. Metaphor is more powerful poetically than analogy, since it involves the polarity of inner and outer. Consider the image for the waves in each case. Heaney uses a churn, that is, a machine for making butter. This is an analogue. The similarity is in the world. On the other hand, 'Breakers turning spurned the shingle' introduces inner states. Spurning implies pride, not only in the height, the hauteur, of waves, poised above the shingle, but also the pride of the men, setting out, against the odds. Every word is layered. 'Breakers' can refer not only to the surf but also to conflict; turning overtly describes the revolution of the waves, but covertly it suggests the gaze of the men, turning their eyes from the shore toward the desolate vastness they are about to cross.

It was the sound of Coleridge's voice that entranced Hazlitt – like 'an eagle dallying with the wind'.[11] He found that Wordsworth also had a remarkable voice, a fact he discovered a few months after his meeting with Coleridge, who had invited him to visit him and Wordsworth. Hazlitt described Wordsworth's voice as 'a mixture of clear gushing . . . a deep gutteral, and strong tincture of the northern burr, like the crust on wine'.[12] Without this voice his poetry is diminished, its power of feeling fades.

The voice is as if an embodiment of text, just as the songs and dances that accompany the story telling in Australian Aboriginal culture is an embodiment of a 'dreaming'.

The body was in Coleridge's conversation. On the morning after his sermon, Coleridge left Shrewsbury setting out on one of his long walks. Hazlitt walked with him for 6 miles, while Coleridge talked: 'In digressing, in dilating, in passing from subject to subject, he appeared to me to float on air, to slide on ice.'[13] His associative, non-linear pattern of thought was accompanied by a similar trajectory of his body. 'I observed that he continually crossed one on the way by shifting from one side of the foot-path to the other. . . . He seemed unable to keep on in a strait line.'[14] It was as if for Coleridge the stream of consciousness was as much a bodily experience as a psychic, its wandering form directing his path. His body was part of his vocal expression.

Rhythm and the music of conversation

The transformative conversation is one of feeling. It is not *about* feeling but feeling is in the words. To the degree that this form of conversation expresses and evokes emotion, it is poetic. This is not to say that weeping, raging, or laughing are poetic expressions. These are uni-dimensional affects. The particular kind of conversation that brings about an enlargement of a personal state of existing is one in which a latent complexity of feeling is realized. The antinomial structure of the poetic form is able to accommodate such complexity. It is as if mankind has devised a special way of representing and so bringing into being, the complex feeling states that are at the core of the higher order consciousness, which is the evolutionary destiny of *Homo sapiens*.

Such a feeling is in the body, felt sometimes as a kind of rhythm. It is necessarily represented by an analogue of this feeling, which has a musical quality. Since each feeling has its own form, no stereotypic, pre-arranged rhythm is capable of giving it representation.

Conversational patterns have a rhythmic complexity that far exceeds the conversational structures of traditional poetry. In order to have a greater expressive power, Shakespeare brought about a revolution in the metrical patterning of English verse.[15] The traditional iambic pentameter was loosened so that the rhythmic beat of the words more nearly resembled conversation. In order further to increase the naturalness of the speech of his players, he gave up the strict rules of rhyme. These modifications are found in late works such as 'The Tempest', which is regarded as the most verbally musical of Shakespeare's plays. In this work, for example, Prospero's 'dark, backward and abysm of time' conveys and evokes, not only through imagery but also by the sounds of words and their rhythm, a feeling that may come upon us from time to time, of the ominous, of a momentary sensing of the vastness and mystery of time.

Shakespeare's revolution was overturned during the heightened rationality of the enlightenment. Wordsworth, however, reinstituted what Shakespeare had begun, 'totally discarding', as Hazlitt put it, 'the artifices of poetic diction, and making use of only such words as had probably been common in the most ordinary language since the days of Henry II'.[16]

Writing more than two centuries after Wordsworth's 'manifesto', T. S. Eliot argued that the kind of rhythm found in the complex, irregular patternings of natural conversation, which he called a music,[17] is the most effective way by which a poet conveys feeling.

The best means of expressing feeling is the ordinary language of a country, spoken by all. It has its own peculiar rhythms and sounds, which evoke the particularity, the essence, of that culture.[18] Such an expression, in a different language, cannot reproduce the same feeling.[19]

In another paper elaborating the notion that feeling is the basis and origin of poetry, Eliot pondered how a poem begins.[20] The starting point may be nothing more definite than a feeling of movement, the sense of 'a rhythm not yet clothed in words'.[21] This rhythm should not come from conventional or traditional systems of versification. Rather, it must resemble and fit a state, which is not merely mental but held within it the totality of the self, including the body. Like a piece of music, it both conveys and evokes the emergent feeling it seeks to represent. This 'music' will be that of a distilled and refined form of conversation.

W. H. Auden noted a similar experience of poetic genesis in the work of Paul Valéry, who described how 'Le Cimetière Marin' began: 'My intention was no more than a rhythmic figure, empty and filled with meaningless syllables, which obsessed me for some time.' His pondering on this form led to the realization that it

> required the potential poem to be monologue of 'self' in which the simplest and most enduring themes of my affective and intellectual life, as they imposed themselves on my adolescence, associated with the sea and the light in a particular spot on the Mediterranean coast were called up.[22]

The resultant poem, with its basis in rhythm and the music of the voice, manifests the feeling of a certain state of mind and, at the same time, evokes that state.

An inner voice

In a certain kind of poetry, the poet does not at first, know what the poem is 'about'. The writing is a form of discovery. The effort to find the right words and how they should be said, is towards a representation of a half-known or barely known state in order that it become more fully known and, in this way, 'real'. The poet embarking on this quest is engaged in a kind of inner conversation. Some of W. H. Auden's poetic expressions, which are very varied, had this form.

Wystan Auden arrived at Oxford in 1925, resolved to become a great poet. He searched for a model. The romantics did not impress him. He found Wordsworth 'a most bleak old bore'.[23] Instead, he became fascinated by the beat and sound of Anglo-Saxon poetry in poems such as 'The Seafarer' and 'The Wanderer', introduced to him by the young professor of Anglo-Saxon, J. R. R. Tolkien whose recitations left him 'spell-bound'.[24] In the following year, he found another formative influence, Eliot's 'The Waste Land', which had been published in 1922. Reading Eliot's *Poems 1909–1925* led him to tear up all the poems he had so far written and to tell his tutor that he now knew how he wanted to write.[25] Further influences included Emily Dickinson and Thomas Hardy. He had arrived at the view, like Eliot, that poetry was essentially musical and that its form must be dictated by the 'conversational speech of everyday'.[26]

His talent seemed to emerge fully formed. His first works were published in 1928, when he was 21. They included: 'Taller Today', which began

> Taller today, we remember similar evenings,
> Walking together in a windless orchard
> Where the brook runs over the gravel, far from the glacier.

Auden had no clear idea of what the poem 'meant'. He could only say that it 'seemed to be part of something'.[27] Several other short lyrics written at about the same time came out of this unformulated sense or mood, which seemed to involve memories of landscape and an important relationship. This poem can be seen as an attempt by the poet to represent to himself the nature of this feeling by means of rhythm and imagery.

The simplicity of these lines is deceptive. The stanza begins with a condensation. 'Taller today' might refer to a memory of childhood; it might equally refer to a sense of well-being, with which comes a feeling of enhanced amplitude of personal being. The imagery of the stanza has a subtle antimonial structure, created by the final phrase, 'far from the glacier', without which the stanza would be mundane. The cold stasis of the glacier is the polar opposite of a state 'where the brook runs over the gravel'. An antinomial structure, as previously remarked, is a feature of great poetry. It creates an inexplicable feeling of significance, sometimes amounting to a bodily feeling, a shiver. It is also, as Jung would argue, the structure of self.

The tone and rhythm is conversational. The voice is double, speaking of the 'we', as if to the poet himself but also to the other. For Auden, the characteristic style of 'Modern' poetry is an intimate tone of voice, the speech of one person addressing one person, not a large audience.[28]

This stanza is part of an attempt to represent a frail and evanescent feeling, which Wood Jones might have called a 'little emotion', (see Chapter 6) a state of mind for which no word exists and can only be 'realized' by means of rhythm and imagery. Auden seemed to have a particular flair for making such representations in the interpersonal sphere. After Auden's death, Oliver Sacks described how Auden had been like a mirror for him, as if showing him to himself in the manner of a therapist:

> I feel, in many ways, that Wystan understood me better than I understood myself. . . . He became a living mirror for me – someone who could detect and encourage the perception of new vistas, images and trains-of-thought long before I myself was conscious of them. And if he did this with me, he did it with a hundred others. He showed us ourselves, he drew us into greater possibilities of being – 'self-actualization', to use the current, trendy word – by being himself, wise and tolerant and affectionate as Socrates, completely devoid of censoriousness and moralizing, yet deeply, purely and passionately ethical.[29]

Sacks' experience was not an isolated one. For example, while lecturing at Anne Arbor, Auden spent much time at the home of one of the faculty members. By talking with this man's wife 'he helped her (she believed) to overcome allergies from which she was suffering. As a result of this she was able to have another child . . . the child was given the Christian names "Wystan Auden"'.[30]

Auden very quickly came to be regarded as the finest English poet of his time, Eliot being American. But he did not grow. Auden himself spoke of 'decline' as if knowing that his extraordinary talent had not been properly fulfilled. He even abandoned, at least to some degree, his original program, returning to a formalistic rhyming structure. Some of his poetry was written as if to amuse himself. He liked to play.[31] In a poem written about 1940[32] for his then friend Benjamin Britten, Auden appeared to represent himself not only to Britten but also to himself.

> I cannot grow;
> I have no shadow
> To run away from,
> I only play
>
> I cannot err;
> There is no creature
> Whom I belong to,
> Whom I could wrong.

In this poem the self-representation is not of the kind necessary to the transformation described by Wolfgang Pauli, in which the 'second meaning' comes from the symbolic order. What Auden could do for others, like Sacks, he could not do for himself. Nor would it be done by others. He did not find, the poem seems to say, an adequate 'alter' who, in conversation could show himself to himself by means of 'forms of feeling' having a structure resonant with the poetic.

Notes

1 Hazlitt, W. (1991, pp. 212–213).
2 Hazlitt, W. (1991, pp. 212–213).
3 Hazlitt, W. (1991, p. 211).
4 Hazlitt, W. (1991, pp. 211–212).
5 Hazlitt, W. (1991, p. 212).
6 Hazlitt, W. (1991, p. 213).
7 Paz, O. (1979, p. 91), translation R. Meares.
8 Tolkien, J. R. R. (1950).
9 Heaney, S. (1999, lines 212–214).
10 Aristotle (1941, pp. 1455–1487).
11 Hazlitt, W. (1991, p. 213).
12 Hazlitt, W. (1991, pp. 224–225).
13 Hazlitt, W. (1991, p. 218).
14 Hazlitt, W. (1991, p. 218).
15 Graves (1961, p. 379; Wright, 1988, p. 140).
16 Hazlitt, W. (1991, p. 228).
17 Eliot, T. S. (1942, p. 29).
18 Eliot, T. S. (1945, p. 19).
19 Eliot, T. S. (1945, p. 19).
20 Eliot, T. S. (1953, p. 98).
21 Eliot, T. S. (1942, p. 38).
22 Auden, W. H. (2010, pp. 191–192).
23 Carpenter, H. (1992, p. 54).
24 Carpenter, H. (1992, p. 55).
25 Carpenter, H. (1992, p. 57).
26 Auden, W. H. (1989, p. 24).
27 Carpenter, H. (1992, p. 79).
28 Auden, W. H. (1989, p. 84).
29 Carpenter, H. (1992, p. 426).
30 Auden, W. H. (1989, p. 89).
31 Carpenter, H. (1992, pp. 319–320).
32 Song II from 'Anthem for St. Cecilia's Day'.

6

LITTLE EMOTIONS

Frederic Wood Jones

Frederic Wood Jones (1879–1954) was one of the greatest anatomists of his generation. Some said the greatest. His talent for research was recognized early when, as a medical student, he published original scientific observations. On graduation, he seemed destined for a prestigious academic role, but instead, chose to become a medical officer in the Cocos Islands. His friend, Le Gros Clark, said of Wood Jones that he was essentially 'a wanderer and a seeker after adventure'.[1] He took away from his year-long stay in the Cocos Islands a wife and the basis of a 'remarkable book'[2] entitled 'Corals and Atolls'. It was a forerunner to the epigenetic revolution in evolutionary thinking that began a decade or so ago and which is implicit in the main theme of this book. Wood Jones studied corals as living animals and demonstrated that genetic expression is influenced by environmental circumstances.

Wood Jones held professorships in London, Adelaide, Melbourne and Hawaii, leaving behind him, in each case, a legendary reputation as a brilliant teacher and as a man of charm, humanity and vigour. Although an anatomist, his focus was always on the world of the living and in particular, the peculiar beauty of the processes of evolution in which the smallest details of a creature's make-up may have a significant adaptive value. Observations of such details appeared not only in his scientific contributions but also in a series of what he called 'Unscientific Essays'. They have a curiously Montaigne-like quality. Montaigne had written, as a note 'To the Reader', 'I desire to be seen in my simple, natural everyday guise, without effort and artifice.'[3] His prose, like that of Wood Jones, reflects that desire. Both men warn their readers of the triviality of their enterprise. Wood Jones wrote:

> These pages are the products of idle moments . . . some passed in London, some in Australia, and some upon a coral island. The products of these idle moments had no purpose, and they represent no more than a desire for the expression of things too trivial and too inexact to be reckoned as scientific.[4]

The titles of the essays of these two men show their similarity of style. Examples include, 'Of idleness', 'Of the custom of wearing clothes', 'Of friendship'

(Montaigne) and 'Of longing', 'In praise of the unnecessary', 'Of words and little emotions' (Wood Jones).

Little emotions

In the last named of these essays, Wood Jones wrote of the importance in human life of what he called 'little emotions', subtle feelings for which there may not be words.[5] These feelings, which are barely contemplated in a research sense, perhaps as too minor to be given such consideration, are the feeling of life going on. Unless they have some means of representation they will wither and sink to the bottom of consciousness, so diminishing not only an emotional range but also the differentiation in feelings, which through their expression, contribute to the connectedness among people. The lexicon does not contain words for the expression of all feelings. 'Unofficial', spontaneously generated slang words are invented. They often have an analogical basis. Wood Jones thought that children were especially good at coining these new words. He cited one example from a collection known as 'Berkshire Babble'. The word was 'creamy', meaning 'the desire to squeeze a little fat cat or a baby'.[6]

The representations that give form to a nebulous feeling state are not only made by words alone. As we speak in ordinary conversation, a series of 'pictures' of feelings are created by the face, the tone of the voice and the gestures of the speaker. These are fundamental elements of the interplay, as they are of the proto-conversation.

These picturing functions are used by the caregiver in a way that gives a shape and reality to her baby's nebulous feeling state. An experimental study using the visual cliff is a well-known example. The babies, who were at the crawling stage, were placed on the 'shallow' side, while their mothers were opposite them, on the deep side. The babies then began to crawl over the glass floor towards their mothers. At some point, perhaps mid-way, the infants stopped and looked down, seeing a space yawning below them. They then looked up towards their mothers, who had been instructed to show on their faces either fear or pleasure. If she showed pleasure, they knew all was well and continued towards her. If, however, she looked afraid, they scuttled back to the shallow side.[7]

During the interplay, the infant's experience, which was amorphous and undefined, becomes distinct and discrete. It is differentiated from a vague and more extensive original state. The differentiation has occurred in the same mother–infant situation as that which fosters integration, in which there is a connection, a sense of fit between the baby's immediate reality and the mother's re-presentation of it. Although differentiation and integration can be abstractly conceived as separate mechanisms in the process of maturation, they are woven together, going on at the same time.

It is not only the mother's face that provides the requisite 'picture' but also her voice. That the human voice has the power of expressing finely differentiated feelings is illustrated by the Roman Jakobson experiment, in which an actor could portray by the sound of the voice, up to fifty different emotional states. A mother making the sound 'Ooh' when her baby sees something strange and new, shapes the sound in a particular way, with her voice rising and falling. She can convey, for example, interest, awe, wonder, fear, surprise and excitement. This representation may be so developed, we might almost say so sophisticated, that all of these emotions can be differentiated by means of a single expression.[8]

Musicality, feeling and the infant

The way in which a mother can convey complex feeling states by the use of her voice resembles the musical as observed in previous chapters. There is evidence to suggest that babies have the capacity to respond to the voice as if it were music. Babies are innately musical. Isabelle Peretz and Krista Hyde[9] report that babies are sensitive to musical scales and a regular tempo. The brain appears to be equipped with musically specific neural networks, which are related to the neurology of language but distinguishable from it. Peretz and Hyde cite evidence suggesting that 'musical training or implicit learning of music theory appears unnecessary to acquire sophisticated knowledge of syntax-like relationships among tones, chords and keys'.[10] Burkhard Maess and his colleagues (2001) found that Broca's area, the part of the brain responsible for the production of speech, is involved in the processing of musical syntax.[11]

The baby responds to the musicality of the human voice in the first days of life or even earlier. By 2 weeks a certain rhythmic way of using the voice can calm and soothe the baby. By 5 weeks, the mother's voice is preferred.[12] The period of 6–9 months seems to mark a period of particular advancement not only in babies' capacity to differentiate emotions but also in their musical discernment. Peretz and Hyde observed, using evidence from other workers, that infants of this age 'process consonant intervals better than dissonant intervals'.[13] One wonders whether differentiation of feeling might be analogous to the recognition of a musical pattern, the discernment of a kind of leitmotiv, i.e. a theme, or short musical phrase, which recurs at the appearance of 'a particular, situation or sentiment'.[14]

The infant's sensitivity to vocal stimuli is remarkable. For example, Eimas and colleagues showed that 1-month-old babies could discriminate English phonemes and moreover, that this distinction was categorical.[15] These results have been replicated in later studies. Older infants are able to distinguish between the prosodic qualities of speech.

Although both face and voice are the main ways in which feeling is conveyed to the infant, the possibility arises that one of these may be dominant. Fernald, among others, has argued that it is the voice.

> At the age of 5-months, when infants are not yet showing consistent selective responsiveness to positive and negative facial expressions, infants do respond differentially to positive and negative vocal expressions, suggesting that the voice is more powerful than the face as a social stimulus.[16]

Wolff had described how the baby's smile is triggered first by the voice and then by the face.[17]

The complexity of feeling: a hierarchy

Wood Jones' expression, 'little emotions', suggests a refinement, a capacity to distinguish and convey in the ordinary interplay of conversation, feelings that might be swamped by other, 'bigger' emotions or neglected as inexpressible. The possibilities of emotional connection are enhanced when the other finds a way of 'picturing' one's states for which there may not be precise words.

Different languages do not all have the same number of words that can be used to express 'little emotions'. It is implicit in this observation that certain cultures may have developed a greater refinement in their ways of expressing what cannot be easily expressed, so enhancing the possibilities of 'meeting', in the Buberian sense, in which 'all real living is meeting'.[18]

Wood Jones' 'little emotions' refers to a class of emotional life that is not minor or trivial but which can be contrasted with 'big emotions', those which James called the 'coarser emotions'.[19] These emotions are more powerful, more 'hard-wired', than the frail and fleeting states to which Wood Jones draws our attention. Fear, as any politician will tell you, overrides those feelings that are the basis of altruism. 'Little emotions' are not faint awarenesses of coarser 'emotions'.[20] They are a different category of experience.

When Wood Jones gave examples of what he meant by 'little emotions', he spoke of feelings. Feelings and emotions are often used as synonyms, but there are important differences between them, which are apparent in ordinary conversation. Someone says: 'You hurt my feelings'. He does not say: 'You hurt my emotions'. However, when we see a person behave in a certain way we may say that he is 'tired and emotional'. The word emotion has cognitive and behavioural connotations, while feelings relate to that which is personal and inner. Put simply, feelings are 'subjective' while emotions are 'objective'.

At the core of every form of consciousness is a feeling, however muted, which gives to each particular state of consciousness its peculiar character. A feeling is not a simple state. It varies in terms of complexity, which can be conceived in terms of a hierarchy that is, of course, the same as a hierarchy of consciousness. A developmental and evolutionary theory of the origins of self depends upon an integrated system of levels.

All 'levels' in a notional hierarchy of feeling are based in the body. 'Every one of the bodily changes,' James remarked, 'whatsoever it may be, is FELT, acutely or obscurely, the moment it occurs.'[21] James goes on to say that 'If the reader has never paid attention to the matter, he will be both interested and astonished to learn how many different bodily feelings he can detect in himself as characteristic of his various emotional moods.'[22]

A well-known catalogue of emotional states came from Silvan Tomkins, who identified nine different affects. They are disgust, dissmell, pleasure, distress, interest, startle, fear, shame and joy.[23] Affects are defined by *The Oxford Companion to the Mind* as 'a term used in psychology for a feeling or emotion particularly one leading to action'.[24]

Tomkins' list, which has been influential, has no homogeneous origins in development or neurobiology. The first six of the nine are manifest soon after birth while the other three, – anger, fear and shame – appear later in the notional hierarchy. It is notional in the sense that the brain does not operate in tiers but as a totally co-ordinated system in which later evolved behaviours and functions have within them elements of the earlier functions. They are 'compounded' to use Jackson's term.

Seven levels can be coarsely distinguished in this hierarchy of complexity. At each level the affect, feeling or emotion is part of a relationship with the environment that may, at the higher levels, be internal. Most fundamental and at the bottom of all the emotional states, which appear later, are those manifest in the newly born. All later feelings have at their core something of the original affects of pleasure/non-distress or distress/pain. For example, shame and humiliation has a neurological basis very similar to the pain produced by a noxious stimulus.[25] The emergence of emotions and feelings is played out as two main themes – positive and negative.

The development of feelings involves a growing complexity, from level to level. The level of complexity of the feeling is manifest in the complexity of the environmental situation that evokes it. The form of interplay between environment and the brain-mind system determines a form of consciousness, which is also a feeling state. Since these three things – the feeling, the form of consciousness and the form of relationship – are all part of the same system, to speak of one is almost to speak of the other two.

The simplest form of feelings – Tomkins' basic six – has the simplest environmental correlate, a single stimulus. The second stage in emotional development at 2–4 months sees the first appearance of anger. It is induced by circumstances more complex than a single stimulus, such as a pinprick or an unpleasant taste. Campos and Sternberg found that anger could be discerned by 2 months and that by 4 months infants regularly became angry in response to arm restraint.[26] This affect can be triggered by the non-human environment. An example, comes from an experimental study by Margaret Sullivan and Michael Lewis.[27] Infants of about 17 weeks learnt to move their arms to make interesting things happen. Their wrists had been connected by a ribbon to a machine, which was triggered by a pull on the ribbon. Its activation resulted in music and a slide show. When the ribbon was disconnected from the machine and their arm movements no longer had any effect, the infants typically displayed frustration and anger. Alternatively, some of the infants exhibited the posture of sadness.

Another feeling that arises at this time can only be evoked by the human environment. At about 2–3 months the proto-conversation becomes established as a game between mother and child, which generates a particular kind of pleasure in both partners that neither could gain alone.

The third stage of complexity is evident at about 7–8 months when anxiety is displayed. It seems to be related to the child developing some conceptual awareness of herself as a distinct entity. This awareness becomes more complicated at the fourth level, between 1½ and 2 years of age, when the 'social emotions' emerge.[28] The appearance of shame, embarrassment and guilt at this stage depends upon the child's awareness of herself as a person in relation to others. It is an aspect of the formation of identity, of 'who I am' in a social situation. This is indicated by the child's recognition of herself in a mirror or in a photograph at about 18 months of age.[29] That these emotions are in the body is evident in the characteristic blushing that accompanies shame and embarrassment. It is at and beyond the fourth stage and the age of about 4 that the 'little emotions' become increasingly important. Whereas the emotions described so far are single states, the 'little emotions' are a complex, a mixture of earlier emotions out of which something new emerges. The kind of relationship that inspires their feelings is also and necessarily, complex. There may be no known 'meaning' provided for them by the environment, as in the case of affects. There is no snake, eagle, or leopard to be seen; no stereotypic situation of frustration or exposure is apparent. In order for these feelings to have some 'meaning', which allows them to be 'real' and so to enter a system of personal reality, a 'picturing' of them is needed. Words, used in a particular way, are required in addition to the more fundamental means of representation given by the face and the sound of the voice.

Complex feeling states are at the heart of higher order consciousness. Their 'realization', I believe, is necessary to its emergence.

It is a very long time in terms of developmental achievement between the ages of 2 and 4, when self makes its appearance. It may be equivalent to millions of years of evolutionary history.

The state of self is one not only of duality but, in its more mature form, multiplicity. It is made of a co-ordination of several feeling states and scenes. It can only come into being when there exists a representation of this somewhat nebulous experience, like an answering voice, giving it shape. The co-ordination between previously disconnected aspects of psychic life is, in this way facilitated. It is through this co-ordination, I am proposing, that the reflective capacity is created.

The fifth level: reflective feeling

The fifth major step in development in the complexity of feeling is that which occurs when the concept of 'innerness' is achieved at about 4 years of age. Autobiographical memory is discovered. With this development, feeling states may seem almost entirely 'inner' and can be triggered by inner events alone. The new extension of the memory system, in which episodes from the past can be brought before 'the eyes of the mind' signals a liberation from the environment and the birth of self.

This is the stage when 'little emotions', which might also be called 'reflective feelings', can be represented, in language, by the child herself. An enormous change in human life has taken place with their appearance. They are, as remarked earlier, a different category of experience, in a number of ways.

Their creation depends upon the differentiation and integration of earlier affective and emotional states, yet this integration is not an amalgam or aggregate, but a unified state, analogous to a musical phrase. It is for the individual experiencing it, new and unique.

These complex feeling states are central to a form of consciousness that is also new in evolutionary terms. Their realization may be central to its emergence.

Although a complex feeling may be evoked by the environment, it is not yoked to external events in the same way that the affects and social emotions are. 'Reflective feelings' have no apparent adaptive value, yet the experience of Coleridge's words was for Hazlitt a crucial event in his life. His experience was an illustration of 'little emotion' or 'reflective feeling' writ large.

This kind of feeling state does not necessarily trigger any characteristic response, behaviour, posture or facial expression as do the affects and social emotions. There may be no overt manifestation of the 'inner' experience. Others can only know of it through the use of words. Since there are, in the main, no words for these states, they have to be 'made up', using figurative language, like Hazlitt did. They depended upon analogy and metaphor. The experience is now tripartite. In the earlier state there were two elements – the environmental stimulus and the subject's behavioural response. In this new condition, a third element, that of words, is necessary for the response to be known by others.

An example of this new condition is provided by a little boy of about 3½. He is walking with his mother past a room from which come the sounds of men who are drinking. He says to his mother, not having full command of consonants: 'Dem boys got dirty boices'. Using the analogy/metaphor of 'dirty', he represents the feeling invoked in him by the coarse male voices. The choice of 'dirty' implies a complexity of feeling.

Like affects of fear and disgust, the boy's feeling is triggered by an environmental event and stimulus. His response, however, is more complex than these affects alone. It has connections to fear and disgust but is a larger constellation of colours and tones of feeling. There are remnants in the response of an original primitive feeling state, namely touch. The sounds and the voices are rough and grating. They are also distasteful. His 'analogical representation' of his feeling is precise. It is also creative, in the manner of a poet.

Although mixed feelings would have been part of the infant's experience, the child could represent them only by 'outer' means, by signs in the voice, the face and posture. Now, through words, they can be more adequately 'pictured', so becoming part of a new form of relatedness in which the form exchange is between 'inner' and 'outer'. 'Little emotions', we might say, are the coins of intimacy.

A single word could not encompass the whole range of the boy's experience. Nevertheless, as a 'form of feeling' the word 'dirty' served better than most.

It did not include, however, the feeling of fear, which was not exactly fear since he was with his mother and felt safe. It was really more a foreboding. He could, perhaps, have used the word 'dark' but this would have excluded the sense of roughness. A poet might use both words, as Shakespeare often did, a practice observed by Frank Kermode in his commentary on Shakespeare's use of hendiadys, in which a single idea is expressed by the use of two words with related meanings joined together by 'and'. [30]

Such an incident seems trivial yet the accrual of such experiences leads to outcomes that confer upon the individual advantage in terms of survival and adaption to the environment, which are only evident in the long term. A crucial element in this story is the presence of the mother.

A major issue in thinking about this incident is a consideration of how it might facilitate the emergence of a sense of personal reality. In the proto-conversation, this process has begun with the analogical representation made by the mother. The interplay in this new phase of development involves representation created not only by the sound of the voice but also by the meanings of words. A 'picturing' expression fashioned in this way has the effect of 'shaping' a vague and amorphous experiential state into something that feels 'real', as if having substance. Shakespeare gives an intriguing abbreviated account of this process, using Theseus in *A Midsummer Night Dream* to speak his words:

> as imagination bodies forth
> The forms of things unknown, the poet's pen
> Turns them to shapes and gives to airy nothing
> A local habitation and a name.[31]

A 'local habitation' is not merely pretty language. It is exact. The poet uses the things of the world, our local habitat, which we all know, to give shape and a figurative solidity to something nebulous or ethereal. What was airy-nothing is now embodied.

Reality and response

The question now arises: has the boy, by means of his analogical representation, made 'real' his feeling evoked by the voices? Here we turn to research evidence.

In a seminal study, Margaret Tessler, working with Katherine Nelson[32] recorded the talk of mothers and their 4-year-old children when they visited a natural history museum, where the exhibits included, among other creatures, squirrels and monkeys. On being asked afterwards what they remembered of their visit, children only remembered what had been spoken about in a conversation with their mother, in which their observations were jointly discussed. If squirrels were spoken about but not monkeys, it was as if there were no monkeys there. When what was seen was mentioned only by mother, even if it concerned a fact spoken of with educational intent, it was not remembered. If the child made mention of something

('The squirrel is digging') and received no reply, there was no memory of the event or thing. 'Real' in this study is what happened as depicted in conversation.

Another question now arises: What kind of conversation is it that promotes 'realisation?' An answer is suggested by a study from M. E. Pip.[33] It involved 5-year-old children who took part in a novel 'pirate' event. Nelson and Fivush describe it as follows:

> All children experienced exactly the same activities, but for some children the event was fully narrated as the event unfolded (now we are going to make the magic map. First we have to mix these colors . . ., etc.) while some children were provided only 'empty language'. ('Now we're going to do this'.)[34]

Children were subsequently asked to recall the event verbally and to act it out after returning to the pirate room where all the objects were available. Children exposed to the narrative condition performed better both at verbal recall and in re-enactment of the event.

This study suggests that what becomes 'real' and so is remembered, is best encountered as a story, for example, of the squirrel storing nuts for winter. These two studies taken together suggest that a conversation with the structure of story, that is, one in that the individual elements are connected and pictured, is the setting in which 'realisation' is most likely to take place. We now return to the boy.

Would his experience have become 'real' if he had simply spoken as if to himself? The answer, if we follow Tessler and Nelson, is no. If there had been no response, his feeling would have been that his words were meaningless. He would be left with a question, a doubt: What was really happening in that room?

How then should the mother have responded? The most important feature of what she says should be that it connects. It might be thought that a suitable counterpart to the boy's analogue of 'dirty', which would enhance the reality of the experience, would concern something actual, give some information perhaps. This response might work but it is likely to be a disappointment, since it would not link to the boy's feeling and so would fail to connect. The progression towards a personal reality is paradoxical, moving from the real to the unreal, the imagined. This movement is opposite to the direction towards a scientific reality in which the imagined, the hypothesis, is compared with an actual counterpart. In ordinary life, however, where the individual has the traits of both artist and scientist, there is a back and forth movement between the two positions.

So, what did the mother actually do? She laughed and said 'yes' in a way that made him feel that he had been understood. He realized that she was delighted and amused by his expression, in this way giving it validation. Something very interesting has happened in this little exchange. The structure of the proto-conversation has been reversed. Rather than the mother 'picturing' the immediate reality of her child, it is the child who does the depicting. He says what is in her mind and, in doing so, evokes pleasure in the mother that might resemble, in a small way, the pleasure of the infant when what the mother represents in her face and voice 'connects' with the baby's experience.

This reversal of the original relation is an essential element in the developmental process. The child has taken over for himself the role of representing. He requires, however, the answering voices that says 'yes', which Hazlitt was never able to hear and which gives affirmation, a validation of the 'picture' of a state that is 'inner'.

If we were to imagine that the boy was living tens of thousands of years ago, we can envisage at least two ways in which an accrual of such incidents might give him an evolutional advantage. First, his survival depends upon his bond with his mother particularly of her bonding with him. Just as the proto-conversation – an interplay involving analogical connectedness – engenders pleasure, even joy, this new form of interplay also creates pleasure and so seems likely to promote the ties between mother and child beyond the effect of the attachment system. The second advantage is more general. It concerns the evolutionary advantage that comes with the development of self, which is potentiated by the effect of such interchanges. The advantage comes through the capacity of an individual self to participate in, through co-ordination with other selves, the creation of tribal structure and culture. Culture, I argue in later chapters, is made of a network of stories, which gives to *Homo sapiens* an immense evolutionary advantage.

The sixth level: the movement of time

Those affects and emotions that appear in the first two years of life simply happen to the developing child. They are not reflected upon. The 'little emotions', of the kind exemplified by the little boy and the 'dirty' voices, are more complex. It is as if, interposed between the event and the response, is thought. The structure of this experience can be figuratively conceived as double. There is, however, a 'doubling' beyond this, which comes in the years following the discovery of inner life at about 4 years old. It depends upon the experience of time.

Hughlings Jackson was perhaps the first neuroscientist to remark on this state. As an example, he described the following experience: 'A smell, say of roses, I now have makes me think of a room where I passed much of my time as a child.'[35] Two kinds of doubleness are evident. First, there is the duality that can be abstractly distinguished in the process of thought. Second, there are two spaces in which the experience occurs, one in the present and another in the past. Jackson called this state, presumably jocularly, 'mental diplopia'.

'Mental diplopia' is accompanied by a barely describable feeling, one of Wood Jones' 'little emotions'. Jackson said of this kind of double awareness that it resembled those times 'when the scent of hay or the caw of rooks rouses in us vague pleasurable feelings'.[36] Virginia Woolf spoke of a similar pleasure, of feeling 'the present sliding over the depths of the past'.[37] The most extended and evocative descriptions of this experience have been given by Marcel Proust. His search for lost time seemed to reflect some profound need, a quest for a personal core.

The sense of time is an extremely complex matter. Much of the timing that is involved in human function is unconscious and automatic, involving the integrated activity of a number of 'biological clocks' operating at various levels from milliseconds to months. Each of these 'clocks', although functioning as part of a larger overall system, is underpinned by entirely different neural mechanisms.[38] Research has focused on judgments of short periods of time. The most accurately perceived interval is only about 700 milliseconds.[39]

Within the limited window of a second or so, the estimation of duration is incredibly precise. It is possible, for example, to sense the difference between two piano players playing the same piece on the basis of the time spaces between notes. Unsurprisingly, the system of the brain that underpins the timing and rhythm of movements, the basal-ganglial striatal system, has been shown to be necessary to this fine perceptual capability.[40] Also unsurprisingly, an illness involving pathology of this system, Parkinson's disease, causes patients with this illness to have timing deficits around 300 to 600 milliseconds.[41] The cerebellum is also crucial to sub-second timing.[42]

Sub-second timing is likely to depend upon distinct neural systems. Judgement of longer time intervals, even as short as 12 seconds are prone to considerable error.[43] The sense of time, however, associated with the complexity of feeling that emerges after the discovery of capacity to reflect upon 'inner' events is very rarely a subject of research. Rather than a perception, or a judgement, it is a feeling. William James spoke of it. He wrote: 'The smallest effective pulse of consciousness, whatever else it may be consciousness of, is also consciousness of passing time.'[44] This sense, which is always with us in varying degrees, seems likely to become increasingly developed after about the age of 5, when the experience of the stream of consciousness is first encountered.[45]

The stream of consciousness, as James colourfully describe it, includes both a past and a future:

> The practically organized present is no knife-edge, but a saddle-back, with a certain breadth of its own on which we sit perched, and from which we look in two directions into time. The unit of composition of our perception of time is a duration, with a bow and a stern, as it were – a rearward – and a forward-looking end.[46]

This experience, in which there is an implicit sense of moving into a future is one of mature consciousness. It develops after the age of 4.

Piaget saw the development of time as a reflection of the capacity to organize disconnected spaces. He wrote:

> Space suffices in the co-ordination of simultaneous positions, but as soon as displacements are introduced, they bring in their train distinct and therefore successive spatial states whose co-ordination is nothing other than time itself. Space is a still of time, while time is space in motion.[47]

Time as succession is not clearly evident till about the age of 4. Piaget remarked that it makes no sense to speak to a child of 3 about next week. The development, however, of the complex experience described by James, in which the present includes a future is hard to demonstrate. Nevertheless, using Piaget's image of time as the co-ordination of temporarily disconnected spaces, inferences can be made. Friedman[48] used such a method in a study of 261 children aged between 4 and 10 in which he estimated their judgement of future distance by means such as pointing at a spatial scale.

Friedman found that children of 4 failed to differentiate future distances while children of 5 could distinguish events occurring in weeks or months from events taking place many months in the future. These children, however, like younger children, confused the near future with the recent past. Between 6 and 8 the future was more differentiated but events more than a few months into the future were collapsed together. Beyond this age, fairly accurate judgements were made.

A crucial element of the Jamesian description of the present moment is a sense of not only a future but also a past. The notion, however, that the past is connected to the present is not entertained by 3-year-olds. Nearing the age of 4, however, an understanding is achieved that recent events determine the present.[49]

Fellows and Farah found that 'a normal future time perspective depends upon the ventromedial frontal lobes'.[50] Ventromedial function is not fixed but continues to develop during life, with an important advancement during adolescence. Indirect evidence suggests that it may continue to develop, if all goes well, until old age. This evidence includes a report from Lea Williams, Kerri Brown and others entitled: 'The mellow years?'[51] In a study concerning subjects whose age range covered seven decades, they showed that ventro-medial prefrontal function, which is associated with the development of self,[52] increased as the years went by. This finding suggests that the complexity of the time experience will increase as the years go by. It will be a central aspect of a consciousness, which is also one of increasing complexity. The time experience is a feeling and not a judgement or a perception, although these arise out of the feeling.

Durée

The philosopher Henri Bergson called the feeling of the passage of time 'durée'.[53] He distinguished it from the perception of succession of distinct elements. Rather, it is 'a flux of fleeting shades merging into each other' in 'an endless flow'. His conception is remarkably Jamesian.

Bergson believed that 'durée' is the hallmark of mature human consciousness. Using his criterion as a milestone, we conclude that, although the state of human consciousness we call self is identified by a reflective awareness of inner events, it cannot be considered mature until it involves a second duality, which is penetrated by a sense of the movement of time. This idea leads us, once again, to the paradoxical realization that what we sense as most real to us, may not be real at all or, at least, half real and half unreal – like play. Durée is illusory. It is not an objective measure of clock-time but an experience in which the passage of time is variable, sometimes going quickly, sometimes slowly. It is not a product of any particular neural system but of how the brain is working, as a whole, at a particular moment. Durée is also illusory in that it is an experience of a moment, which includes the future, which does not exist. It is always moving towards something, like the Jamesian stream: [54] 'Durée is the continuous progress of the past which gnaws into the future and which swells as it advances.'[55]

The 'endless flow' that is the feeling of the passage of time is perhaps the most important of the little emotions. This is an experience of time that is beyond the simple difference between the 'spaces' of 'now' and 'then' of the Piagetian experiments, in which time moves as a thing or a person moves, from place to place. In durée, however, there are more than two spaces. The past is a number of spaces. There is, then, a multiplicity of spaces unified in a single experience, in a figurative 'layering'.

Layering is illustrated by considering the feeling of sadness. The sadness of the little girl of 4 to 5 months, indicated by her slumped and dejected posture when she can no longer make interesting things happen, is a single feeling evoked by a discrete event. The kind of feeling state characteristic of the sixth level of complexity is not made of a single feeling. Kierkegaard, for example, described an antinomial feeling state, which he called 'my melancholy'.

> Besides my other numerous circle of acquaintances I have one more intimate confidante – my melancholy. In the midst of my joy, in the midst of my work, she waves to me, calls me to one side, even though physically I stay put. My melancholy is the most faithful mistress I have known, what wonder, then, that I love her in return.[56]

Francoise Sagan described something similar at the beginning of her novel *Bonjour Tristesse*. 'A strange melancholy pervades me to which I hesitate to give the grave and beautiful name of sorrow. . . . Today it envelops me like a silken web.'[57] Robert Burton, in his famous exploration of the subject also observed the paradox involved in certain kinds of melancholy. He found beauty to be a 'cause' of melancholy.[58]

Sadness in maturity takes different forms depending on different mixtures making up a unified multiplicity of feeling states. The difference between grief and nostalgia is an example. Both states involve loss. Contained within grief are two main states. There is the initial state of a response to loss of a loved one – pain, severe distress and psychological disorganization. As time goes on, through the process of mourning, a more complex frame of mind develops in which the pain of the past is infused with the positive experience associated with the person who is gone.

Nostalgia is primarily pleasurable, although it is a state of sadness involving longing. There are, however, states of complexity beyond nostalgia, which resembles this condition but differs from it as Kierkegaard's melancholy differs from a child's sadness. Such states are exemplified by the strange mood evoked by Chekhovian drama, which has often been called nostalgic but for which no word properly exists.

Chekhov's poetic art has a peculiar enchantment, an effect that is difficult to describe. An atmosphere is created out of provincial failure, resignation and even despair, which includes the opposite of these conditions. It is intimated in the final scene of 'Uncle Vanya' when Sofia, an unattractive woman whose dreams of love have never been fulfilled, speaks:

> We shall go on living, Uncle Vanya. We shall live on through a great, great line of days, of long evenings; we shall patiently endure the trials our fate brings us; we shall toil for others, now and when we are old, without rest; and when our time comes we shall die submissively, and there beyond the grave we shall say that we have suffered, that we have wept, that our lives were bitter, and God will take pity upon us, and I and you, uncle, dear uncle, shall see a life that is luminous, beautiful, splendid . . . In your life you have not known any joy, but wait, Uncle Vanya, wait . . . We shall have rest.[59]

Here, mingled together in the single experience of this moment, are other moments from the past and in the future. In Chekhov one finds a juxtaposition of opposites as in the form of lyric poetry. Despair co-exists with hope; the tragic is also comic. Such reconciliations of opposites engenders a mood that cannot exactly be defined but which is frail and evanescent, including the opposites but also something beyond them. In a certain kind of melancholy there is both sadness and beauty.

The way in which the contradictory feelings are brought together to create a mood larger that the individual feelings alone depends upon a particular structuring of sound and a musicality exemplified in a characteristic use of triple clauses: 'we shall say that we have suffered, that we have wept, that our lives were bitter'.[60]

The voices in Chekhov have an interior quality. Some of the conversation is wandering, desultory, contradictory, the speakers speaking as if half to themselves, as if no one will understand. The characters are as if condemned to their own peculiar forms of loneliness. It might be supposed that the depiction of such frailty would be associated with vulnerability. The opposite, however, is the case. Chekhov himself was a very resilient man. The states he portrays are those that predict resilience. Bodner and colleagues, for example, found that old people who were able to integrate positive and negative feeling had a higher level of self-esteem than those who could not. The author concluded that the capacity to experience a high degree of complexity of feeling contributes to resilience and mitigates against diminishing self-esteem in the elderly.[61] Other studies suggest that nostalgia is a buffer against existential threat.[62]

The sixth level: memory and poetic consciousness

The form of consciousness depicted by Chekhov is that of human maturity. It is, in essence, that of self, portrayed in a mode that parallels that of James and Bergson. Since this experience of personal existing is characterized by the feeling of time it must also be characterized by a certain kind of memory. There is no name for it. It is a faculty more complex than autobiographical memory, which the child gains about the time 'innerness' is discovered, at the age of 4 or 5. The child of this age can remember and describe events which had taken place 6 months earlier.[63] Autobiographical memory is tested by asking the subject to bring up in memory and describe an event in their past associated with a particular entity, for example, a river.[64] This capacity is more complicated than the memory of facts, which Tulving[65] had called 'semantic' and which is first demonstrated at about 9 months. Nevertheless, it is memory of a similar kind in that it can be conceived as cognitive, to do with thought rather than feeling. It is a memory of the episodes in which the facts were gathered.

Madelaine Lucas has called the kind of memory implicit in durée 'poetic memory'. It is poetic in that its structure is made by resemblance, by analogical correspondence between scenes experienced at various times in the past. They are brought together in the present in a figurative 'superimposition'. This is the experience of the synchronic to which we shall come in a later chapter. 'Poetic memory' is larger than autobiographical memory, just as autobiographical memory is larger than semantic. Higher forms of memory include all other forms of memory. Through exile, travel or migration, nostalgia becomes complicated because, as Bohm argues:

> Memory, no longer has a single anchor in the native city but unfolds through superimposition of native and foreign lands.[66]
>
> The image of a superimposition suggests that the nostalgic narrative that engages with multiple dimensions of place and time is like a double-exposure – there is no clear distinction between past and present, home and abroad, imaginary and real, truth and fiction.[67]

The notion of double-exposure resonates with Jackson's 'mental diplopia'.

Lucas describes the environmental context in which 'poetic memory' arises as largely interior, a form of inner conversation. Lucas is able to discover this form of consciousness in a certain kind of writing resembling Conrad's quest for 'utterance', discussed in the following chapter.

The seventh level: a sense of the spirit

The seventh level of feeling is not often achieved and the achievement is not maintained, lasting minutes, 'or at most an hour or two', so William James believed.[68] It will only be touched upon briefly, since discussion of it is beyond the scope of this book. It can be understood as a transient ascent in a hierarchy of feeling beyond that described in 'poetic memory'.[69] In his *Varieties of Religious Experience*, William James likened it to mystical experience. It may arise through a more than usual co-ordination of mind-brain processes and unification of consciousness resulting in a sense 'of vastness, of union'.[70]

This state is, supremely, of a positive feeling that has the quality of 'ineffability' – 'no adequate account of it can be given in words'.[71] Like all feelings, it is the basis of a particular reality. As James famously remarked:

> Individuality is founded on feeling; and the recesses of feeling, the darker, blinder strata of character, are the only places in the world in which we can catch real fact in the making, and directly perceive how events happen, and how work is actually done.[72]

Concluding remarks: a hypothesis about the significance of complex feeling states

This chapter has been concerned with the notion of the brain-mind system as a series of dynamically co-ordinated 'layers' build up through the course of evolutionary history. Seven such notional layers can be distinguished in terms of the development of complex feelings, this being indicated not only by the form of the feelings themselves but also by the relative complexity of the subject's relationship with the environment, outer or inner, in which the feeling is embedded.

Since every form of consciousness involves some kind of feeling, this hierarchy is also a hierarchy of consciousness, which at the same time implies a hierarchy of forms of relatedness.

Ordinary mature consciousness in a resting state, currently called the default mode, is at the reflective level, which is the fifth tier in the conception put forward here. Consciousness, however, is not a static nor a unitary state but constantly shifting in adaption to environmental demands, including those of the body. Descent down the hierarchy is associated with an increase in such demands. The least complex forms of consciousness might reflect the effect of traumatic impacts. Ascent in the hierarchy is associated with increasing interiority.

The main focus of the chapter has been on the significance and nature of the shift from the level of consciousness of a 2-year-old – level four – to that of a 4-year-old – level five. Level four might be that achieved by the higher non-human primates. The question being asked is: how is the jump between levels made, not only in human development but also as an evolutionary process.

The answer I believe, lies in the 'picturing' of 'little emotions', half-formed complex feelings for which no specific name usually exists. Such 'picturing', by means of analogic/metaphoric language, makes 'real' this nebulous state. It also, and most importantly, creates coherence. States that do not usually go together are co-ordinated in a single representation. A series of such representation potentiates the movement towards a more co-ordinated form of consciousness out of which can emerge the enlargement of a personal 'view' brought about by the emergence of the reflective function.

The process of 'picturing' is a continuation and enlargement, by means of a particular kind of language, of the kind of picturing that began in early life. Its stereotypic form is the proto-conversation. The large kind of picturing provided by symbolic language does not supersede the earlier means of re-representation – the voice, the face and associated gestures – but includes them in a patterned mode of responding that might be compared with music.

It is notable that, whereas in early life it is the care-giver who creates this patterning, the child gaining the capacity for language becomes a participant in the process of verbal re-representation, even at times taking the primary role.

Finally, this chapter has implicitly approached the problem posed by Hughlings Jackson when he proposed that the reflective consciousness peculiar to the human primate, which he called 'self', had evolved as the outcome of a higher degree of co-ordination of brain elements than was occurring earlier in evolutionary history. How then did this happen and how to does it happen in the development of an individual life? An answer follows Vygotsky's postulate that the functions of higher order consciousness require a 'sociogenic' component, beyond the 'biogenic', for proper maturation to occur. 'Sociogenesis' arises in a kind of conversation in which the form of the function to be internalized is shown extracorporeally as an interpersonal activity. This style of conversation is one in which 'forms of feeling' are created that have a unifying or co-ordinating effect that is sensed as a feeling of 'fit'. The co-ordination in this experience includes both 'outer' and 'inner'. The hypothesis suggests that the conversational interplay activates and potentiates the developing co-ordinating faculty of the emergent pre-frontal cortex.

Notes

1 Clark, W. E. Le Gros (1955, p. 256).
2 Clark, W. E. Le Gros (1955, p. 256).
3 Montaigne, M. (1580, p. 1).
4 Wood Jones, F. (1931, p. 5).
5 Wood Jones, F. (1931, pp. 14–24).
6 Wood Jones, F. (1931, p. 21).
7 Sorce *et al.* (1985).
8 Meares and Jones (2009, pp. 509–510).
9 Peretz and Hyde (2003).
10 Shephard and Jordan, 1984; Tillmann *et al.* (2000).
11 Maess, B. *et al.* (2001).
12 Meadow-Orlans, K. P. (1980, p. 6).
13 Schellenberg, E. and Trehub, S. (1996).
14 *Oxford English Dictionary* (1971).
15 Eimas *et al.* (1971).
16 Fernald, A. (1992, p. 408).
17 Wolff, P. (1963).
18 Buber, M. (1937, cited by Hobson, 1985, p. 1).
19 James, W. (1892, p. 374).
20 James, W. (1892, p. 374).

21 James, W. (1892, p. 378).
22 James, W. (1892, p. 378).
23 Tomkins, S. (1962–1963).
24 Gregory, R. L. (2004).
25 Eisenberger *et al.* (2003).
26 Campos and Sternberg (1981, cited by Izard, 1984).
27 Sullivan and Lewis (2003).
28 Lewis, M. (1992).
29 Lewis, M. (1992).
30 Kermode, F. (2000).
31 Act V. Scene 1 (14–17).
32 Tessler and Nelson (1994).
33 Pip, M. E. (1996).
34 Nelson and Fivush (2000).
35 Jackson, H. (1958, vol. II, p. 30).
36 Jackson, H. (1874, pp. 361–362).
37 Woolf, V. (1978, p. 114).
38 Eagleman, D. M. (2008).
39 Fraisse, P. (1963).
40 Pouthas *et al.* (2005).
41 Harrington *et al.* (1998).
42 Lee *et al.* (2007).
43 Gunstad *et al.* (2006).
44 James, W. (1895, p. 157).
45 Flavell, Green and Flavell (1992).
46 James, W. (1890, vol. I, p. 609).
47 Gruber and Vonèche (1977, p. 550, quoting from Piaget, 1969).
48 Friedman, W. J. (2000).
49 Povinelli *et al.* (1999).
50 Fellows and Farah (2005).
51 Williams *et al.* (2006).
52 Damasio, A. R. (1996).
53 Bergson, H. (1913, p. 3).
54 Bergson, H. (1913, p. 4).
55 Bergson, H. (1913, p. 4).
56 Kierkegaard, S. (1843, p. 14).
57 Sagan, F. (1954).
58 Burton, R. (1621, vol. III, pp. 3, 42–64).
59 Chekhov, A. P. (1998).
60 Lafitte, S. (1971, p. 23).
61 Bodner *et al.* (2013).
62 Routledge *et al.* (2012).
63 Nelson, K. (1992).
64 Robinson, J. (1976).
65 Tulving, E. (1972, 1983, 1985).
66 Boym, S. (2001, p. 258).
67 Lucas, M. (2013).
68 James, W. (1902, p. 290).
69 Meares, R. (2012b).
70 James, W. (1902, p. 330).
71 James, W. (1902, p. 289).
72 James, W. (1902, p. 289).

7

EMPATHY AND UTTERANCE

Feeling and the origin of mind

Feeling was neglected by the psychological scientists of the twentieth century, yet for William James, writing during the century before, it was central. The index entry for 'feeling' in his magnum opus, *The Principles of Psychology*, is 'synonym for consciousness in general in this book'. A feeling state of some kind is at the heart of every moment of personal existing.

The subject of feeling has been restored to scientific respectability in recent years by studies such as those of Damasio[1], which demonstrate that feeling conveys 'meaning'. The capacity to discern feelings in the face and voice has become an important area of research.

Although 'hard-wired' affects such as rage and fear emerge with little help from the social environment, certain emotional states may need a particular kind of human responsiveness from the very start of life. One of these states is joy. Those who have been denied the ordinary 'good-enough' care described by Winnicott and who, in adult life, receive a diagnosis of borderline personality disorder, have a joyless existence in which the cardinal feature is a chronic dysphoria, which may have the intensity of pain produced by a noxious stimulus. A possible cause of such a state is a deprivation of those responses from caregivers, given as part of a playful interchange, which 'picture' the baby's positive feeling and which, on repetition, generate an escalation from initial pleasure to the exhibition of excitement and joy.

Such picturing responses are also required for the realization of complex feeling states that the child experiences only in a dim and amorphous way. When language begins to be acquired around 18 months of age, the complexity of feeling states increases. Feelings now are partly 'inner'. The child lives in a personal zone which, at least for some of the time, is neither inner nor outer but both. Winnicott called it 'transitional'. These quasi-inner states cannot be depicted properly by non-verbal means. Words are needed. The picturing may come about as a joint creation, in a conversation between the child and caregiver, like the incident involving 'dirty' voices.

The capacity for reflective awareness, that is, the capacity to experience particular personal states as peculiarly 'inner' and not part of the public domain, is gained at about 4 years old. This development must be an aspect of neurophysiological maturation that, to use Schore's expression, is 'experience dependent'. I am suggesting that the realization of the barely expressible feelings, which are the stuff of ordinary existing, brings into being the reflective function.

This hypothesis suggests that the first form of the reflective function comes from the other, whose expressions form a kind of scaffolding. She functions as an auxiliary 'I'. The process continues into maturity when it becomes internal in a kind of inner conversation. Conrad and Woolf provide examples.

Empathy and utterance

What is being put forward here is the view that the brain function underlying the potential capacity to reflect upon inner events and 'to see in the mind's eye' is activated in the outer world in a conversation in which there is a 'seeing together'. This activity involves the use, by the other, for empathy, in which the other becomes an auxiliary in the process of 'seeing with the mind's eye'.

Empathy is to be distinguished from sympathy. Put at its simplest, the difference is between one state of mind and two. Chimpanzees display sympathy by sitting quietly and sadly with a deceased chimpanzee. They imagine, we suppose, that the bereaved animal feels as they would feel. Empathy depends upon the capacity to imagine a state different to what one would feel and to have sympathy with that experience. Empathy, then, involves a complex doubling, perhaps first described by the Vico, who advocated an approach to history in which the historian tries to imagine, using the capacity for 'fantasia', the minds of those who created the culture being studied.[2] A large part of his thesis, entitled 'The New Science', is devoted to the subject of 'poetic wisdom'.

Empathy cannot be made useful without some participation of the subject. What emerges is co-created. I have used the image of a metaphoric screen as a way of conceiving the process.[3] Both partners attempt, by the use of words, to cast images, at first fragmentary, upon this initially empty space. The subject gives glimpses of such shapes of thought and feeling through spontaneous or half-formed expressions, through shifts in body and facial expression, and by inflections of voice. The other, the co-conversant, has a chance to create an answering picture, which corresponds to what is given. It is larger and endowed, perhaps, with features missing but implicit in one's attempt at representing.

Such conversations may be very simple, as between a child and a parent, or more complex, as between a writer and reader. If one is lucky, they go on through life. Some have remarkable outcomes, one such being the effect upon Bertrand Russell of his meeting with Joseph Conrad in which, as he said, 'we talked with increasing intimacy. We seemed to sink through layer after layer of what was superficial, till gradually both reached the central fire. It was an experience unlike any other I have known.'[4]

Intimacy is the right word for such an encounter. It is a relationship that is independent of sexuality and which involves the sharing of that which is 'inner'.

It is a 'place' in which what Conrad called 'utterance' can be achieved. In Lord Jim, he gives his narrator, Marlow, the following words: 'Are not our lives too short for that full utterance which through all our stammerings is of course our only and abiding intention?'[5] He suggests that the aim and purpose of life is 'utterance', however incomplete and imperfect it may be. Utterance, he implies, is not mere speech. Rather, it is something we strive towards. The urge to find its necessary words was felt intensely by Conrad himself. For him, the metaphoric empathic screen had become internalized. Its virtual form was now embodied in a white sheet of paper. In a letter to Marguerite Poradowska, with whom he corresponded for 30 years, he wrote:

> I begrudge each minute I spend away from paper. I do not say from the pen, for I have written very little, but inspiration comes to me while looking at the paper. Then there are flights out of sight; my thought goes wandering through great spaces filled with vague forms. Everything is still chaos, but, slowly ghosts are transformed into living flesh, floating vapours turn solid, and who knows? – perhaps something will be born from the encounter of indistinct ideas.[6]

This passage suggests something of the quest that, for Conrad, occupied his whole life. For each of us there is an experience, dimly sensed, which is highly valued and peculiarly personal. It is sensed as a core but paradoxically appears on the surface, akin to a shimmer on the Jamesian stream. It is felt as 'oneself'. This feeling has no name. Since it is not tangible nor part of the observable world, it can only be grasped, made 'solid' and real, through its representation, which for Conrad, depended upon the use of words.

Conrad saw more clearly than most the need for transformation of the formless, shadowy, inchoate 'ghosts' of inner life into 'living flesh'. Nevertheless, the need is shared by us all, although consciousness of it may be barely present. The word 'need' is used here in the sense of a biological necessity. The imperative that drove Conrad's life is not one that affects only the gifted. It is an urge that is at the heart of humanity. Its evolutionary purpose, however, is not personal but tribal and communal. It is the means of creating culture that is the outstanding feature of humans and which distinguishes us from the other primates. It is particularly the poet who helps to realise nebulous and barely expressible feeling states. An example comes from W. S. Merwin in a poem entitled: 'Utterance'.[7]

> Sitting over words
> very late I have heard a kind of whispered sighing
> not far
> like a night wind in pines or like the sea in the dark
> the echo of everything that has ever
> been spoken
> still spinning its one syllable between the earth and silence

The 'utterance' is that of the universe, which cannot speak, having but a 'single syllable'. A second 'utterance' is that of the poet who attempts to represent what he 'hears' in this syllable. The poet finds words for an intuition many have shared, of vastness sensed as if in a moment. He acts for the reader as an auxiliary 'I', making 'real' and giving shape to a profound but transient experience of personal existing that might otherwise be lost and pass by as ephemeral.

Virginia Woolf: the realisation of self through 'inner' conversation

Virginia's quest resembled that of Conrad, for whom she had a great regard.[8] The realisation of self is an implicit and main theme in her writing. The intuition that self is a fabric woven out of feelings is central to her work. Like Conrad, what she strove towards depended upon a virtual or inner conversation. She represents, for herself, in words, on a white sheet of paper, those evanescent movements within her that can never be precisely defined but which, when given form in words, become more alive, real and, in a figurative sense, substantial.

She writes about the project she has set herself in various ways. For example, on 5 August 1929, she talks to her diary:

> Why do I write this down? I have not even told Leonard; and whom do I tell when I tell a blank page? The truth is I get nearer feelings in writing than in walking – I think: graze the bone, enjoy the expression; have them out of me; make them a little creditable to myself.[9]

Thinking about the book that became *The Waves*, she asks herself: 'Why write it?':

> Every morning I write a little sketch to amuse myself. I am not saying, I might say, that these sketches have any relevance. I am not trying to tell a story. Yet perhaps it might be done in that way. A mind thinking. They might be islands of light – islands in the stream I am trying to convey: life itself going on. . . . Autobiography it might be called.[10]

This autobiography is not of the usual kind. Writing about 10 years after these extracts were written, she remarks: 'People write what they call "lives" of other people; that is, they collect a number of events, and leave the person to whom it happened unknown.'[11] This unknown is a reality, or at least a personal reality, that differs from the public world of events. She likens it to music. 'If I could catch the feeling I would,' she wrote to her diary, 'the feeling of the singing of the real world, as one is driven by loneliness and silence from the habitable world.'[12] It is this music she tries to capture: 'I am writing to a rhythm not a plot' she said of *The Waves*.[13] Since, however, the music is made of words, *The Waves* became something different – a 'play-poem'.[14]

When Woolf first contemplated the idea underlying *The Waves*, another image of, or analogy for, the mystery of personal reality came to her on 30 September 1926. She communed with her diary:

> I wished to add some remarks to this, on the mystical side of this solitude; how is it not oneself but something in the universe that one's left with. It is this that is frightening and exciting in the midst of my profound gloom, depression, boredom, whatever it is: One sees a fin passing far out.[15]

In February 1931 *The Waves* was finished. She wrote in her diary:

> Here in the few minutes that remain, I must record, heaven be praised, the end of *The Waves*. I wrote the words O Death fifteen minutes ago, having reeled across the last ten pages with some moments of such intensity and intoxication that I seemed only to stumble after my own voice, or almost, after some sort of speaker. . . . But rounded off, completed, the thing stated – how hastily, how fragmentarily I know; but I mean that I have netted that fin in the waste of waters which appeared to me over the marshes out of my window at Rodmell when I was coming to an end of *The Lighthouse*.[16]

Here, the two images of existing, the musicality of words and the fin far out, come together. Some 8 or 9 years later, they had formed the basis of a formulation of her 'philosophy'. As a prelude to a brief statement of this philosophy, she described 'perhaps' the strongest pleasure known to her. It came from a sense of connectedness.

> It is the rapture I get when in writing I seem to be discovering what belongs to what; making a scene come right; making a character come together. From this I reach what I might call a philosophy; at any rate it is a constant idea of mine; that behind the cotton wool is hidden a pattern; that we – I mean all human beings –are connected with this; that the whole world is a work of art; that we are parts of the work of art. Hamlet or a Beethoven quartet is the truth about this vast mass that we call the world. But there is no Shakespeare, there is no Beethoven; certainly and emphatically there is no God; we are the words; we are the music; we are the thing itself.[17]

She was saying that a sense of patterning, akin to music and made with words, is at the heart of us.

'Fit', the body and the feeling of unity

Woolf's observations of her feelings were acute. As these feelings came and went, she was able to identify shifts in her bodily state and in the style of 'conversation' with the world and within herself. For example, in *The Years* she describes two different and contrasting experiences, which arise from 'conversation'.

The first is one of 'fit', in which a feeling of well-being is associated with a harmony, a sense of correspondence between the condition of the world and the sense of the body. Martin is in the vicinity of St Paul's having just heard the ripples of the last stroke of the great clock die away.

> He crossed over and stood with his back against a shop window looking up at the great dome. All the weights in his body seemed to shift. He had a curious sense of something moving in his body in harmony with the building; it righted itself: it came to a full stop, It was exciting – this change of proportion.[18]

The second experience comes later in Martin's day, after he had had lunch and become angry after being cheated by the waiter:

> Again they came out in front of St. Paul's. He looked up. There was the same old man still feeding the sparrows. And there was the cathedral. He wished he could feel again the sense of weights changing in his body and coming to a stop; but the queer thrill of some correspondence between his own body and the stone no longer came to him. He felt nothing but anger.[19]

Martin's experience of his body had changed due to the feeling that comes through a disruption of the interplay between self and world. Anger breaks up the harmony between inner and outer. There is a loss of 'fit'. A kind of ecology is suggested, having three main components of a feeling, a bodily state and an interplay, a kind of conversation. A change in any one changes the other two.

Forms of feeling

Woolf believed that the task of the writer of 'modern fiction', was to discover human reality in the 'flickerings' of psychic life, those half-formed glimpses on the shimmer of the Jamesian stream – small and subtle nuances in the flow of feeling. She wrote:

> Let us record the atoms as they fall in the order in which they fall, let us trace the pattern, however disconnected or incoherent in appearance, which each sight or incident scores upon the consciousness. Let us not take for granted that life exists more fully in what is commonly thought big than what is commonly called small.[20]

A state of mind in which 'life exists more fully' is one of higher order consciousness, a form of mental life characterized by an increase in both its unity and its complexity. Complexity of consciousness can be defined as the number of different elements of which it is comprised. However, for these states to emerge, to become 'real', this focus must not be an inspection, a dissection, or an analysis. Such procedures risk the consequence of fragmentation. Instead, realisation comes in the way of Virginia Woolf's discipline, of finding the words that give shape or the pattern to the disconnected and incoherent. Such a pattern is what Robert Hobson called a 'form of feeling'.

'Forms of feeling', Hobson wrote, 'are elaborations of presentational symbols'.[21] A presentation can be understood as immediate experience. It has no other meaning than how it presents itself. 'A presentation is unique: it is what it is and means what it says.'[22]

Its elaboration is co-created in a generative conversation. As a partner in this interplay 'the therapist needs to be a kind of artist', fashioning an 'envisagement' of an

> elaborated feeling as regards general structure, proportion and rhythm: a total organization. It is not a matter of juxtaposed parts but of interacting elements which convey a pattern, a meaning, a balance which is 'felt' as a complex system.[23]

Notes

1 Damasio, A. R. (1996, 1999).
2 Vico, G. (1744).
3 Meares, R. (1983).
4 Russell, B. (1971).
5 Conrad, J. (1900, p. 225).
6 Karl, F. (1979, p. 330).
7 Merwin, W. S. (1988).
8 Woolf, V. (1925, pp. 282–291).
9 Woolf, V. (1982, p. 239).
10 Woolf, V. (1982, p. 229).
11 Woolf, V. (1978, p. 80).
12 Woolf, V. (1982, p. 260).
13 Woolf, V. (1982, p. 316).
14 Woolf, V. (1982, p. 139).
15 Woolf, V. (1982, p. 113).
16 Woolf, V. (1983, p. 10).
17 Woolf, V. (1978, p. 84).
18 Woolf, V. (1937, p. 244).
19 Woolf, V. (1937, p. 251). I am grateful to Margaret Comstock (1977) who pointed out to me the significance of this anecdote.
20 Woolf, V. (1925, p. 190).
21 Hobson, R. F. (1985, p. 79).
22 Hobson, R. F. (1985, pp. 71–72).
23 Hobson, R. (1985, p. 91).

8

POINTING AND DEPICTING

The great literary critic, I. A. Richards wrote of the 'contrast between discourse which primarily *points* and discourse which in one way or another, in some degree *depicts*', noting that it is 'parallel with many accounts of contrasts between sciences and poetries'.[1] In the preceding chapters we have been concerned with the picturing discourse and its relationship to feeling in the emergence of self. In brief, we have been discussing the growth of symbolization. '*Symbols*,' wrote Hobson, 'unlike signals, *represent* rather that point.'[2]

Although self is created by means of depictions, these depictions cannot speak. They need the other language to make manifest this fundamental and implicit imagery. In talking of the making of mind it is necessary also to consider the development of the discourse that points. This chapter begins a consideration of the pointing discourse, which reflects a mode of consciousness having the quality of intentionality, that is, it is *about* something. The evolution of this form of thought is illustrated by the story of Alice, who is 7–8 months old.

Alice is sitting on her grandmother's knee by a window, at night. 'Look!' exclaims her grandmother, pointing to the sky: 'Stars!' Alice is 7 or 8 months old.

Alice is a bright little girl. She has recently learnt to play the good-bye game the proper way, with her fingers pointing at the other person. Before this she waved good-bye strangely, with her fingers pointing at her own face. In doing this she was demonstrating a cardinal feature of the psychic life of the normally developing child before about 7 months. At this stage, infants seem to conceive (as compared with perceive) others as part of themselves. There is not much difference between 'your world' and 'my world'. Rather, there is only one world, the personal, in which 'how you see me' is much the same as 'how I see you'. In the last few weeks a great change has come about in Alice's development, indicated by the turning of her hand through 180° in playing the good-bye game. Michael Tomasello[3] would call it a 'revolution'. Alice has taken the first step on the path towards the discovery of 'otherness'. Sitting on her grandmother's lap they now gaze together at something that is 'other'.

World-to-be-manipulated

Otherness emerges as a third thing between the child and the caregiver from the earliest days of life, when what is other is a thing. The scene of this emergence is the 'world-to-be-manipulated'.[4] It is the undifferentiated forerunner of two distinct but interwoven themes of development, which are manifest in later life as discourses that either point or depict.

Early in infancy the baby begins to take an interest in those things it can handle while at the same time in an engagement with the mother. These things include clothes, bits of bodies, bottles, bedclothes, toys and so forth. The activity is 'autotelic'. It has no other purpose than the purpose of doing it. It has no 'point'. It is simply play. Indeed, Piaget went so far as to say 'that everything during the first months of life, except feeding and emotions like fear and anger, is play'.[5]

The world-to-be-manipulated becomes more purposeful by the age of 4–5 months when intentional grasping begins.[6] Tom Bower charted the development of this early form of intentional behaviours. He considered the behaviour in terms of reaching for, touching and grasping an object. Babies in the first weeks of life reach for and grasp an object in almost reflex manner. By the age of 20 weeks the behaviours have become selective. 'The reaching component and the grasping component are temporarily quite separate.'[7] The infant does not necessarily grasp what it initially reached for. Older infants in his study tended to touch an object before grasping it.[8]

The relationship between mother, child and things – perhaps simple toys – is triadic in the sense that it does not consist of an oscillation between two different dyads of mother-baby and baby-object. The mother and baby appear to be engaged together in play with the object. This object, however, as the third thing in the relationship is not yet entirely 'other'. It still has an aspect of the personal attached to it. There are, then, two kinds of emergent 'thirdness', one in which the third is sensed as 'other' and a second state in which the third remains partly within personal space. Those things within the latter zone might include a teddy bear, doll, or cuddle rug. They take on special significance for the child, having the capacity to give comfort and soothing. Winnicott called them transitional objects.[9]

The two forms of treating objects involve different qualities of experience and become aspects of different ways of relating to other people, each of which has a characteristic language, a subject to be touched upon in a later chapter.

During the first months of life, when there is nothing beyond the personal domain, the child does not point. Grasping is the characteristic movement. Objects are drawn back towards the child, into the personal sphere.

The mother and baby playing together with a few toys looks a simple scene but when a movie of it comes to be analysed, it is found to be extraordinarily complex. A striking finding, however, is that, as time goes on, the baby's interest in the object increases. In one of our studies, for example, the babies at 3 months directed their gaze at the toys for only 12 per cent of the time while at 6 months, 60 per cent of the gaze was focused on the toys. This trajectory culminates in a differentiation into two developmental pathways, mentioned earlier, that lead to two different kinds of discourse, one analogous to pointing and the other to depicting. The forking into two pathways is manifest at that developmental stage, which Tomasello[10] has called the '9-month revolution'.

Joint attention

About a month after the episode at the window, Alice is being carried by her grandmother, who is walking outdoors in the night. Once again the grandmother points to the sky saying: 'Look! Stars'.[11] Almost in unison, Alice brings her own arm up, parallel to her grandmother's, pointing with her. Another month after this, Alice initiates pointing episodes herself.

Tomasello says of the grandmother's action, citing supporting data, 'that the simple act of pointing to an object for the sole purpose of sharing attention to it is a uniquely human communicative behaviour'.[12] Chimpanzees do not behave in this way. Adult chimpanzees rarely act on objects with 'an apparent attempt of engaging the attention of the infants' whereas human mothers 'primarily manipulate objects with the intent of stimulating, sustaining or enhancing the actions of infants'.[13]

The difference between Pan troglodytes (the chimpanzee) and *Homo sapiens*, in this respect seems to be clear. Whereas human mothers foster joint visual attention on objects,[14] ape mothers do not. Joint usual attention is a bridge between elementary forms of attention and the higher forms of voluntary attention.

The 8-month anxiety

Alice's capacity at the age of 9 months to participate in the pointing game is related to what has been called 'the 8-month anxiety'.[15] It is an indication of a step towards the first appearance of the markers of self at about the age of four. This progression involves a succession of negations in which self emerges, in part, by a realization of that which is not self. At about 7 months, the child becomes aware that he or she is an entity, somewhat distinct from other people. The changed direction of Alice's hand during the good-bye game gives evidence of such awareness. This awareness is related to the first emergence of anxiety in the child's life.

The 8-month anxiety can be understood, again, in part, by considering the nature of anxiety or fear. It is the result of a threat to self. Anxiety, therefore,

> can only arise when the baby has some sense of herself as an entity and some ability to evaluate a threat to this entity. This argument gains support from observations of children who were observed on the visual cliff. Children of 5 and 9 months of age crawled out over a glass flooring, seeing a space emerge below them. Both groups of children had their heart rates recorded while they did this. The younger group was quite aware of what was happening but seemed interested rather than alarmed. This was indicated by a drop in heart rate. The older babies' heart rates

rose, an index of fear.[16] Thus the older children apparently sensed a threat to their existence, whereas the young ones did not.[17]

'Otherness' and self, emerge hand in hand. The pointing game begins, in my view, when the child realizes that there is something beyond self, which is not self, that can be pointed at. This view resembles, in part that of Tomasello, though the language is different. He believes 'that infants begin to engage in joint attentional interactions when they begin to understand other persons as intentional agents like the self'.[18]

The main threat that induces 8-month anxiety is separation from that figure who in the beginning of life was experienced as part of a proto-self. At 8 months this single organism made of two people has been differentiated into two connected parts. Although the child feels she is distinct from others, at the same time she experiences the particular other, the attachment figure, in a special way. The caregiver is imbued with a feeling of the personal. In this way, he or she is not entirely other. Rather, this person is sensed as a necessary part of the child's personal existing, a loss of which would threaten that existence. Kohut would have called the other experienced in this way a 'self-object'.[19] There are now two different relationships with others – one in which the feeling of the personal is still attached to the other and a second in which this is not so. These different kinds of relatedness underlie the two developmental themes relating to pointing and depicting.

The 8-month anxiety is a complicated developmental shift that cannot be explained entirely by the beginning of a conceptual distinction between self and other. The fear of strangers, which is a part of this period of anxiety, may depend upon something else, involving a match-mismatch process.

The peekaboo game and object permanence

At about 9 months, soon after the occasion of pointing at the stars in tandem with her grandmother, Alice has invented a new game for herself. In this game, she lies in bed and covers her face with the sheet, laughing as she does it. Then she suddenly pulls down the sheet, revealing herself, laughing even more delightedly at the amazed expressions of her parents' faces and voices. 'Ooh! There you are!' they exclaim. She shows that she still does not have the sense that 'how I see you' is not the same as 'how you see me'.

Alice's behaviour in this game reflects a development of what Piaget called the concept of object permanence, a main stage of which occurs between the ages of 8 and 10 months. Before this step is reached the child behaves as if objects have no permanent existence. When something disappears from view the infant acts as if it were no longer in the world. If a child of 4 or 5 months is playing with a toy for which it previously reached and grasped and which is now placed under a sheet or the coverlet of a bed, the child does not search for it. It is as if it has gone forever. It is between 8 or 10 months, according to Piaget that the child searches for an object screened from its vision in this way.[20] It now acts as if an object, although no longer visible, must still exist. This behaviour has implications that support the view that at about 7–8 months the infant discovers an awareness of itself as an entity. As Lewis and Gunn remark: 'If an infant knows that objects exist, he must also know that he exists as separate from objects. It would be reasonable to assume that knowledge of others, self and objects develop at the same time.'[21] Object permanence is not properly established until 18 months.

Alice's new game is a variant of the peekaboo game, which her parents had played with her earlier in her infancy. At first, she was a rather passive partner but now, just as she has done with pointing, she has become the agent.

The peekaboo game is played with infants in many cultures and may even be universal.[22] An essential contribution to the game is the parent's voice, which is used rather in the way that it is used in the proto-conversation. Anne Fernald and Daniella O'Neill speak of 'the "lyrics" of the peekaboo routine'. [23] There is, in this routine, a kind of musicality. Jerome Bruner has written at length about the possible contribution of the peekaboo game to the later development of language, noting that it has a structure resembling the reciprocal character of conversation. 'Timing' of the parental response is particularly important.[24] Bruner remarked that 'a game, in its way, is a little proto-conversation'.[25]This proto-conversation can be seen as an elaboration of and development from, the proto-conversational game played first at about two months.

Imitation

The undifferentiated 'world-to-be-manipulated involving mother, child and the space between, as an embryonic inner space, forks at the 9-month revolution'. It becomes differentiated into two distinct developmental pathways. One of these, manifest in the pointing game, moves towards intentional consciousness. The other leads towards symbolization. At the 9-month stage, the latter pathway is reflected in another game. It is imitation. Tomasello and his colleagues have demonstrated that joint attention and imitation emerge hand-in-hand.[26] They followed 24 children from 9 to 15 month of age, assessing them every month. In terms of assessment measure, they were 'joint engagement, gaze following, point following, imitation of instrumental acts, imitation of arbitrary acts, reaction to social obstacles, use of imperative gestures and use of declarative gestures'.[27] The measures, then, reflected three main capacities – joint attention, imitation and gesture. They tended to emerge together: 'All of these skills emerge in close developmental synchrony for individual children, with nearly 80 per cent of the infants mastering all nine tasks within a four-month window.' [28,29] Both joint attention and imitation were displayed by Alice as she and her grandmother pointed at the stars.

The observation that the behaviours of joint attention, imitation and gesture are linked together developmentally seems important. Although these categories of behaviour are treated as separate research subjects, the implication that they are closely related makes intuitive sense. The three categories can be seen, in a broad way, to reflect the world that is other, the world that is self and the interplay between them. These are the basic components of an emergent human consciousness.

The notion that the measures used by Tomasello and his colleagues to investigate the nature of the '9-month revolution' make up these three groupings needs some explanation. For two of these groups, however, little more needs to be said beyond what has already been mentioned. Joint attention, as displayed in the pointing game, is the first manifestation of the child's encounter with otherness, something beyond personal space. Gesture has a part to play in the development and presumably the evolution of human communication. It is the third group of behaviours involving imitation for which an adaptive purpose cannot easily be found. Earlier psychologists, of whom the most prominent, perhaps, was Karl Groos,[30] postulated that the behaviour represents the rehearsal and practice of roles necessary in later life. Piaget rejected this proposal, pointing out that imitative behaviours very often have nothing to do with adult roles. This kind of behaviour may be performed simply for the child's own amusement. It is autotelic and most clearly displayed after the age of 2. Piaget suggested that it is related to 'assimilation to the self'.[31] It has a role in the creation of self-function and the development of symbolization.

Not all imitations performed by humans are autotelic. Some have a clear purpose. The person, child or adult, copies another person with the aim of being able to perform the actions of this other person. This observation leads to the idea that there are two kinds of imitation evident in child behaviour. One is autotelic and related to the emergence of self. The other is purposeful. It is involved in learning behaviours, which are adaptive in that they are helpful in dealing with the environment, including the social environment.

A case for distinguishing between the copying (of which chimpanzees are capable) and the imitation performed by children has been made by Tomasello. The difference is used to support his theory of the evolution of human consciousness, stated as follows: 'I have alighted upon the hypothesis that human beings evolved a new way of identifying with and understanding conspecifics as intentional beings.'[32]

Tomasello called the copying performed by chimpanzees 'emulation' to contrast this behaviour with the imitation of children. Chimpanzees replicate the activity of the other without identification. An illustration of the effect of identification is given by the following experiment, reported by Gergely and colleagues.[33] Infants of 14 months watched an experimenter perform the action of switching on a lamp with the forehead with hands behind the back. Half the children watched the experimenter with hands free and the other half when they were bound. The children were asked to perform the same action as the experimenter. 69 per cent of the hands-free watchers attempted to turn on the lamp with their foreheads, assuming the experimenter's behaviour was intentional. Of the subjects watching the experimenter with hands constrained only 21 per cent used the forehead solution. Most of them used their hands, because they realized the model could not do anything else but perform the odd way of lighting the lamp. The findings suggested that these children showed an awareness of intentionality.

Children suffering from autism who, it is supposed, suffer a deficiency in the sense of self, also emulate but do not imitate. They are good at copying novel actions performed by others but they do not show identification with the person performing the tasks. Peter Hobson and his colleague Tony Lee were able to demonstrate this in creatively designed experiments.[34] For example, the experimenter put a pipe rack to his shoulder as if it were a musical instrument and strummed it with a stick. Half the children in their group of subjects were shown Tony Lee strumming 'in a harsh way, making a staccato sound, and half saw him use a graceful and gentle strumming action'.[35] Most of the non-autistic children performed the action as the experimenter had but only a few of those with autism did so. They merely strummed, as if not identifying with the feeling that might be involved in playing with the imaginary musical instrument.

The analyses of the tapes of the subjects attempt at imitation gave further indication of failure of identification in the autistic group of subjects. Most of the children without autism were able to put themselves in the place of the experimenter, acting as if they were him. For example, they put the pipe rack to their shoulders. Few of the children with autism did so. They merely copied a strumming action.

The behaviours of the children involved in this experiment illustrate the doubling involved in imitation. The child pretends to be someone else, play acting, knowing, at the same time, who she really is. It is as if, in a limited way, using the body, she can be two people at the same time. Emulation, on the other hand, involves no such co-ordination of two different consciousnesses. Only one is involved. The behaviour of the other is appropriated for oneself.

Alice's action in copying her grandmother's pointing at the stars is the forerunner and the point at which they begin to diverge, of two different themes of development. The theme of pointing develops into, and becomes internalized as, intentional consciousness; the depiction involved in imitation is a step towards symbolization.

Notes

1 Richards, I. A. (1976, p. 117).
2 Hobson, R. (1985, p. 66).
3 Tomasello, M. (2000).
4 Meares, R. (1993, p. 33; 2005, p. 27).
5 Piaget, J. (1951, p. 90).
6 Piaget, J. (1952).
7 Bower, T. (1974, p. 154).
8 Bower, T. (1974, p. 163).
9 Winnicot, D. W. (1974).
10 Tomasello, M. (2000).
11 Penman *et al.* (1981).
12 Tomasello, M. (2000, p. 63).

13 Bard and Vauclair (1984, p. 181).
14 Collis, G. (1981).
15 Spitz, R. (1965).
16 Schwartz *et al.* (1973).
17 Meares, R. (1993, p. 54; 2005, p. 46).
18 Tomasello, M. (2000, p. 68).
19 Kohut, H. (1971, 1977).
20 Piaget, J. (1954).
21 Lewis and Gunn (1978, p. 211).
22 Fernald and O'Neill (1993).
23 Fernald and O'Neill (1993).
24 Bruner, J. (1975, 1993); Bruner and Sherwood (1976).
25 Bruner, J. (1983, p. 47).
26 Carpenter *et al.* (1998).
27 Tomasello, M. (1999, p. 93).
28 Tomasello, M. (1999, p. 93).
29 Something that looks like imitation can be seen in videos of the proto-conversation. This behaviour differs from imitation distal to the model to be imitated. The behaviours of the neonate reported by Meltzoff and Moore (1977) may be different again. Meltzoff and Moore followed their initial paper with a series of similar observations, reviewed by Anisfeld (1996), demonstrating mirror-like responding in a baby to a close-up adult face protruding its tongue and opening its mouth and making other gestures. These responses are best explained, Anisfeld has argued, by a process other than imitation. They more closely resemble echopraxia, in which the object makes involuntary movements, which mirror those of the person who confronts him. It occurs in severe cases of schizophrenia. It is a reflexive behaviour having a possible basis in an absence of the sense of self.
30 Groos, K. (1898, p. 190).
31 Piaget, J. (1969, p. 494).
32 Tomasello, M. (1999, pp. 204–205).
33 Gergely *et al.* (2002).
34 Hobson, R. P. (2004, pp. 215–223), Hobson and Lee (1999).
35 Hobson, R. P. (2004, p. 218).

9

MYTH AND PROTO-MYTH

The 'revolution' in the child's sense of herself and her world that occurs at 7–9 months is followed by another revolution at 18 months, which is equally if not more portentous. It is at this point that language use begins. At the same time children become social, begin to have an awareness of who they are in relationship to other people. Identity emerges. Soon after this the child can say 'that's me', pointing at a photograph. Emotions necessary to the regulation of proper social conduct emerge. Michael Lewis has studied the appearance of shame, embarrassment and guilt, pointing out their relationship to the discovery of personal identity.[1]

These are large issues, with an extensive literature beyond the scope of this discussion. My focus is upon the evolution of self and those aspects of emotion, language and relationship relevant to its emergence. During this new period of development there are further steps toward selfhood. Once again negation is involved. It is now explicit. When children reach the age of 2, they start to use the word 'no' in a way that asserts their own distinctness as individual persons. They demonstrate to others that they are agents in their own world, with the capacity for choice.[2] Alice, for example, who is now 2 years old, tells her parents, when they take her to visit her grandparents: 'You are not my family, Nanna is my family'. Her parents are amused. Their response was similar a year later when they walked with Alice in a park and reached a point where the pathway forked. As they stepped towards the pathway going left, Alice said 'No, this way', choosing to go right. Children of this age who say 'no' more often than their peers at this age are likely to be developmentally advanced.[3] Parental skills are required in negotiating behaviour that looks like simple defiance. Rather, it should be treated as a game.

With the enhancement of the proto-self come other changes, including the diminishment of the normal separation anxiety,[4] which was first evident at about 7 months and reached a peak at 18 months.[5] Those children whose background has included the 'good-enough' mothering advocated by Winnicott, in which periods of conversational play have occurred, are likely to be able to cope with separation from parents well enough to attend pre-school. Those without this background make up a significant proportion of children whose normal fear of separation from parents is prolonged. Lack of separation impedes the growth of 'otherness'. The other, or the object to speak psychoanalytically, is discovered through its absence. Without 'otherness' there is no self, a state characterized by a feeling of ownership, which separates my world from your world. As self grows separation fears fade.[6]

Self begins to emerge in the phase of language acquisition, not only by negation and the furthering of 'otherness' but also in a positive way, by the child's discovery of the capacity to represent a nascent self to itself. This depends on make-believe, on pretend play. It seems strange to find that what is most central to us rests on so apparently flimsy basis, without obvious adaptive purpose or the process of reason.

At about 18 months, or perhaps a bit earlier,[7] the child might do such things as use a banana as a telephone. The representing object resembles the shape of that which it represents. As the play develops, the representing actions may begin to tell a little story. For example, a 3-year-old girl, Lucy, creates a tale about rabbits. She uses glasses lying on their sides for the burrows and white tissues rolled up for the rabbits. She demonstrates the use of analogical thought. The objects chosen to stand for the elements of her mini-narrative have shapes similar to those elements. Children with autism do not play in this way. They cannot pretend.[8] They can, however, play in the sense of doing a puzzle, of fitting things together.[9]

Lucy's story is apparently private, told only to herself. She is at an almost empty restaurant with her mother, grandparents and some friends. She has moved away to another table where she sits with her back to the others, apparently oblivious of their presence. She continues to play when her mother comes over. 'It's a bunny', she says of a white paper ball. The murmuring tone of her voice does not change. It seems that her mother is included in her world that is private. She speaks in a particular way, which we might call quasi-intimate. If one of the friends, who was a stranger, came over to her table to see what was going on, Lucy would have stopped the play and spoken to the person in a different way, which was more truly public.

Like a dream, the story Lucy tells is related in some way to her experiences of the life she lives. The analogical process, again like a dream, has processed the material so that it emerges as if in a code. The playing child, of course, does not know this. All she knows is that what she is doing is interesting and she likes doing it. It does not matter that neither she nor anybody else knows what the story 'means'. It is the process that is important.

At one level, the story might 'mean' that rabbits, like people, can leave the place where they live and go out to visit other places, like restaurants. Freud might call this 'manifest content'. There is, however, likely to be another story, or stories, underlying this, more fundamental and of greater consequence, involving perhaps the dramas of family life. No one of these stories overrides the rest. Each is a reality of its own, which when combined with the others creates, like a poem, a larger reality different from but encompassing its constituents.

Lucy has now reached the age between say 3½ and 5½, when symbolization is achieved. She will soon be able, if asked by an experimenter, to tell her story by means of objects other than those that showed resemblances to the elements of her story.[10] She will no longer be constrained by the physical attributes of the representing object. The representing object can now be arbitrarily selected. Very soon a story can be told in imagination without the physical presence of representing objects. Symbols are used instead.[11] The child's thought is no longer constrained by environmental immediacies, a developmental attainment beyond that of other primates. The capacity to use symbols has been seen by many authorities as the hallmark of the kind of consciousness that is peculiarly human. Ernst Cassirer called the human primate 'animal symbolicum'.[12] A number of writers have used the term *Homo symbolicus*. They include Mircea Eliade,[13] and Henshilwood and d'Errico.[14] Deacon calls humankind 'the symbolic species'.[15]

Lucy's narrative might be seen as co-created, an interplay with what the environment makes available and a personal world of feelings, memories, desires and so forth. She uses that in the environment capable of being used for representational purposes. The availability of choice determines, at least in part, which elements of her experience come to be represented.

The scene of symbolic play is a crucial step along the pathway to self. This was the view of Piaget. The representations that the child makes during this play are not to be conceived as rehearsals for adult roles, as Karl Groos,[16] among others, might have supposed. Lucy, for example, is not preparing to become a rabbit farmer. Her behaviour, Piaget believed, refers 'to a pole of assimilation to the self'.[17]

> In symbolic play this systematic assimilation takes the form of a particular use of the semiotic function – namely, the creation of symbols at will in order to express everything in the child's life experience that cannot be formulated and assimilated by language alone.[18]

The representations are made for the emergent self and not for someone else. It is a 'symbolism centering on the self'. [19]

The girl who creates a narrative from analogic representations is not only on her way to selfhood she is also on the verge of becoming a cultural creature. In fact she is already part of culture in the way that Clifford Geertz spoke about it. He wrote: 'Believing, like Max Weber, that man is an animal suspended in webs of significance he himself has spun, I take culture to be those webs.'[20]

These webs are spun in language, or the equivalents of language and, most fundamentally, they consist of stories. As Lucy plays, she is talking and the story she tells, which is her own, uses material that is not her own but that is cultural. Lucy lives in the city. She has never seen a rabbit. What she knows of the animal has comes from stories.

The story she is telling is for herself alone. It is embryonically 'inner', derived, in its originality, from an emergent mind or self. This inner material is partly public and partly an aspect of mind or self, appearing in the outer world, laid out on a restaurant table. It is a proto-myth. Lucy's creation is the forerunner of the rituals and stories that are at the heart of human culture and human uniqueness.[21] Multiple stories, which have the form of symbolic play, but greatly elaborated, make up the fabric of culture. The various patternings made by these interwoven threads of narrative both manifest and constitute the 'mind' of these societies.

Before elaborating this viewpoint it is necessary to confront the difficult word 'culture', which, like 'mind' and 'personality', is not easy to define. Kroeber and Kluckhohn reviewed various attempts at definition and found over 160, reflecting a dozen different conceptual approaches.[22]

An approach to an adequate definition must begin with a study of what seems fundamental to culture. Like personality, the expressions of culture are shifting and various. Also like personality, it is to be identified by what is enduring. The several hundred Australian Aboriginal cultures are regarded as the most enduring in the planet, having been in continuous existence for perhaps 60, 000 years. Rock carvings, 20,000 to 40,000 years old have been found depicting people dancing in ceremonies in which the body decoration is similar to that which would be worn in the present day. The essential unit of this culture is a story, which Spencer and Gillen in trying to translate the untranslatable, called a 'dreaming'.[23]

The dream time

A dreaming is a myth that is of both practical and religious significance. There is a multitude of these individual dreamings related to a unifying myth concerning the creation of man and the world. Before this time, The Dream Time, the earth was peopled by creatures who were not human but who nevertheless behaved in human ways.[24] Like ordinary human beings, they had failings and virtues, pleasures and sufferings. Suddenly this period ended. All these creatures, who resembled plants and animals, were, at a stroke, frozen into particular places in the landscape. The various features of the landscape contain not only beings but also their stories. Aborigines believe these mythical beings to be their ancestors, whose presence they sense in the features of the natural world. A dreaming is a story of one of these ancestors. It is owned by a particular group of people whose responsibility is to keep the story alive.

The natural world, in this system, is the sphere of the sacred. The Dreaming, however, links not only nature and spirit but also a wide range of day-to-day activities, including the laws and values of society, which the ancestral beings laid down. The stories of the dreaming contain information of a practical nature, e.g. to do with the waterholes and sources of food. The Dreaming is thus constantly being lived so that past and present co-exist. Living within the Dreaming involves the Dream Journey in which the wandering course of an ancestral being's story is followed throughout the year over large tracts of country. This journeying not only involves roaming from one food site to another as the seasons change. It is also a sacred journey. At intervals during the wandering, the primordial world-creating story is retold and re-enacted in rituals of dancing and song. The Aborigines live in a highly symbolic world in which the landscape is part of themselves. Stanner,[25] who has given one of the best descriptions of the mysterious concept of the Dreaming, remarks that it is a symbolic complex of 'one flesh-one-spirit-one country-one Dreaming'.[26]

This system operates like a vast extra-corporeal memory system, which gives to aboriginal society an evolutionary advantage. It can be conceived in Darwinian terms as a highly sophisticated means of survival and adaptation to the conditions of a harsh country. Individual dreamings concerning, for example, yams and honey ants, provide different threads of the multiple informational strands that make up the 'web' of culture that surrounds aboriginal society. Its encyclopaedic potential is suggested by Dianne Johnson, an expert in aboriginal astronomy, in describing the place of the night sky in this system.

> The night sky is still significant to Indigenous people. It is viewed as being a series of multi-layered interconnecting maps, and its meanings operate at many levels simultaneously. When, for example, the night sky is viewed as a seasonal calendar, this does not exclude meanings it has in mythology or social relationships – indeed these meanings frequently elaborate the seasonal symbolism, representing simply a shift in emphasis. The use of stars for seasonal voyaging does not exclude their meanings in the context of terrestrial landscape. Knowing them as belonging to the place of the dead does not preclude seeing them also as celestial campfires. In addition, the celestial landscape is intrinsically linked with the terrestrial one: most of the myths that involve the stars have their dramatic starting points or episodes on the earth. Thus many sky-based ancestral heroes and heroines are also associated with particular places in the earthly landscape . . . Across the continent, the sky-world is seen as the dwelling place of many ancestral spirits and creation heroes and heroines, those personified sources of energy, which inform and give meaning to natural and cultural life. The sky-world is a vast, bountiful, and lively place, from which the sky-people can travel along shamanic pathways.[27]

Drawing on the account of William Stanbridge who, in the 1850s, had become friendly with the now lost Boorong people in North Western Victoria, John Morieson has studied the astronomy created by these people. It gives further evidence of the encyclopedic role of aboriginal stories. At least 40 creatures, both human and non-human, were distinguished in the constellations of the night sky. Their stories had survival value not only as navigational aids but also relating to food sources. For example, Morieson was able to identify in the night sky Neilloan, the malleefowl, as a bird in profile, in what Europeans call the Vega constellation.

> When the Boorong observed the disappearance of Neilloan from the sky they would know that the laying season had begun and they might head off for malleefowl country for a change of diet and an easily obtained

> egg supply. And while they were there another aspect would unfold. The Aboriginal parent and child would observe much about the daily life of the malleefowl that was applicable to their own behaviour . . . the malleefowl provides an excellent role model for human behaviour in that they mate for life, demonstrate specialized gender responsibilities, demonstrate teamwork and co-operation.[28]

Myth and meaning

With the advent of writing, the means of storing and transmitting information across generations, which the mythological system of culture provided, became irrelevant. Simpler means were now available. The intricate apparatus creating a symbolic realization of the natural world was allowed to fall into decrepitude. The literate world of Aristotle, as G. S. Kirk put it, was 'demythologicalized'.[29]

By the time of the Romans, as Cassirer points out, the myths were regarded as allegories, some of which, as he said, 'seem to be extremely naïve'.[30] This view of myth has persisted to present day. In this viewpoint, myths are parables to be used as guides to human behaviour. Such 'explanations of mythical phenomena,' wrote Cassirer, 'become in the end an entire negation of these phenomena. The mythical world appears as an artificial world, as a pretense for something else.'[31]

Until the twentieth century much theorizing about the nature, origin and function of myth depended upon the evidence of Greco-Roman myths. The stories were presumably handed down from an earlier time. Elements relating to the environment and man's adaption to the natural world began to be omitted. Kirk, in his book on the meaning and function of myth, points out that, what might be called a degradation of myth in Greek culture, was regarded in Victorian times and by those writing later in the spirit of that age, as an improvement. Those writing from a nineteenth-century viewpoint included the Swedish philologist and mythographer, Martin Nilsson and Herbert Jennings Rose whose *Handbook of Greek Mythology*, which first appeared in 1928, has become a standard work, going into six editions. Kirk quotes from Nilsson as evidence that Nilsson believed that Greek myths were superior to the earlier stories from which they were derived and which, in my view, would have had functions similar to a 'dreaming'. Nilsson asserted that a systematic analysis will show 'how the special talent of the Greeks, their rationalism, led to selection, elimination and remoulding of the excessively fantastic folktale motifs'.[32] Rose put forward a similar view.[33] Kirk concludes that Greek mythology is a 'censored, derivative and literary affair . . . seriously short of the qualities of imaginative unreason that are normally associated with mythos'.[34] He believed the original forms of Greek myth

> lay in the far distant past, not in the eighth century BC or the ninth, not even in the Mycenaean Age or perhaps the Bronze Age as a whole, but possibly far back in the Neolithic Age, at a time, indeed, when the term 'Greek' has almost no meaning.[35]

The myth of Narcissus

An illustration of how the literate version might differ from its original form is given by the Narcissus myth, the essentials of which are summarized by Rose:

> A beautiful youth, son of Cephisus (the Boeotian River) and Liriope, a nymph. He loved no one till he saw his own reflection in water and fell in love with that; finally he pined away, died, and was turned into the flower of like name. The story may arise from the magical danger of seeing one's own image in a mirror (see Frazer), but Ovid gives an explanation (his own?) of it; Narcissus was punished for his cruelty to Echo. Hera had deprived her of normal speech because her chatter prevented the goddess catching Zeus at his amours with the other nymphs; she could only repeat what others said. She tried to make love to Narcissus with fragments of his own speech, but he repulsed her and she so wasted away with grief that there was nothing left of her but her voice.[36]

In this account, the story concerns a person. In a 'dreaming' it would also concern the plant. The Polish anthropologist, Bronislaw Malinowski (1884–1942) makes this point. Having studied pre-literate cultures in both New Guinea and the Trobriand Islands, he wrote: 'Every myth possesses as its kernel or ultimate reality some natural phenomenon or other, elaborately woven into a tale to an extent which almost masks and obliterates it.'[37] The tribal memory of the ancient hunter-gatherer world needed to include information about plants not only as food sources, but as the basis of folk medicine. This memory system was impressively large. Lévi-Strauss cites the findings of H. C. Conklin, an ethnographer specializing in taxonomy. 'The Hanunóo classify their local plant world, at the lowest (terminal) level of contrast, into more than 1800 mutually exclusive folk taxa, while botanists divide the same flora – in terms of species – into less than 1300 scientific taxa.'[38] From a botanical perspective the hunter-gathering system was highly scientific.

A myth having the form of a 'dreaming' would have recorded the medicinal properties of a plant such as the narcissus, the name of which signals its effects. *Narke* is a Greek word meaning numbness. The verb *nakhon* means to stupefy. It is now known that the bulb of the narcissus contains a toxic alkaloid, which in small quantities is an emetic but in large doses is narcotic,[39] having deadening and stupefying effects that can be fatal.

The original myth would have recorded, as the Greek version does, where the plant is found. The preferred habitat of daffodils is as Wordsworth described it in his famous poem, 'along the lake, beneath the trees'.

An essential aspect of an original myth is its analogical structuring. Its starting point is typically some analogical resemblance between the shape of some element in the environment and the being, who will be the centrepiece of the story. The narcissus is that analogue. It is likely that the myth *concerns narcissus poeticus*, which is more potent than the usually encountered narcissus pseudonarcissus. It is also white, like a pale face. Hanging over the water on its stem – a stem or a stick is often used in symbolic play to represent a person – it may have looked to pre-historic man like a lovelorn youth.

The literate version of the Narcissus myth maintains, to this point, the basic elements of the hypothetical earlier form. It is when one comes to 'meaning' that the problems arrive. It may be that a myth has no 'meaning' at all. This was the view of Jane Ellen Harrison (1850–1928), a pioneer female academic, feminist and classical scholar, who was a central figure in the brilliant 'Cambridge Group', who were developing an approach to Greek religion and myth inspired by Frazer of *Golden Bough* fame. She believed that a myth is simply a representation, 'another form of utterance, of expression'.[40] At its most fundamental level, it can be compared with a particular kind of poem, which has an intensity, a mood and sense of significance but no 'meaning'.

In a very influential essay Lévi-Strauss approached the problem of meaning in a novel and very interesting way. He states: 'If there is a meaning to be found in mythology, it cannot reside in the isolated elements which enter into the composition of a myth, but only in the way those elements are combined.'[41] Following this viewpoint, Frazer's supposition concerning the origin of the narcissus myth, referred to in Rose's summary, is to be rejected. It is based on a single feature of the myth, the reflected image. Frazer found that in many cultures there was a belief that 'a person's reflection in water or a mirror is his soul'. He wrote that it was a maxim in 'ancient Greece not to look at one's reflection in water' and that 'they feared that the water spirits would drag the person's reflection or soul under water, leaving him soulless to perish. This was probably the origin of the classical story of the beautiful Narcissus'.[42] A consideration of the myth, however, suggests that Frazer's idea cannot be discarded entirely.

The Lévi-Strauss approach, involving the way the constituents of the myth are combined, is intriguing. He deemed each constituent to consist of a *relation*, defined in the shortest possible sentence.[43] These units were to be arranged in a manner resembling an orchestral score. A horizontal axis, the diachronic, is made up of the events of the story as they move through time. The second, the synchronic, consists of vertical columns of events, or relationships, which resemble each other. Since these repetitions of similarity are extracted from the time stream they are timeless. Lévi-Strauss noted that this was the particular quality of myth, which always refers to events alleged to have taken place a long time ago. 'What gives myth an operational value is that the specific pattern described is timeless; it explains the present and the past as well as the future.'[44]

The two axes replicate those used by Lévi-Strauss to analyse the structure of a particular culture as a whole. He borrowed the terminology of diachronic and synchronic from Saussure, whose study was language. Lévi-Strauss seemed to be saying that a myth, a culture and a text can each be analysed in the same way since each is a product of the human mind, which tends to organize the world, with which it is in constant interplay, in a stereotypic fashion.

We return to the question of the 'meaning' of myth. Lévi-Strauss remarked that if we want to tell its story we read along the diachronic axis but 'if we want to *understand* the myth, then we will have to . . . read from left to right, column after column, each one being considered as a unit'.[45]As myth is told and retold, it will change in passing from generation to generation. Consequently, it will have a number of variants. 'Accordingly', Lévi-Strauss said, 'We define the myth in all its versions'.[46] When the various versions are analysed together, a version of the myth emerges that has greater validity than any single version. The practice can be compared with the system used in clinical neurophysiology to extract from other brain activity going on at the same time, the electrical patterning specifically related to a particular event. This event, a stimulus of some kind, is presented repeatedly and those segments of electrical patterns immediately following the stimuli are averaged. The averaging amplifies the elements related to the event and neutralizes extraneous elements. If Ovid's story of Narcissus is combined with the other main version, of Pausanias, a clearer set of Lévi-Strauss columns can be discerned.

In the Pausanias version, Echo is replaced by a twin sister, who dies. Narcissus is bereft by the loss and wanders in search of solace and of a replacement for her. He comes to a pool where he is transfixed by the reflected image of his likeness, which is also the likeness of is sister. He withers and dies. Putting the two versions together we arrive at several repetitions, or analogous relations, which make up the following columns: responding/non-responding; withering/death; birth/rebirth. In the first column, the relation of responding is personified by Echo before Hera's curse. An engaging conversationalist, she would have been able to represent Narcissus to himself. So also would the twin-sister, who 'knew' him. Non-responding is the relation inflicted on Echo by the curse. She cannot give to Narcissus what he needs, being able only to repeat the last words he speaks. The reflected image is similarly useless. Withering, a depletion of life, follows non-responding and rejection – the fate of both Echo and Narcissus. The myth seen in this way might be seen as an allegory of the idea that one comes to know oneself through particular responses of other people. Deprivation of this kind of responsiveness, for a young person, leads to an emotional and psychological withering, a failure of mind or self to grow.

The final column is derived from the details of the birth and death of Narcissus. His mother was the blue nymph, Liriope. Liriope is a grassy plant with a blue-purple flower. Its preferred habitat is damp, fertile soil, as found on a riverbank. Her union at the water's edge with Cephisus, the longest river in Boeotia, results in the birth of Narcissus. His death comes at the same site, as he gazes into the water. The beautiful flower arises at the place of his death, a renewal of life.

With this analysis, the myth now comes to have the sense of a poem made of two main polarities. Such polarities, or binary opposites, are principal features of Lévi-Strauss structures. The two polarities are related – responding (life) is the opposite of non-responding (death).

Lévi-Strauss based his way of understanding the organization of the various elements of hunter-gather culture and what he called 'totemic' thought, on Saussure's distinction between syntagmatic and paradigmatic relations, conceived as 'horizontal and vertical',[47] a distinction, it seemed, to which he was introduced by Jakobson. Both Jakobson and Lévi-Strauss were refugees from Nazi persecution of Jews in World War II when they met in New York, in 1942. Lévi-Strauss was 34 and Jakobson 12 years older. Jakobson proved to be both an inspiration and something of a mentor to the younger man. 'The discipline practiced by Jakobson enthralled me like a detective story,' Lévi-Strauss remembered. 'I had the feeling I was taking part in a great adventure of the mind.'[48] Yet in 'The Savage Mind' there is only one brief mention of Jakobson. Neither 'metaphor' nor 'metonym' appear in the index. His emphasis was now on 'discontinuous oppositions'. Chiding Boas for puzzling about a system of classification in hunter-gatherer culture, Lévi-Strauss wrote:

> To have recognized it he need only, contrary to a commonly held position, have been prepared, instead of reducing the story or myth to a mere narrative, to try to discover the scheme of discontinuous oppositions governing its organization behind the mythical discourse.[49]

The details of the birth and death of Narcissus locate the story in a particular landscape, the countryside of the province of Boeotia,[50] which is in the central part of Greece. In this way, the myth resembles a 'dreaming', which is tied to a specific geography, to specific rock formations, streams, water-holes and so forth. The story, which is magical and unreal, has its basis in the real, that which is visible, solid and in which the storyteller lives his or her daily life. In this way, the mythical story resembles the child's symbolic play, which depends on the paradoxical co-existences of real/unreal and serious/unserious.

Since the particularity of the landscape and the plants and animals within it, provides the starting point and basis for a 'dreaming', which I am suggesting is the forerunner of the myths of literate culture, then the third version of the Narcissus story referred to by Rose and written by Conon, cannot be regarded as a true variant of the tale set in Boeotia by Ovid and Pausanias. A central character in the very brief Conon account is Amenius, which is a river in Arcadia,[51] a province on the Peloponnesian peninsula south of Boeotia.

The Conon story is also discrepant in that it does not adhere to the analogical laws governing myth. In this account a youth, also called Narcissus, stabs himself to death. A flower springs up from his blood spilt on the ground. Such a flower, following the law of analogical correspondence upon which Lévi-Strauss structuring depends, should be red rather than white. For example, in the myth of Adonis, at the season when it is enacted, the river Adonis turns red.

> At that season the red earth washed down from the mountains by the rain tinges the water of the river, and even the sea, for a great way with a blood-red hue, and the crimson stain was believed to be the blood of Adonis, annually wounded to death by the boar on Mount Lebanon. Again, the scarlet anemone is said to have sprung from the blood of Adonis.[52]

Narcissus may have been a vegetation god akin to Adonis.

In stories such as these, a resemblance is shown between a 'dreaming' and a Greek myth. Like Narcissus, Echo, Liriope and Cephius, the creatures of a 'dreaming' not only appear as real features of the natural environment, they are also inhabitants of a divine domain in which they have human characteristics. Two realities co-exist. The myth, to use the terminology of Wolgang Iser, is a fiction made of the real and the imaginary. [53] So also is the personal myth to which we shall come in the final chapter.

Lévi-Strauss projected a clear idea of where meaning is to be found in a text such as a myth. He suggested, in directing us to find meaning in his columns of resemblance, that meaning is to be found in the synchronic dimension of a mythical text. In this he was following the viewpoint of Saussure, of which Frederic Jameson has the following to say:

> Saussure's separation of the synchronic from the diachronic, of historical from structural research, is equally absolute, and contains a methodological presupposition which is just as peremptory a value judgement: 'to the degree that something is meaningful, it will be found in the synchronic'.[54]

Jameson's implicit point is that there are different forms of understanding and that the diachronic and synchronic are 'two mutually exclusive forms of understanding'.[55] Later on in his consideration of structuralism, Jameson quotes from Lévi-Strauss' 'Tristes Tropiques' a passage that encapsulates a problem associated with the structuralist approach. Lévi-Strauss had the conviction

> that understanding consists in the *reduction* of one type of reality to another; the true reality is never what is manifest on the surface, and that the nature of truth may be measured by the degree to which it tries to elude you. . . . that the passage between the two orders [of lived experience and of reality] is discontinuous; that is in order to reach the real, one must repudiate the existential, only to reintegrate it later on in an objective synthesis from which all sentimentality has been eliminated.[56]

This desiccated view of human reality harks back to Plato and a doctrine that devalues the ordinary experience of living, in favour of mysterious immutable forms lying behind the veil of appearance and that are seen as true reality. This doctrine has some validity when applied to non-living forms such as the relics of preliterate myth that have come down to us through such chronicles as Ovid's. Lévi-Strauss' brilliant method allows us to discover that embedded in the myth of Narcissus is the story of a vegetation God, like that of Adonis and Hyacinth, an emblem of the annual cycle of birth, death and renewal. But this is not the 'truth' of the myth. It is part of it.

Living myth is played out in rituals in which the story is enacted through dancing, song and communal representation. It is a *feeling based reality* in which the present contains experiences which are not of the present, but which enhance it. Reality is in the existential. It can be conceived in terms of a metaphor derived from the mathematician Bernhard Riemann (1826–1866) who put forward the idea of a multi-layered surface.

Human reality is layered, having the structure of a language. This view has been developed by the linguist Michael Halliday (1973a) and illustrated by studies of particular texts including stories. He writes that 'Language, by the multiplicity of its functions, possesses a fugue-like quality, but which a number of themes unfold simultaneously.'[57] The structural layers of language – phonological, lexical, syntactical and contextual– provide different elements of 'meaning'. The 'truth' of the text comes through its realization in the co-ordination of these layers. It is the poet who is able to create such co-ordinations. This idea is important in psychotherapy in which the therapist should, in my view, approach the text of the conversation not in the manner of Platonist or mid-twentieth century Freudian but with the sensibility of a poet. The therapeutic aim is the facilitation of the 'realization' of an immediate reality by a participation in the co-ordination of its 'layers' through the creation of forms of relatedness, which are analogical.

One can imagine a similar kind of co-ordination occurring in the rituals that would have been enacted in telling the story of Narcissus. He was the centre of a cult in ancient Boeotia, where shrines were dedicated to him.[58] Such a celebration, ceremony, or festival would not have been an objective reality bereft of 'sentimentality', to use a Lévi-Strauss term. Rather it would have been an emotion charged affair. Frazer describes the scenes of the festivals where the death of Adonis was 'annually mourned, with bitter wailing, chiefly by the women . . . women attired as mourners, with streaming hair and bared breasts, bore the image of the dead Adonis to the sea-shore and committed it to the waves'.[59] As the story unfolded in such a setting, intricacies of personal relationships, such as that of Narcissus and Echo, and of Echo and Hera, become intertwined with universal events.

The various festivities that celebrated or enacted the stories of the gods were linked by relationships between the gods, who formed a mythical community and family within and above the mortal communities and families that they mirrored. Hera, for example, the vengeful and jealous matriarch, the queen of the sky, appears in a number of the stories of the Greek gods. She was important in Boeotia, where a major festival celebrated her marriage to Zeus.[60] This network of divine creatures inhabiting the same landscape as the mortals, created through their stories a web of communal reality that would have had a unifying effect on society. In this way, the Greek myths preserved one of the functions of an original mythic structure, tribal coherence.

Two kinds of human languages

When G. S. Kirk came to the end of his inquiry into the nature of myth he could come to no firm conclusion about its origin. Nevertheless he did venture the suggestion that what may be important is a 'special kind of imagination that I have called, with no great precision or subtlety, "fantasy"'.[61] He also believed that Jung's ideas may have some value. He did not, however, connect these two.

Jung distinguished between two forms of thought, which he called 'fantasy thinking' and 'directed thinking'. Directed thinking is linear and directed towards a goal. 'The thinking leads to action on the external world. It takes place in words or substitute motor signs. . . . Directed thinking has the purpose of adaption to the environment'.[62]

Directed thought can be considered logical – it 'involves a causal sequence'. Fantasy thinking, on the other hand, is analogical. It is non-linear and apparently not directed towards any purpose or goal. It is autotelic. Rather than words it depends on images. Whereas directed thinking is oriented towards the outer world, fantasy thinking is concerned with that which is inner. Hobson's description of the process shows it akin to the dream. The images that compose it:

> show features of condensation and displacement, without a clear recognition of opposites. There is little fatigue in the process, the effortless direction of thought being determined by subjective affect with association based on analogy. A great deal of the process goes on in the 'half-shadows' or unconsciously.[63]

Fantasy thinking, for which I will substitute the term analogical process, is prominent in reverie. It is characteristically positively toned. It is switched off by alerting events in the environment and by negative, reactive emotions, when directed-thinking becomes dominant.

Jean Piaget is among a number of writers who have made a distinction between two forms of thought. He spoke of '*directed* or intelligent thought and *undirected* or, as Bleuler proposes to call it, *autistic* thought'.[64] They are governed by different laws, the law of symbolism being the guide for undirected thought. Piaget noted that an intuition or awareness arrived at by means of the reverie style of thinking is very difficult to translate into the communicable language of directed thought. Arguments 'connected with some schema of visual imagery or based on some sort of analogy' seem almost 'incommunicable'.[65] The two thought forms represent 'we may even say, without paradox, two different logics'.[66] The undirected thought form, the analogic process, Piaget identified with 'mythological thought'.[67]

(The most famous distinction between two modes of mental function, Freud's, is not equivalent to that of Jung and Piaget since the form of thought which they call undirected is, in Freud's conception, directed in disguise. It always has a goal, which is necessarily decoded. It can always be 'translated into a rational process'.[68] Other theoretical assumptions compound the difference.)

Piaget observed that the two different modes of mental function are clearly distinct in early childhood and manifest in language. When engaged in symbolic play the child chatters, using a form of language that is structurally different from the way in which she talks with other people. Vygotsky investigated these two languages in greater detail. They are the precursors of what he called 'social speech' and 'inner speech'.[69]

Vygotsky discovered in the speech of the child the dream-like process of condensation, which Hobson and Jung had found in the imagery of analogical thought. Not only do words sometimes combine in a kind of 'agglutination' so also do their senses. The senses of different words flow into one another – literally 'influence' one another. He called it 'an influx of sense'.[70]

The language is typically one of predicates. The sentences are abbreviated, often incomplete and lacking a subject. They are not, in the usual sense, syntactical. It seems that the chattering of the child, in speaking this way, is contributing to the representation of the imagery of thought. It is made 'visible' by the use of analogue and is, in some way, an aspect of the embryonically inner life of the child.

Social speech has characteristics that are the opposite of inner speech. The sentences are largely syntactical and have a subject. 'I' and 'you' are used. Moreover, the 'influx of sense' found in 'inner speech' is not apparent. Words have a single, discrete meaning while in the language of inner speech they may have 'layers'.

Syntax is sequential, moving words toward the goal of 'meaning'. In this way, social speech is linear, a language of succession. In reflecting a particular kind of mental function, it might be conceived like the ticking of the seconds of a clock, an image of time in which one discrete moment follows another. It is the language of Saussure's diachronic dimension.

Inner speech is the synchronic, the axis of simultaneity. 'Meaning', in this dimension, is of a different kind to that portrayed in the diachronic. 'Meaning' here is a representation. The way the child uses words in symbolic play is like adding colour to a picture. Since a picture is made of many elements tending all to become part of one thing, this kind of mental function is characterized by continuities while the diachronic mode of the social is composed of discontinuous units.

The influential linguist, Roman Jakobson used Saussure's concept of the two axes structuring language to differentiate modes of figurative language. He wrote of:

> two basic modes of arrangement used in verbal behaviour: *selection* and *combination*. . . . The selection is produced on the base of equivalence, similarity and dissimilarity, synonymity and anonymity, while the combination, the buildup and the sequence, is based on contiguity.[71]

Metonym is the characteristic figure of speech in the mode of contingulty and metaphor is fundamental to the system of similarity.[72] Jakobson observed that the 'study of poetric tropes has been directed mainly towards metaphor and the so-called realistic literature, intimately tied with the metonymic principle',[73] although the distinction is not absolute.

Jakobson also acknowledged the significance of Gerard Manley Hopkins as 'an outstanding searcher in the science of poetic language'.[74] Whereas Saussure's discovery of the two axes was linguistic, for Hopkins it was poetic. In studying Greek lyric art in the early 1880s he concluded that

> in any lyric passage of the tragic poets . . . there are usually . . . two strains of thought running together and like counterpointed, the overthought that which everybody, editors, see . . . the other, the underthought, conveyed chiefly in the choice of metaphors etc. used and often only half realized by the poet himself, not necessarily having any connection with the subject in hand . . . Perhaps I ought to say that the underthought is commonly an echo or shadow of the overthought, something like canons and repetitions in music.[75]

The right brain/left brain

Those writing on the two forms of thought did not, in the main, attempt to relate this distinction to different types of brain function. Jakobson was an exception. He used the writings of Hughlings Jackson as a basis for the understanding of what he called a 'contiguity disorder'.

Jackson was a pioneer in showing that the two hemispheres of the brain had different functions. He described this difference as it was reflected in language. Jackson had remarked that 'the process of verbalizing is dual; the second "half" of it being speech'.[76] The first part is imagery. Antonio Damasio, the first person in the current era to attempt a neural model of self, confirms Jackson's view of the 'dual process' of verbalizing. He wrote that 'images are probably the main content of our thoughts' and that 'most of the words we use in our inner speech, before speaking or writing a sentence, exist as auditory or visual images'.[77]

Jackson noted that 'extensive damage in a certain region of the left hemisphere will destroy speech altogether'.[78] The person so afflicted 'cannot propositionize'.[79] He cannot use syntax to draw words together to create meaning. Jackson saw syntax as like a movement, making a parallel between speech and the sequencing of muscular activity necessary to perform a movement.[80]

Although the person with left hemisphere damage is speechless they are not wordless. Speech can be triggered. Jackson considered that words were available to both hemispheres but used in different ways. Words can be used in an automatic way by the right hemisphere. The patient can say 'good-bye' in an appropriate context but cannot reproduce the words voluntarily.

The right hemisphere seems to be particularly related to emotional and to musical expression. A patient may swear when vexed and utter interjections that have an emotional basis. Short syntactical sentences can be emitted under the pressure of high emotion. For example, a 'patient's wife . . . affirmed that her husband, otherwise always speechless, said: "God bless you, my dear"'. Jackson noted that 'there are two modes of expression, one emotional and the other intellectual. By one we show what we feel, and by the other we tell what we think.'[81]

Jackson remarked that: 'The chief significance of the duality lies, I think in its bearing on what is most fundamental in mental operations – the double process of tracing relations of likeness and unlikeness.'[82] It was left to Jakobson to point out that there are two forms of these relations – metonymic and metaphoric. Jackson suggested that the right-side was particularly concerned with 'recognition' that is with the detection of 'likeness'.[83] The implicit story made by these images may be different although related to the verbal expression. It may have a mythical structure as illustrated in the final chapter. This idea anticipates modern theories of the origin of propositional speech (see the following chapter).

The detection of similarity between two patterns is not inevitable. It is a choice. Similarity, the finding of an analogue, is a selection. Gerald Edelman, it will be recalled, distinguishes 'two main modes of thought – logic and selectionism (or pattern recognition)'. The latter mode is analogical and 'pre-metaphorical'. [84] His use of the term 'selectionism' provides an interesting resonance with Jakobson's dichotomy of selection/combination.

Concluding remarks

This chapter has been concerned with the developmental theme of 'depicting' as it evolves from the scene of symbolic play to its cultural expression in myth and its enactment. It is argued that the evolution of *Homo sapiens*' capacity to create myth gave to a group of people an evolutionary advantage. It depends upon a mode of thought dependent upon imagery and analogical connectedness between its elements.

Notes

1 Lewis and Gunn (1978), Lewis, M. (1992).
2 Crockenberg and Litman (1990).
3 Vaughn, Kopp and Krakow (1984).
4 Meares, R. (1986).
5 Kagan, J. (1972).
6 Meares, R. (1986).
7 Hobson, R. P. (1993, p. 145); Uzgiris, I. (1991, p. 226).
8 Baron-Cohen, S. (1987).
9 Kasari *et al.* (1993).
10 Elder and Pederson (1978).
11 Overton and Jackson (1973).
12 Cassirer, E. (1944, p. 26).
13 Eliade, M. (1959).
14 Henshilwood and d'Errico (2013).
15 Deacon, T. (1997).
16 Groos, K. (1898, 1901).
17 Piaget, J. (1966, p. 494).
18 Piaget, J. (1966, p. 494).
19 Piaget, J. (1966, p. 494).
20 Geertz, C. (1973).
21 Merker, B. (2009).

22 Kroeber and Kluckhohn (1952).
23 Spencer and Gillen (1899).
24 Mountford, C. (1973, p. 9).
25 Stanner, W. E. H. (1979).
26 Cited by Cowan, J. (1992, p. 4).
27 Johnson, D. (2000, p. 25).
28 Morieson, J. (2008, pp. 260–261).
29 Kirk, G. S. (1973, p. 281).
30 Cassirer, E. (1944, pp. 73–74).
31 Cassirer, E. (1944, p. 74).
32 Kirk, G. S. (1973, p. 242).
33 Kirk, G. S. (1973, pp. 242–243).
34 Kirk, G. S. (1973, p. 241).
35 Kirk, G. S. (1973, p. 242).
36 Rose (1978, p. 722). (Ov. Met. 3.342 ff.)
37 Malinowski, B. (1926, p. 12).
38 Lévi-Strauss, C. (1966, p. 253).
39 Cooper and Johnson (1984).
40 Harrison, J. E. (1912, p. 16).
41 Lévi-Strauss, C. (1968, p. 210).
42 Frazer, J. (1922, p. 192).
43 Lévi-Strauss, C. (1968a, p. 211).
44 Lévi-Strauss, C. (1968a, p. 209).
45 Lévi-Strauss, C. (1968a, p. 214).
46 Lévi-Strauss, C. (1968a, p. 217).
47 Lévi-Strauss, C. (1966, p. 149).
48 Cited by Wilcken, P. (2010, pp. 139–140).
49 Lévi-Strauss, C. (1966, p. 136).
50 Schachter, A. (1966).
51 Graves, R. (1955).
52 Frazer, J. (1922, p. 136).
53 Iser, W. (1993).
54 Jameson, F. (1974, p. 5).
55 Jameson, F. (1974, p. 5).
56 Lévi-Strauss, C. (1955, pp. 48–49, cited by Jameson, 1974, pp. 142–314).
57 Halliday, M. A. K. (1973b, p. 279).
58 Zimmerman, C. (1944, p. 18).
59 Frazer, J. (1922, p. 335).
60 Frazer, J. (1922, p. 143).
61 Kirk, G. S. (1973, p. 268).
62 Hobson, R. (1971, p. 86).
63 Hobson, R. (1971, p. 86).
64 Piaget, J. (1959, p. 43).
65 Piaget, J. (1959, p. 46).
66 Piaget, J. (1959, p. 46).
67 Piaget, J. (1959, p. 45).
68 Freud, S. (1932, p. 247).
69 Laplanche and Pontalis (1973).
70 Vygotsky, L. S. (1962, p. 147).
71 Jakobson, R. (1960a, p. 358).
72 Jakobson, R. (1971).
73 Jakobson, R. (1960a, p. 375).
74 Jakobson, R. (1960a, pp. 358–359).

75 Cited by White, N. (1995, p. 338).
76 Jackson, H. (1878–1879, p. 129).
77 Damasio, A. R. (1996, pp. 106–104).
78 Jackson, H. J. (1874, p. 129).
79 Jackson, H. J. (1874, p. 131).
80 Jackson, H. J. (1874, p. 137).
81 Jackson, H. J. (1874, p. 121).
82 Jackson, H. J. (1874, p. 129).
83 Jackson, H. J. (1874, p. 142).
84 Edelman, G. (2004, p. 147).

10

ACTION PATTERNS AND THE EVOLUTION OF LANGUAGE

The previous chapter concerned the part of language that depicts, a kind of language that cannot 'propositionize'. This chapter approaches the mystery of the other aspect of conversation that is the vehicle of, and can make connected, the incomplete utterances of the language of depiction. This second, propositioning, syntactical type of speech has the figurative structure of 'pointing'. It has the quality of intentionality. In making possible a connected series of depictions, or scenes, it provides the skeletal basis of a story, which is a larger form of picturing.

The widely used metaphor of 'pointing' to describe the identifying component of intentional consciousness suggests that its precursor was an activity involving the hand. The idea that mind, or self, might have evolved as a consequence of the capacity for a hand movement is not new. The social anthropologist Edward Tylor, for example, suggested that 'gesture language' was the precursor of human speech, used together with expression feature, emotional tone, musical rhythm and intonation.[1] He believed that 'word-language not only followed gesture-language but grew out of it'. He gives as his main example the origin of numerals. [2]

Gestures, however, do not merely point. Spontaneous hand movements, of which we are barely conscious, represent a state of mind as we speak. Two politicians, interviewed at different times on television, display this universal tendency. One holds his hands in front of him, palms facing, forearms at right angles to his body. Sometimes the hands move closer, sometimes farther apart. At other times, they move up and down in a chopping motion. The other man uses his hands in a more fluid way and not always together. Sometimes his hand and arm move in a sinuous fashion as if sculpting the air. On occasions his fist is clenched. At others he wags his finger in emphasis. These men 'depict', involuntarily, different states of mind. It is not hard to guess who is the conservative of this pair. These gestures show a co-ordination of two different kinds of language, one involving words and the other wordless.

The Gestural theory of language: the mirror neuron hypothesis

The search for the origins of intentional consciousness is interwoven with attempts to understand the evolution of language, which, in its propositioning form, is left hemispheric. The observation that the control of fine movements of the hand is also, in the typical case, dependent on left hemispheric function gives rise to a hypothesis that the evolution of language is related to dexterity, to the skilled use of the hand. Proponents of this idea give particular significance to primate and hominid tool use[3] and to grasping movements, which depend upon the action of an opposable thumb necessary to constructional abilities. Impetus has been given to this line of inquiry by the discovery of mirror neurons.

Rizzolatti and his colleagues have discovered that the grasping movement has intriguing neurophysiological correlates. They noticed that when it is performed or observed by a monkey, specific neurons in the rostral part of the ventral premotor cortex (area F5) discharge. Importantly, it was found that 'the discharge correlates with an action, rather than the individual movements that form it'.[4] In an article entitled 'Language within our grasp', Rizzolatti and Michael Arbib propose that 'such an observation/execution matching system provides, a necessary bridge from "doing" to "communicating"'.[5] They propose, in short, that the specific neurons in the F5 area, the mirror neuron system, mark 'the beginning of intentional communication'. [6]

Their thesis gains plausibility from evidence that the F5 area in monkeys is the homologue of Broca's area in humans. Broca's area is necessary to the articulation of speech.[7] Rizzolatti and Arbib cite reports of other scientists, which show that:

> The motor properties of human Broca's area do not relate only to speech: recent PET data indicate the Broca's area might also become active during the execution of hand or arm movements, during mental imagery of hand grasping movement (mostly area 44) and during tasks involving hand-mental rotations (areas 44 and 45).[8]

They cite, in addition, observations that movements of the mouth and face trigger mirror neurons. In summary, these reports suggest a close relationship between hand movements and those movements necessary to the capacity for speech.

Rizzolatti and Arbib note that their thesis resembles that of Michael Corballis who writes on the 'The Gestural Origins of Language'.[9]

The idea that gesture could be the origin of language is a plausible one. Certain pieces of evidence, however, might seem to threaten its validity. For example, if gesture is the forerunner of language it should be closely linked to sign language, this being a complex series of gestures used for communication. This linkage, however, could not be demonstrated in three deaf people who used sign language and had unilateral brain damage to the left hemisphere. Although the damage caused aphasia for sign language, gesture was retained.[10] The possibility that gesture and the ability to speak are independent of each other is further supported by the observation that those who suffer aphasia as a result of damage to Broca's area retain their use of gesture, which they use in an attempt to improve their deficient capacity to communicate.[11]

A possible explanation for the retention of gesture in the context of a loss of sign language is Jacksonian and to be found in the hierarchial structure of consciousness. Gesture can be a largely automatic function, as exemplified in the behaviour of the two politicians mentioned earlier. Language emerges later than gesture in evolution and in human development. It is both voluntary and the outcome of learning. In damage to the brain-mind system, late evolved, voluntary functions are the first to be lost while more primitive and automatic functions may be retained.

It is difficult to discount the possibility that mirror neurons have some part to play in the evolution of language since they are so closely related to Brocca's area, which is necessary to the delivery of language. They cannot, however, explain the complexity of language, as Moro has argued, pointing out that the characteristic of recursion in human language cannot be solely evolved through mirror neurons.[12] Recursion is the process of embedding relative clauses in a sentence. What seems more likely, at least to me, is that the functions of the hand and the vocal tract developed in parallel in the service of a larger and more fundamental system, which was envisaged by the anatomist Frederic Wood Jones in his classic work, *The Principles of Anatomy as Seen in the Hand.*

In this book, Wood Jones expresses his impatience with his contemporaries extolling the marvels of the mechanism. He observed that although the human hand had become a better grasping instrument than the hands of the higher primates, this does not make the human hand remarkable. What is remarkable is the range of movements of which the human hand is capable. 'It is not the hand which is perfect, but the whole nervous mechanism by which movements of the hand are evoked, co-ordinated, and controlled.'[13]

This chapter cannot encompass the huge area of the evolution of language. Instead a particular path is taken through this field guided by an idea of Wood Jones, which is resonant with recent research data. He spoke of neural patternings, 'which we imagine to constitute a pictured movement, or an action pattern' for a complex, learned movement, of which the articulation of speech is one example.[14]

Evolution and manual grasping

Before proceeding to Wood Jones' view, it is useful to consider, in the briefest way, the evolutionary background to the manual dexterity of *Homo sapiens*. The ideas prevailing about the emergence of the human from an earlier primate line of descent are based on variations of the 'savannah hypothesis'.

It is a story beginning about 8–10 million years ago (mya) with a climate change affecting Africa, in which a period of aridity caused the tropical forest to die back.[15] The animals who lived in the forest canopies and who included our primate ancestors, found their 'manner of procuring subsistence' under threat. Some, perhaps the less robust, who were less able to compete for the limited food resources, were forced out of their habitat to find food further afield. They needed to travel. Those who survived developed the capacity to walk upright, a capacity that Rodman and McHenry demonstrated, is 'much more efficient than bipedal or quadrupedal locomotion in the chimpanzee'. Their line of descent split off from that of chimpanzees' 7 to 5 mya.[16]

Adoption of bipedalism allowed the evolving creature to use her hands. As a consequence, tool use was possible. With tool use, so the story goes, came an increase in brain size leading eventually to the enhanced intellectual prowess and characteristic consciousness of *Homo sapiens*.

It is a story particularly appealing to the Western tradition, raised on a myth in which the first of mankind are cast out of their original paradise to wander the wilderness. It is also an old story in scientific terms. Its essentials had been proposed by Lamarck in 1809.[17] It was also put forward by Darwin, as evidenced in the following widely quoted remark:

> As soon as some member of the great series of the primates came, owing to a change in its manner of procuring subsistence, or to a change in the conditions of its native country, to live somewhat less on trees and more on the ground, its manner of progression would have been modified, and in this case it would have had to become either more strictly quadrupedal or bipedal.[18]

The savannah story gained credence from the discovery by the Australian paleoanthropologist, Raymond Dart, published in 1925, of the remains of an early humanoid in South Africa – *Australopithecus africanus*. This find supported belief that mankind's origin was on the open plains.

The 'savannah hypothesis' has problems, including the relation of climate change to human evolution.[19] These matters, however, are beyond the limits of this discussion. My focus is on a prevailing idea that early man's capacity to grasp was the turning point, which led to the human mind. Richard Leakey, writing with Roger Lewin, developed a clear and modern account of the savannah hypothesis in which he points out that, rather than prehension, the outstanding anatomical changes in those creatures who were the forerunners of *Homo sapiens* are those related to the ability to walk and run.[20]

The capacity for prehension is not unique to the *Homo* genus but is found in other primates. Napier observed that there are two prehensile movements, which he called 'power grip' and 'precision grip'.[21] These two grips he found to be well developed in the earliest species of the *Homo* genus, which he and co-authors named *Homo habilis*.[22] They noted that in this hominid the thumb 'is well developed and fully opposable and the hand is capable not only of a power grip but of, at the least, a simple and usually well-developed precision grip'. The typical power grip resembles a clenched fist; the precision grip is a pinching movement between the thumb and index finger used, for example, in picking berries. *Homo habilis*, who first appeared on the planet about 2.3 mya, was believed to be the first creature to make tools, this ability being attributed to his hand.

The rather simple story, however, of man the tool-maker, *Homo faber*, became more complicated with later reports. One, from the Hadar site in Ethiopia, suggested that the predecessors to *Homo habilis*, the *australopithecus*, had a hand very similar to the hand of *Homo habilis*. The authors of this report wrote: 'new results indicate *australopithecus afarensis* possessed overall manual proportions, including an increased thumb/hand relationship that, contrary to previous reports, is fully human and would have pad-to-pad human-like precision grip capability'.[23] They go on to say 'since *australopithecus afarensis* predates the appearance of stone tools in the archeological record, the above-mentioned conclusions permit a confident refutation of the null hypothesis that human-like manual proportions are an adaption to stone-tool-making and thus alternative explanations, must be therefore sought'.[24]

Australopithecus afarensis lived about 3–4 million years ago. Lucy is the best known of their fossil skeletons. She lived 3.2 mya and was found at the Hadar site in Ethiopia in 1974 by Donald Johanson and his colleagues who, to celebrate their find, that night repeatedly played 'Lucy in the Sky with Diamonds'.

Her brain size was about the same as a chimpanzee. The brain size of *Homo habilis* was somewhat larger. At about 600 cc. it was 50 per cent larger than the brain of *australopithecus*, the difference seeming to support a hypothesis that a larger brain makes it possible to conceive tool construction and use. The hypothesis, however, is challenged by a more recent finding, in Ethiopia's Afar Depression, of the fossils of an *australopithecus* species, which its discoverers named 'garhi,' which means 'surprise' This creature, like Lucy, was gracile and short, a bit over 4 feet tall. Its brain size was also about the same as Lucy at 450 cc. The fossils, however, were more recent than Lucy's, being dated at 2.5 mya. The 'surprise' was that nearby these remains were found stone tools, dated at 2.6 mya. Before the surprise fossils were found, it was supposed that the earliest hominid to use stone tools was *Homo habilis*. The tools of *Australopithecus garhi* pre-dated those made by *Homo habilis* by 100,000 to 200,000 years.[25] These data do not support the notion that hominid tool use of the kind was the outcome of a larger brain. Nor does it support the reverse hypothesis.

It seems that a larger brain was not necessary to the production of Oldowan stone axes, named after the gorge where they were first discovered by Louis Leakey in the 1930s. They were not complicated to make. One stone was used to chip a second stone so that it fractured, causing a sharp edge to fall off. This implement could be used to chop flesh off a bone found in scavenging.

This kind of tool usage is not very different from the opportunistic way chimpanzees use objects in the environment to serve an immediate purpose. Some of these techniques, often devised merely for play, are ingenious, as Luria and Vygotsky demonstrate drawing on the works Wolfgang Kohler (1886–1941) and Karl Buhler (1879–1963).[26] Chimpanzees can, for example, use sticks as levers and construct elongated reaching poles by piecing together two pieces of bamboo. Chimpanzees have been observed using sticks in hunting, in a manner that has been supposed to be uniquely human.[27]

The social origins of large brains

Wood Jones had remarked that it is not the anatomy of the hand that makes *Homo sapiens* remarkable but the way that hand can be used, which depends upon the brain. How the human brain emerged is the problem to be solved as we confront the puzzle of evolution. The question arises: If the larger brain of *Homo habilis* was not related to tool use or bipedalism, how had it come about? The answer may be social. Clusters of Oldowan tools have been found in many places beyond East Africa, including South Africa, Georgia, Spain and the Middle East. There seems, then, to have been what some have called an 'Oldowan industry', a kind of tradition transmitted between groups of proto-humans. Such a network, however tenuous, would have involved a co-ordination between various of our ancestors, which greatly exceeded that which can be demonstrated in modern chimpanzees.

The notion that a network of individuals who are able to co-operate and that is larger than those found in other primates, is an essential feature of the pre-history of humanity. It leads to a hypothesis. This theory proposes that the complex co-ordination of the social group is necessarily related to a system of complex co-ordination in the elements of the brain function of the members of the group. Individual brains evolve in parallel with the evolution of the complexity and size of the social group in a continuing interplay between environment and the brain. A system of complex co-ordination in the brain depends upon the frontal association areas. It is the prefrontal and frontal cortices that increase most in size as encephalization grows from the 450 cc of the *australopithecus* to the 1250 cc of the modern human.

The hypothesis regarding a correlation between brain size and social group was framed and tested by Robin Dunbar. The test is complicated by the fact that brain size varies with body size. In order to overcome this difficulty, Dunbar used an 'encephalization quotient' devised by Jerison[28] to calculate relative brain size in different primates. In studies[29] summarized in an engaging book, Dunbar showed that in primates 'group size is found to be a function of relative neocortical volume, but the ecological variables are not'.[30]

The important feature of Dunbar's hypothesis is its focus on complexity with an increase in group size. Social animals have an increasing number of relationships into which they enter and deal with in different ways. He suggested that the 'number of neocortical neurons limits the organism's information processing capacity and that this then limits the number of relationships that an individual can monitor simultaneously. When a group's size reaches this limit, it becomes unstable and begins to fragment.'[31]

In a later paper, Dunbar, with Susanne Schultz, developed the idea that the neocortical size of a primate exceeds that necessary for the simple tasks of its survival. They drew on work by Byrne and Whiten[32] to support their view that it is the complexity of the social life of primates that might be related to their unusually large brains. 'The computational demands requiring a larger brain' are made not only by the intricacies of group function but also by those of 'pair bonding'.[33]

Running man

The next development in the evolution of the *Homo* genus and the human brain may have been facilitated by climate change. Susanne Schultz, together with geographer Mark Maslin, has argued that human evolution involves pulsed speciation driven by climate change. The climate of the Rift Valley appears to have undergone extreme oscillations in which conditions changed from arid to very wet. During the latter periods huge freshwater lakes were created and surrounded by lush vegetation supporting plentiful game. During one of these pulses a major new species in the *Homo* line of descent appeared. This was *Homo erectus*, whose earliest fossilized remains are about 1.8 million years old. The lakes also appeared at about this time.[34]

Homo erectus was the first of the *Homo* line to have an essentially modern human form. He was about human height, slender, with long legs. He was built for running. He was certainly mobile, being the first of the *Homo* genus to migrate beyond Africa into Eurasia, or so it is generally believed.

Running has not been regarded as a major feature in human evolution, until recently. A major figure in a change in this viewpoint has been Daniel Lieberman. He demonstrated that although early man cannot compete with many other animals as a sprinter, he could outrun them over long distances. The body of *Homo erectus* was particularly suited to endurance running. Lieberman and his colleague Dennis Bramble wrote that no primates other than humans are capable of endurance running.[35] Groups of runners, acting in a co-ordinated way, could chase much faster animals for hours, eventually running them to a near stand-still, when they could be killed. *Homo erectus* was an effective hunter. Whereas earlier members of the *Homo* genus and *australopithecus* were opportunistic omnivores, often relying on grasses and scavenging, *Homo erectus* hunted large animals such as gazelles.[36]

Homo erectus had a considerably larger brain than his predecessors – 850 cc. This evolved to a size approaching that of early humans – 1100 cc. This brain, which devoured energy, required a food intake rich in nutrients such as those found in brain tissue. *Homo erectus* scavenged for skulls of other animals killed by predators in order to extract from them this fatty, nutrient-rich tissue in order to support the needs of their own brains and their endurance running.[37] Tools were needed to break skulls and to perform the butchering of hunted animals. At the time when *Homo erectus* appeared (I am using the term *Homo erectus* as Richard Leakey does, to include the species *Homo ergaster* who is sometimes distinguished from *erectus*), an advancement in the sophistication of stone axes became evident. These newer axes are given the name Acheulian, after the site of Saint-Acheul, in France where they were first found 1.7 mya, This axe had a typically teardrop shape. It was a proper fabrication, the work of a craftsman.[38] Such implements have been found in widely separated parts of the world, in Africa, Asia and Europe. The new axes do not seem to be related to any major change in the anatomy of the hand. They can, perhaps, be attributed to the larger brain of *Homo erectus*.

Homo erectus would have had some form of language, necessary to the co-ordination of a tribal organization, more complex than that of the creatures who came before him.[39] It would also be needed in the co-operation required for the hunting of an animal like a gazelle, in which the distances between the hunters would have made communication merely by gesture ineffective. Furthermore, *Homo erectus* had discovered the use of fire, cooking and even, it seems, the concept of the hearth, which would have potentiated the possibility of communicative activity. It is generally believed that *Homo erectus* had the capacity for a primitive, human-like kind of speech, at least in the last part of his era, although he may not have developed the human vocal tract, which provides extra 'vocal space' to humans relative to other primates. The human vocal tract, having a longer pharyngeal section than chimpanzees and Neanderthals, is not found in the early *Homo erectus*.[40]

Broca's area in the evolution of language

If language had been available to *Homo erectus*, evidence of this capability should be found in cranial markings. The language areas of the brain in humans, Broca's and Wernecke's, have associated indentations on the inner surface of the skull. In the human, they are larger on the left, consistent with the observation that language use in right-handed humans is dependent upon left hemispheric function. Broca's area is also larger on the left in *Homo erectus*. For example, in a specimen recently discovered in Java – Sambungmacan 3 – brain symmetry included a marked asymmetry in Broca's cap.[41]

Since language is associated with left hemispheric dominance, it might be supposed that if *Homo erectus* had some capacity for speech, he would be right-handed. Nicholas Toth studied the way in which stone axes were made and found that right-handed, that, is left hemispheric dominant, individuals were most likely to have been the craftsman during a period 1.4 to 1.9 mya, the evolutionary point at which *Homo erectus* appeared.[42]

Whereas there is evidence that *Homo erectus* had some human-like capacity for language, as shown in the asymmetry of Broca's area, this evidence is lacking in chimpanzees. A recent study from Natalie Schenker and her colleagues found that there was no 'significant population-level asymmetry for any measures of areas 44 and 45 in chimpanzees'.[43] These areas make up Broca's area in humans. This finding overturned and superseded an earlier report from William Hopkins, a co-author with the Schenker paper, in which it was concluded that asymmetry for Broca's area is found in the brains of chimpanzees.[44]

Broca's area: 'action patterns' and pictured movement

I have so far been using the term Broca's area as a kind of shorthand, which needs to be explained. In the past, Broca's area has been considered a 'language centre'. There is, however, no 'centre' for language. Rather, language is delivered by the co-ordination of a number of neural circuits involving different parts of the brain. The proper function of the network includes the activity of Broca's and Wernicke's areas.

A second misconception concerning these specific areas is that their activity is directed towards the sole function of speech. The circuitry relating to Broca's area, however, is not language specific. For example, a PET study found that linguistic and melodic phrases produce almost identical patterns of left hemispheric activity, including activation of Broca's area.[45] As the authors of this study remark, music and language lie side by side in the brain. Music, however, is not only processed in Broca's area but also right hemispherically.[46] Whereas transcranial magnetic stimulation applied to the left frontal lobe produces speech arrest, the capacity to produce song is retained.[47] A realisation is growing that Broca's area does not subserve a single function such as speech or music. Rather, it is part of a system having the function of creating the function 'of action patterns' and 'pictured movements'. In using these images, Wood Jones drew on the work of Hughlings Jackson and his dictum that 'movements, not muscles, are represented in the cerebral cortex'.[48]

Wood Jones was focusing on movements produced by the hand, the complexity of which depends upon their cortical representation, a process that is more extensive in *Homo sapiens* than in any other primate. These representations are patterns of the movements of muscle necessary to particular movements. Such patterns are also the basis of dance, music and of language, the fundamental elements of human culture, and so of mind. This idea is consistent with the viewpoint of Jackson who 'in his writings turns back and forth between muscular co-ordination and mental experience as if for him they were but aspects of a single theme'.[49]

Jackson's ideas are intriguing. They suggest that the first form of thoughts, in an evolutionary sense, were movements. He considered that the brain 'thinks' not in terms of muscles but of movements, i.e. patterns of muscular co-ordination. Such patterns, are the forerunners of the larger patterns that make up mental processes. He likened these patternings to a kind of language, a syntax. In an article reprinted in Brain in 1915 he wrote: 'In this article the term perception is used for a *process*, for a "proposition of images" as speech is used for propositions, i.e. particular inter-relations of words.'[50] An idea resembling Jackson's but greatly developed, was put forward by Karl Lashley in a classic paper delivered in 1951. The paper deals with 'the logical and orderly arrangement of thought and action'.[51] Lashley related serial order in action to the use of syntax in a sentence. He pointed out that simple associative chains cannot account for language, the sequencing of which resembles music. Lashley believed that, in a way that we do not understand and which is mostly unconscious, the organization – of the sentence or musical phrase – is made in advance, like a 'pictured movement' or an 'action pattern', to use Wood Jones' expressions. Lashley saw the organization of the action pattern as hierarchial – multilayered and operative at several levels. The highest level concerns the overall intention of the proposition that is to be spoken. Lower levels involve the choice of syntax and, at a fundamental level, the choice of sounds to be uttered.

Similar ideas have been developed, in recent times, by William Calvin. He argues human language has its origins in the fluency of the whole body, not merely the hand and arm, in the making of, say, a topspin forehand. He sees the sequence of muscle activity involved in throwing as an analogue of the syntactical structuring of language.[52]

In a primitive language such as that of the vervet monkeys, studied by Cheney and Seyfarth, different sounds have the effect of creating a specific response in those animals that hear them. The sounds have particular meanings, referring, for example, to the proximity of leopards, eagles and snakes.[53] These meanings are single and complete. It is a language of signs. They do not connect with each other. William Calvin makes a similar point about chimpanzees:

> Wild chimpanzees use about three dozen different vocalizations to convey about three dozen different meanings. They may repeat a sound to intensify its meaning but they do not string together these sounds to add a new word to the vocabulary. Speakers of English use about three dozen vocalizations, called phonemes. Yet only their combinations have content: we string together meaningless sounds to make meaning for words.[54]

This difference between the human and the chimpanzee is also apparent in muscular involvement, so Calvin believes. Whereas a chimpanzee flings an object, a spear thrower or a baseball pitcher is doing something requiring very fine adjustments to a complex task. He is implicitly suggesting that *Homo sapiens* has a greater capacity for co-ordinating the muscle movements involved in fine or skilled movement than other primates.

If we are to follow the ideas of Jackson, Lashley and Calvin we are led to a possible solution of the puzzle posed by what Chomsky called 'universal grammar'.[55] The origins of our innate ability to structure sounds, which make meaning according to principles that have never been 'learnt', in the behaviourist sense, but which must be part of our phylogenetic history, is an evolutionary mystery. It seems to have no evolutionary predecessors. The notion, however, that the serial ordering of muscle activity involved in skilled behaviour is an analogue of the syntactical structuring of language suggests a solution to the puzzle. Neurocircuitry originally underpinning motor control is taken over for the purposes of language. The fact that neural tissue can alter its primary function has gathered evidence in recent years with growing evidence of neuroplasticity.[56] The suggestion that neural networks responsible for the creation of 'action patterns' governing movement are the larval forms of the systems necessary to language makes sense in Jacksonian terms. He did not believe that a human function could emerge in evolution with no predecessors, out of the blue, as if tacked on to the brain. Rather, functions that appear late in evolution come into being through the recruitment and elaboration of existing systems.

Finally, Calvin's analogue of throwing seems particularly relevant to the main theme of this chapter, which concerns the kinds of consciousness that 'points', i.e. intentional. Throwing 'points'. It is directed at a goal.

Disconnectedness and Broca's damage

In the previous section it was implied that Broca's area may be involved in the creation of 'action patterns', or more particularly the syntactical arrangements necessary to the formation of speech. This is consistent with clinical observation. Damage to Broca's area causes a loss of fluency. The muscles involved in speech do not properly co-ordinate while comprehension is relatively intact: 'Speech is characteristically sparse, slow and hesitant, with marked disturbances of rhythm, inflexion and articulation . . . There is a marked impairment of syntax. . . . Reading out aloud will show a halting, jerky flow, with slurring and occasional mispronunciations.'[57]

Disconnectedness in function due to damage to Broca's area is not confined to language. It has an effect on the more fundamental function of the sequencing of movement. Patrick Fazio in Ferrara, together with his colleagues led by Luciano Fadiga, showed that this may be so. They asked a group of six patients suffering Broca's aphasia and who had no symptoms relating to movement, to reorder a series of pictures, which were stills of a simple action, e.g. a man grasping a bottle, they had previously seen in a short movie. The patients could not reorder the stills into their correct temporal sequence. On the other hand, they correctly ordered clips taken from a non-human action, e.g. a bicycle falling over. The inference from these observations is that the sequencing association with Broca's area is specific to human activity as is the activity of mirror neurons.[58]

An equally intriguing study comes from Thomas Bak working with John Hodges group at Cambridge.[59] They studied a man and his son who had a selective deficit in the processing of verbs. This was associated with a movement disorder. The authors of this report note that Hauk and colleagues had found words that mean actions involving the face, hands, or feet activated the motor and premotor cortex along the motor strip, suggesting that 'action concepts are automatically activated when these words are being read or heard'.[60] Such a finding is consistent with the idea that language, even at the presyntactical level of words alone, has its precursors in actions. In support of this idea, they cite their own work on motor neuron disease, believed to be exclusively a disorder of the motor system, which show that it is associated with a selective deficit in processing verbs.[61]

The organization of language, as reflected in syntax, is not dependent upon Broca's area alone but on a larger system of neurocircuitry, involving many areas of the brain, which includes Broca's area. This is evident in findings relating to the FOX P2 gene.

The FOX P2 gene is a widely distributed gene, found not only in primates but also mice.[62] It is a transcription gene, that is, it has the effect of facilitating the expression of other genes. It seems likely to be involved in neural plasticity.[63] Great interest, even excitement, has been generated by the recent discovery that a mutation of this gene causes severe speech and language defects.

The discovery was made by the geneticists Simon Fisher and Anthony Monaco, who investigated the basis of such a malady recurring over three generations in a

London family, called the KE family.[64] The investigators found the cause to be one of classical Mendelian inheritance, involving a single, autosomal dominant gene. This disorder involved, most prominently, syntax. The affected subjects could not process words according to grammatical rules. They could not properly comprehend sentences in which recursion was a feature, i.e., involving embedded relative clauses. In addition, the sufferers of the syndrome could not 'form intelligible speech and had defects in the ability to move the mouth and face not associated with speaking'.[65] In a later paper, these investigators showed that in the brains of affected individuals, the caudate was bilaterally reduced in size. This nucleus is a key element of the system necessary to the co-ordination of movement.[66] Detailed studies of these patients showed that they had a particular difficulty in performing sequential movements.[67]

The investigators concluded that the mutation of FPX P2 in the KE family had interfered with its promotional effect on other genes at an embryonic level, resulting in a failure in development of the neural pathways necessary to human speech.[68]

Music and the neurocircuitry of language

The neural basis of language, as noted earlier in the chapter, is very similar to that of music. In reviewing this evidence Luciano Fadiga and his colleagues concluded that the inferior frontal gyrus and ventral premotor cortex, the brain regions constituting Broca's area, are

> activated in tasks other than language production. Specifically, a growing number of studies report the involvement of these two regions in language comprehension, action execution and observation, and music execution and listening. Recently, the actual involvement in these two areas in representing abstract hierarchial structures has also been demonstrated. Language, music and action share a syntactical structure.[69]

In his book *Musicophilia* Oliver Sacks points out that the temporal lobes, the frontal lobes, the basal ganglia and the cerebellum are 'all parts of the brain activated in the perception of "real" music'.[70] Brown and colleagues show that these structures are also those that are involved in speech.[71]

The cerebellar contribution to this system is particularly important. Reciprocal connections link the cerebellum to the prefrontal cortex and the motor cortex. The parts of the cerebellum associated with the prefrontal loops are relatively larger in humans than in chimpanzees, suggesting an evolutionary expansion favouring the association areas. The authors of this report speculate that the selective expansion of the prefrontal projecting cerebellum lobules may contribute to the development of the higher order mental functions in humans.[72]

Lesions of the cerebellum may produce the syndrome of asynergia in which a movement is broken up into its elements leading to weakness, slowness and jerkiness. Speech is affected. It has a characteristic scanning quality. 'Full-blown agrammatism' has been described following cerebellar infarction.[73]

The close association between the neural bases of language and music suggest that they may have evolved together, or perhaps, and this seems more likely, music-like vocalization preceded the use of words. This it seems, was the view of Darwin. Music is one of those human activities and abilities for which, like play, there is no apparent biological purpose. They are autotelic – conducted for their own purpose and no other. Accordingly, Darwin remarked that our musical faculty 'must be marked among the most mysterious with which he is endowed'.[74] It seems, however, to be fundamental to the emergence of human consciousness. The dynamic structuring of the proto-conversation and the subsequent babbling of the infant are proto-languages made of the patternings of the sounds that can be seen as the forerunners of both language and music, each having the properties of melody, phrasing and rhythm.

The proto-conversation, then, might be called a 'musilanguage'.[75] Darwin's intuition was that the cadences of the voice, displayed by primates such as the gibbons, might be the forerunner of the human power to express emotion by the use of words: 'we must suppose that the rhythms and cadences of oratory are derived from previously developed musical powers'. He further supposed 'that musical tones and rhythm were used by our half-human ancestors, during the season of courtship'.[76] Tecumseh Fetch has written extensively on the neglect of Darwin's hypothesis on the musical origins of emotionally expressive language.

Ellen Dissanyake[77] seems to have been the first to suggest that the rhythms, phrasing and patterns of cadence shown in the highly co-ordinated game of the proto-conversation provided the first forms of activity that contributed to the later development of music. Steven Mithen has made a similar suggestion.[78]

Darwin's remark about the gibbon's song and the evolution of language implies that *Homo sapiens* may be descended from an ancestor shared with gibbons, or of one of the other primates who sing. There are only four – Indri, Tarsius, Calicebus and Hylobate (i.e. gibbons). They make up 6 per cent of primate genera. The possibility of man's descent in this way is plausible.

Gibbons are monogamous unlike most other primates. Whereas they can sing, as man does, chimpanzees only bark and grunt. Moreover, gibbons are bipedal – they can stand fully upright, unlike the knuckle-walking chimpanzee. They are slight, fast and agile. Finally, of those primates having an opposable thumb, theirs is the one with the longest thumb, making it more nearly like man's than other primates. However, it is their singing ability that separates them from other primates. They tend to sing in duets, lasting up to half an hour. Solos are given by males, uninterrupted for 2 hours. The songs are patterned, like music.[79] Esther Clark and her colleagues found that syntactic differences in these songs are meaningful to con-specifics.[80] They believe that their study 'provides the first evidence of referential signaling in a free-ranging ape species, based on a communication system that uses combinational rules'.[81]

During the 1920s Wood Jones proposed that mankind derived from an ancestor shared by another of the singing primates, the tarsier, a tiny creature with enormous eyes, found in Indonesia: 'We have pictured the members of the proto-human stock to be forms which had progressed from a primitive tarsoid stage in the general direction of primitive Gibbon.'[82] Over the twentieth century evidence accrued that, on the contrary, humans are descended from a primate ancestor we share with chimpanzees and bonobos. To his colleagues, Wood Jones' persistence with his theory appeared quixotic and harmful to his reputation. It may, however, have been no co-incidence that his wife's ancestry, like that of the tarsier and the gibbon, was South East Asian. He was very fond of his wife, to whom he dedicated all his books. He might have enjoyed the story he composed, based on the hard evidence of comparative anatomy, in which the origin of mankind, the actual Eden, was the homeland of his wife.

Language and resonance

Muscles do not grow by themselves. They develop through interaction with the world. Immobility of a limb results in fibrotic changes in the muscle that cause it to lose its function. In the same way, language emerges in an interplay such as that of the proto-conversation. Just as the child appropriates from the mother the role of analogical representing, she takes on for herself the function of resonance to its own vocalization with the development of babbling.

The kind of babbling produced by most infants develops, so that between 7 and 10 months they begin to produce sounds resembling those used in spoken languages. This type of vocalisation is called 'reduplicated' or 'syllabic babbling'. Progression to this stage of babbling depends, so it seems, on a resonance between the child's utterance and his or her hearing the sound created. On the other hand deprivation of babbling may profoundly disturb language and development.

The latter effect was exemplified in the story of a child who had been tracheotomized. She was generally aphonic between the ages of 0.5 and 1.8 years. She was cognitively and socially normal, with near normal comprehension of language. Following the removal of the cannula from her trachea, her utterances revealed a tenth of the canonical syllables that might be expected in normally developing infants. In this way, she was like a congenitally deaf child. Two months later (1.10), she produced only a handful of different words.

The proto-conversation, then, appears to have within it the first forms of the developmental themes of two different kinds of language, arising from different types of interaction with the environment. One is sequential and syntactical, evolving from the patterning of a series of muscular movements and the other symbolic, depending upon analogical representation, a form of resonance. The former is obviously the more robust since it is difficult to avoid physical interaction with the environment. The development of the latter theme is more uncertain, depending as it does upon a certain kind of relatedness with others, which has the quality of 'innerness'.

Notes

1 Tylor, E. B. (1871, vol. I, p. 163).
2 Tylor, E. B. (1871, vol. I, pp. 146, 147ff).
3 Gibson and Ingold (1993).
4 Rizzolatti and Arbib (1998, p. 188).
5 Rizzolatti and Arbib (1998, p. 188).
6 Rizzolatti and Arbib (1998, p. 191).
7 Rizzolatti and Arbib (1998, p. 189).
8 Rizzolatti and Arbib (1998, p. 189).
9 Corballis, M. (2003).
10 Poizner, Bellugi and Iragui (1984).
11 David and Kopelman (2009, p. 51).
12 Moro, A. (2008, p. 257).
13 Wood Jones, F. (1920, p. 236).
14 Wood Jones, F. (1920, p. 244).
15 Vrba, E. S. (1995).
16 Rodman and McHenry (1980).
17 Edited by Bender, Tobias and Bender (2012).
18 Darwin, C. (1871, vol. I, pp. 140–141).
19 E.g. Behrensmeyer, A. K. (2006).
20 Leakey and Lewin (1992, p. 81ff).
21 Napier, J. R. (1980, p. 197).
22 Leakey, Tobias and Napier (1964).
23 Alba *et al.* (2003, p. 225).
24 Alba *et al.* (2003, p. 225).
25 Asfaw *et al.* (1999); de Heinzelin *et al.* (1999).
26 Luria and Vygotsky (1992, pp. 5–14).
27 Pruetz and Bertolani (2007).
28 Jerison, H. J. (1973).
29 Dunbar, R. (1992, 1993).
30 Dunbar, R. (1996).
31 Dunbar, R. (1992, p. 469).
32 Byrne and Whiten (1988).
33 Dunbar and Schultz (2007).
34 Schultz and Maslin (2013).
35 Lieberman and Bramble (2007).
36 Ferraro *et al.* (2013).
37 Ferraro *et al.* (2013).
38 Gibbons, A. (2000).
39 Leakey and Lewin (1992).
40 Lieberman and McCarthy (2007).
41 Broadfield *et al.* (2001).
42 Toth, N. (1985).
43 Schenker *et al.* (2010).
44 Cantalupo and Hopkins (2001).
45 Brown *et al.* (2006).
46 Maess *et al.* (2001).
47 Stewart *et al.* (2001).
48 Wood Jones, F. (1920, p. 240).
49 Sherrington, C. S., cited by Compston, A. (2007, p. 886).
50 Jackson, H. J. (1958, vol. II, p. 165n).
51 Lashley, K. (1951, p. 112).

52 Calvin, W. H. (2004, pp. 87, 95).
53 Cheney and Seyfarth (1990).
54 Calvin, W. H. (2006).
55 Chomsky, N. (1972, 2006).
56 Doidge, N. (2007).
57 David and Kopelman (2009, pp. 50–51).
58 Fazio *et al.* (2009).
59 Bak *et al.* (2001).
60 Hauk *et al.* (2004, p. 322).
61 Bak *et al.* (2001).
62 Enard *et al.* (2002).
63 Fisher and Scharff (2009).
64 Lai *et al.* (2001).
65 Vargha-Khadem *et al.* (1995).
66 Vargha-Khadem *et al.* (1998).
67 Watkins *et al.* (2002).
68 Lai *et al.* (2003).
69 Fadiga *et al.* (2009).
70 Sacks, O. (2008, p. 57).
71 Brown *et al.* (2006).
72 Balsters *et al.* (2010).
73 Beaton and Marien (2010).
74 Darwin, C. (1871a, p. 867).
75 Brown, S. (2000).
76 Darwin, C. (1871a, p. 871).
77 Dissanyake, E. (2000, 2009).
78 Mithen, S. (2005).
79 Geissman and Orgeldinger (2000); Marshall and Marshall (1976).
80 Clarke *et al.* (2006).
81 Wood Jones, F. (1929, p. 351).
82 Locke and Pearson (1990).

11

THE DOUBLENESS OF SHAKESPEARE

The two previous chapters have concerned the two kinds of language, syntactical and symbolic, which make up human speech. At about the age of 4, they are integrated in ordinary conversation so that the syntactical mode becomes the vehicle for the symbolic, which cannot speak for itself. The interweaving of two modes presumably resembles a greater level of co-ordination between the right and left hemispheres than could be achieved earlier in life.

The resultant speech form can be seen as double. It is illustrated here by a single extract from *Antony and Cleopatra*, 'one of Shakespeare's late plays in which his conversational style is most fully developed'.[1] As he gazes at her dead body, Caesar says of Cleopatra:

> she looks like sleep,
> as she would catch another Antony
> In her strong toil of grace.[2]

The 'baffling splendour'[3] of those words has intrigued many people. Like Hobson's 'minute particulars' in which a single word or phrase can be found to show, in miniature, the essence of a world of personal being, a contemplation of 'her strong toil of grace' gives intimations of something much larger than a few words can encompass. Amplification of these few words will depend upon a 'conversation' between the reader and the text. Every reader will engage with the mini-universe of the text in a different way.

What is being conveyed is both real and unreal, as in the analogical/metaphoric process. The reader's role in experiencing what 'double' words convey has been pointed out by Donald Davidson, in a famous article entitled 'What Metaphors Mean'. The essay begins as follows:

> Metaphor is the dreamwork of language and, like all dreamwork, its interpretation reflects as much on the interpreter as on the originator. The interpretation of dreams requires collaboration between a dreamer and a waker, even if they be the same person; and the act of interpretation is

> itself a work of imagination. So too understanding a metaphor is as much a creative endeavor as making a metaphor, and as little guided by rules.[4]

In listening to Shakespeare's words it is necessary to attain a 'symbolical attitude' in which what is expressed is understood not only as real but also the creation of an analogical movement of mind, in which things that are not usually connected become connected in the manner of dream. The reality, then, of 'her strong toil of grace' is co-created, the outcome of a certain kind of 'conversation' in which the reader or the listener becomes immersed imaginatively in the associations of what is written or been heard.

So, to begin – the word 'toil'. It means a trap. It is, however, a special kind of snare, having shades and contrasts within its meaning. Partridge tells us that the word toil comes from the old French *toile* meaning a cloth, a spider's web, whence *toiles*, which are nets, their meaning in English. Their purpose was to capture wild beasts, such as a stag.[5] The net, however, had a smaller more delicate form as a *toilette*, used for keeping toilet accessories clean. This usage led to the word referring to the act of dressing and adorning oneself, and finally, to clothes and adornments.

The work 'toil' is linked in Caesar's speech to another word, which has an opposite connotation. Whereas 'toil' has associations that are delicate and feminine, 'strong' has the masculine implication of power. The second meaning of 'toil' implies a polarity, between 'passive' and 'active'. A toil, as a net, catches its prey passively, but 'toil' also denotes struggle and tumult, a fight. Hence, a spell of hard and continuous exertion – as in the high passion of prolonged sexual activity.

Scholars such as George Steiner[6] detect a further doubling in 'toil', evoked by its sound alone. It may trigger associations with 'coil' or 'thrall' or, perhaps, both together.

'Grace' is also a word having layers of meaning. It means not only charm and attractiveness but also a great deal more. A second main meaning concerns 'favour', which can be conferred by a superior, or allotted to one by fortune and providence and 'may be said with reference to God'.[7] In *Henry VI*, Shakespeare uses the word in this sense: 'Chosen from above by inspiration of Celestial Grace.'[8]

The implication of a god-like status for Cleopatra brings other associations to mind. Caesar knows that Cleopatra identifies with the goddess, Isis and gives audiences dressed as her.[9] To her people she is the embodiment of Isis, a principal Egyptian deity. This element of her story, which seems crucial to Shakespeare's creation of Cleopatra, is frequently neglected by commentators on the play. So great an authority as Bradley, for example, understands the pattern of the play in terms of Greek mythology rather than Egyptian.[10] Without Isis, the doubleness of Shakespeare's creation is lost. Cleopatra is both a woman, beguiling and manipulative, and a goddess, somewhere floating above the human world. Isis was thought of as the moon goddess, at least by the Romans, who would have provided the information Shakespeare used in fashioning his portrait of Cleopatra. When Antony dies she says:

The odds is gone
And there is nothing left remarkable
Beneath the visiting moon.[11]

As if she were the moon, coming and going like a human being, but overseeing from on high the world below.

The myth of Isis tells the story of an enchantress, a mistress of magic who was able to piece together and re-animate the body of the king, her husband, Osiris, after he had been dismembered. Their son, Horus, as heir to the throne, became the re-incarnated Osiris on his ascent to the kingship. Every pharaoh was considered the embodiment of Horus and, at the same time, every pharaoh was Osiris, the occupier of the throne whose wife was Isis.[12] Isis was, therefore, both wife and mother to the King. For Cleopatra the situation became compounded because she was also the occupier of the throne. Cleopatra reinforced popular identification of her with Isis, for example, by having a coin struck when her son was born depicting him as Horus.[13] Horus was the sky god, who had the form of a falcon whose eyes were the sun and the moon. Shakespeare paints Antony as Horus in the eyes of Cleopatra. She speaks of her relationship with Antony as above the ordinarily mortal, as if conducted in the sky. She says: 'His face was as the heavens and therein struck a sun and moon.'[14]

In casting herself as Isis, Cleopatra created an illusion into which others were drawn. Caesar, it seems, was not immune. Although belittling her role as Isis (a posture that was necessary to discouragement of the cult of Isis, which was growing in Rome) his words in gazing upon her in death suggests that her 'strong toil of grace' was not merely female attractiveness but also the power of someone who could bestow upon a recipient the favour of her divine grace. The words evoke the sense of a love played out in a region vaster than the ordinarily mortal and made by the union of two zones, the carnal and celestial. A number of commentators have speculated that Shakespeare's model for Cleopatra was the Dark Lady of the Sonnets.

Shakespeare illustrates, to a high degree, the co-ordination, as in the creation of self, between the two kinds of language envisaged by Vygotsky and which he called 'social speech' and 'inner speech'. 'Inner speech', in reflecting right hemispheric function, does not have words of its own. Words are as if 'borrowed' from the left hemisphere and used in a different way, as things are used in symbolic play, to portray a barely expressible idea or feeling. In this way, the words selected are double and the person choosing them has a vision in which more than one thing can be seen in a single image. For example, the pathologist and poet Miroslav Holub can peer down a microscope at a group of cells and say: 'Here too are cemeteries, fame, and snow.'[15]

Caesar's words can be written in a way that illustrates the conceptions of James and Saussure, which portray the two modes of thought, manifest in language, co-ordinated as orthogonal axes:

She would catch another Antony

in
her
strong
toil
of
grace

Along the horizontal axis, the elements are connected as they are connected in the world. The vertical axis, however, consists of elements that are not entirely in the world. They are abstract and symbolic, connected by other means.

The horizontal axis, the diachronic, tells of a public reality. It shows Cleopatra in an alluring posture, evoking the image of a high-class courtesan, which is how the Romans saw her, as a 'strumpet'. The portrait made by the synchronic axis is of a private reality, both personal and intimate, known only to Cleopatra and her lover. It is less defined, and confined, than what is ordinarily conceived as real. 'Meaning' is not circumscribed. Rather, one 'meaning' becomes continuous with another.

The phrase 'in her strong toil of grace',[16] is an example of a kind of recursion, which authorities such as Hauser, Chomsky and Fitch[17] and Corballis[18] see as the defining feature of human language. Recursion refers to a process whereby a sentence can theoretically be infinitely expanded by the inclusion of relative clauses, or their equivalents. Relative clauses typically begin with 'wh'- words such as 'whose' 'which' and 'where'.

The essential feature of recursion in language is that it represents the embedding in a particular stream of thought of other, different, but connected thoughts. The phenomenon is considered inexplicable in terms of the evolution of language. If, however, language is considered as an activity which cannot be conceived as isolated from the rest of mental function, but as an aspect of consciousness, an explanation presents itself. If language and consciousness go hand and hand, not only for communicative purposes but also in evolution, the recursion can be seen as a reflection of the unified multiplicity that is evident in the thought of Shakespeare and that is characteristic of the complexity of human consciousness, or self.

Notes

1 Wright, G. T. (1991).
2 Kermode, F. (2004, p. 47).
3 *Antony and Cleopatra*, V. ii. 344–346. Arden edition.
4 Davidson, D. (1978, pp. 29–46).
5 *Oxford English Dictionary* (1971).
6 Steiner, G. (1980, p. 21).
7 *Oxford English Dictionary* (1971).
8 *Henry VI*, V. iv. 40, cited in Craig, W. J. (1922).

9 *Antony and Cleopatra*, III. vi. 16–18. Arden edition.
10 Bradley, A. C. (1923).
11 *Antony and Cleopatra*, IV. xv. 66–68. Arden edition.
12 Murray (1949, p. 173).
13 Schiff, S. (2010, p. 87).
14 *Antony and Cleopatra*, V. ii. 78–79. Arden edition.
15 Holub, M. (1967, p. 25).
16 Hauser, Chomsky and Fitch (2002).
17 Hauser, Chomsky and Fitch (2002).
18 Corballis, M. (2011).

12

IMPEDIMENTS TO PROTO-CONVERSATION THROUGH BLINDNESS AND DEAFNESS

Testing a hypothesis

At this point in the argument a testing of the main hypothesis can be made. The main hypothesis is that the experience of the proto-conversation is the origin of the activity of pretend play and the 'doubling' of symbolic thought. The hypothesis predicts that impediments to the establishment of the proto-conversation will lead to the developing child having deficiencies in both areas. Children who are born blind and deaf, whose participation in one sensory modality of the proto-conversation is blocked, show such deficiencies.

The effect of blindness

The psychoanalyst Selma Fraiberg took a particular interest in the problem of children who are born blind. In a famous study, she followed the developmental course of ten children who had been blind from birth and who had no other known handicaps or neurological damage. These babies were less than a year old. The aim of the study was not only to discover the effects of blindness on psychological development but also to see whether a sensitively devised program of developmental guidance could improve the babies' outcome. It did, but as Fraiberg pointed out, 'no amount of educational intervention obscured the adaptive problems posed by blindness'.[1] The outstanding deficit found in these infants was a relative failure of 'representational intelligence'.[2]

The problems begin from the earliest days of life. Not only is the baby deprived of usual representations of his feeling states, which help to 'realise' these states, but also of the usual reciprocal interplay with the caregiver, most particularly the mother. The blind baby has virtually 'no sign vocabulary that elicits an automatic response from the mother'.[3] In the case of the sighted baby, in contrast, 'the nonvisual vocabulary of the infant "speaks to" the mother and the mother responds and is rewarded by her baby'.[4] The blind baby lacks 'eye language' and smiling is infrequent. 'The voice, even the voice of the mother does not automatically evoke smiling in blind infants.'[5]

Doctor Fraiberg was struck by the behaviour of her co-workers on their first acquaintance with a blind baby. The expressions of their faces and voices were markedly different from those with sighted children.

> Typically, the visitor's face remains solemn. There is a large vocabulary of expressive behaviour that one does not see in a blind baby at all. The absence of differentiated signs on the baby's face is mirrored in the face of the observer.[6]

The blankness of the observer mirrors what she sees. The proto-conversation cannot get going.

Fraiberg elaborated upon the lack of differentiation in the facial expressions of emotion in the blind baby. She noted that although pleasure and distress can be 'read' by the caregiver, between these states there is lacking that 'tremendous range of modulated affect and attitudes which is normally discerned by human partners through expressive facial signs'.[7] She gives examples in sighted babies of 'attentive', 'longing', 'quizzical', 'doubtful', 'coy' and 'bored' expressions – little emotions – that are not displayed by the blind baby. The means of connection between caregiver and baby are gravely limited. Doctor Fraiberg found that babies brought to her in the second year of life, or later, appeared disconnected from and 'without investment in persons or things. These are children of families for whom no guidance was available in the crucial sensorimotor period.'[8]

An extreme of this state of disconnectedness might produce a condition analogous to autism. Peter Hobson, an expert in autism, sensed that congenital blindness might offer some understanding of the origins of autism. In following up this idea, he visited a school for blind children. He wrote:

> Perhaps the first thing to record is what struck me when I first visited a school for blind children. I was both shocked and moved by what I saw. The shocking thing was to discover just how difficult it is for many young blind children to sustain contact with other people, especially their fellow pupils. It was common to see children sitting quietly by themselves, fiddling with their fingers or rubbing their eyes rocking silently.[9]

Following this experience, he set up with his colleagues, Rachel Brown and others, a study of children who had been blind from birth. It turned out that 10 of the 24 children studied would have satisfied the clinical criteria for autism.[10]

Doctor Fraiberg made a study of another form of connectedness and its vicissitudes in blind children. Whereas the reciprocal interplay between mother and child, dependent upon a mutual 'reading' of the other's face and voice, creates a felt connection between them, a connection with the world comes about in a different way, particularly involving the hand. Fraiberg was impressed by the significance of prehension in the child's development. She saw it as uniting the infant with 'the world "out there"' and also giving 'intentionality to action and a sense of voluntariness'.[11] The hands of the blind children were 'groping in the near void' of their world, 'derailed in the progress by a deficit in the biological plan'.[12] However, with help from her program, this progress was not severely disrupted. The system of intentionality was largely preserved.

An example of this relative preservation was shown by a consideration of the infant's reaching and attaining an object, such as a bell that makes a noise. A sighted child is proficient at this kind of grasping at about 5 months. The blind children did not do it until about 8 months. However, if the bell is hidden behind a screen, sighted children also only attain this milestone at 8 months.

The deficit inflicted by blindness was mainly in the representing, or depicting, system. Fraiberg noticed that the hands of the blind children were used to compensate for this deficiency. She found that although it was difficult to 'read' the feeling states of the blind child in the face, finger movements provided an alternate 'reading'.

As an example of the particular disability of the blind child in the sphere of representation, Doctor Fraiberg describes the case of Kathie. By the age of 2, Kathie, a bright little girl, had a normal language competence, but

> between the ages of 2 ½ and 3 years, Kathie's language and her capacity to represent showed marked deviations from that of the sighted child. In both our detailed home observations and in the reports of the mother, it was very clear that Kathie could not represent herself through a doll or a toy. She could not recreate or invent a situation in play. She could not attend to a story or tell a story herself. She could not spontaneously report an experience.[13]

Kathie could not pretend. She could not perform that kind of double consciousness in which she uses something to represent what it is not. It was not until she was between four and five that she began pretend play with her dolls.

Kathie had a vocabulary equivalent to a sighted child of her age but 'between the ages of 3 and 4, she continued to confuse and reverse pronouns and the concept of I had not emerged as a stable grammatical form'.[14] She said 'you' when she meant 'me', or 'my' when she meant 'your'. It was between 4 and 5 that she used 'I' both as a concept and as a grammatical form.[15] A sighted child might reach this milestone two years earlier.

Doctor Fraiberg understood the delay in using pronouns not as primarily a linguistic delay but as a conceptual one, involving the sense of self. Since the blind child has a reduced sensory awareness of otherness, of the world 'out there', an understandable delay arises in conceiving of a boundary between self and other. Self and other, 'I' and 'you', are not properly distinguished and may be reversible.

In summary, congenital blindness is an impediment of the development of self. This is most evident in the story of Kathie whose self-deficiency was manifest in a number of ways, including a lack in the capacity to create symbols, an ability that distinguishes human consciousness from the consciousness of other primates.

She did not show, at the expected ages, the doubling of consciousness characteristic of self, which is necessary to pretend play. Nor was the dual and co-existing experience of self and not-self clearly established. Above all, she could not 'represent' herself to herself, a failure in 'representational intelligence', consequent, I believe upon the lack of availability of representations of her immediate states by the mother's face. These representations are the necessary precursors to self-representations.

The effects of deafness

Difficulty in representing oneself is also a feature of congenital deafness. This is somewhat different to the case of blindness. A main difference between the effect of blindness and that of deafness is that babies babble, producing sounds in which they can listen to themselves. It might seem that what they are doing is attempting to self-represent. But perhaps they are not doing that at all, perhaps they are simply playing, liking to make noises that sound like language.

All babies babble. The form of the babbling changes as the babies develop, becoming more like language. There are three main stages. Deaf babies do not exhibit the third and last forms of babbling.

Babbling's first stage goes on between 4–6 months, called the 'expansion' stage, during which the infants reproduce single syllables. The next stage, between 7–10 months, is known as the 'canonical' stage. It involves repetitive reduplication of syllables (e.g. baba). The first forms of imitation are seen at 7–10 months, a process in which the child can begin to represent herself as another. The third stage, called the 'jargon' phase, finds the baby producing sounds like those of language. Although deaf babies do not reach the later stage of babbling, they do so if they have been exposed to sign language. In this case, they display 'manual babbling', moving their hands in a repetitive way opening and closing them and moving them up and down in a rhythmic way.[16] Petitto and her colleagues reported finding the same pattern in hearing children taught sign language.[17] This study led her to conclude that babbling is fundamentally a linguistic activity and not merely random noises produced as manifestations of improved motor control over the vocal apparatus.

Sign language may give the developing deaf child an advantage over blind children. For example, a study by Woolfe and colleagues compared deaf native-signing children raised by deaf native-signing parents with deaf late-signing children of hearing parents in terms of a so-called 'theory of mind' test – a 'false-belief' situation. Even though they were younger than the children who learnt sign language late, the children who learnt sign language early in life performed better.[18]

Peterson and Siegal found that deaf children in hearing families, who learned sign language later than children of deaf parents, performed at the same level as autistic children in these tests. The children of deaf parents, however, performed at the same level as normal children.[19]

As was the case for congenital blindness, autism is associated with congenital deafness. Stella Chess had observed this association in congenital deafness as a consequence of rubella. She found that in 243 children with this affliction, 10 could be given the diagnosis of autism and another 8 had a partial autistic picture.[20] However, it would not be firmly inferred that the syndrome of disconnectedness these children displayed was due to deafness, since it was possible that it was due to rubella alone. Nevertheless, studies of children who are born deaf from other causes also tend to show this picture.

Since symbolic play is considered to be a precursor to the development of self, it would be predicted that in deaf children this kind of play would be relatively lacking. An interesting study by Patricia Spencer and Kathryn Meadow-Orlans attempted to elucidate the relationship between play, language and maternal responsiveness in deaf children. The subjects in the study were 43 middle-class mothers and their infants who were reviewed at 9, 12 and 18 months of age. These dyads were made up of three different kinds of pairings. The first, involving normal hearing mothers and their children, gave an indication of ordinary maternal responsiveness. The second group was made up of normal hearing mothers and deaf children. The third cohort consisted of deaf mothers and deaf children. At 18 months, all of the hearing children showed pre-planned representational play but only half of the deaf children with hearing mothers. Language development did not always coincide with emergence of play. Most importantly, it was found that maternal responsiveness was significantly associated with pre-planned play at 18 months.[21]

In a book summarizing research work on the development of deaf children, Kathryn Meadow-Orlans gave further evidence of an impairment in the development of symbolization in deaf children. She noted that children with hearing loss have difficulty in understanding words with a double meaning, for example, 'bank'. They also learn concrete words like 'eat' and 'jump' more easily than abstract words like 'equal to' and 'jealous'.[22] These observations of deficient symbolic thinking in deaf children are given support by Oliver Sacks. He studied the effect of deafness in a boy who was reared without access to sign language. What he found was reported in his book, *Seeing Voices*:

> Joseph saw, categorized, distinguished . . . but he could not, it seemed, go much beyond this, hold abstract ideas in mind, reflect, play and plan. He seemed completely literal – unable to juggle images or hypotheses or possibilities, unable to enter an imaginative or figurative realm.[23]

Since the capacity to imagine is a hallmark of selfness, we can conclude that Joseph did not have access to that experience we call self.

Self as a specific module?

These various data suggest that children deprived of a mother's responsiveness, of an analogical kind and dependent upon her face and voice, results in the children's relative failure to develop the capacity to symbolize, which is necessary to the ordinary development of selfhood. This outcome is consistent with the idea that the development of symbolization is a two-person process, involving a particular kind of 'conversation'. The first form of the symbol, the analogue, comes from 'outside' the baby. The observations of Fraiberg, particularly the account of Kathie's development, have a further implication. Kathie showed a relative preservation of the development of intentional consciousness, the state of mind that 'points'. It is linear, goal-directed and especially concerned with outer events. Her deficiency lay in the symbolizing theme, which concerns the representation, or 'depicting', of inner life. This implies that under certain circumstances an individual may grow up without a self and yet manage the world fairly normally, as if self were a specific 'module' of brain-mind function.

At first sight the idea makes no sense. How can it be said that a person who walks and talks, who has an occupation and who behaves in a rational manner, has no self? Also, the idea seems to have no scientific value. The only way of determining whether or not a person has a self, one might suppose, is subjective, depending on an account of the stream of consciousness or its absence. Such an account might be beyond the capabilities of many of those not having the gifts of William James.

The difficulty, however, of discovering self and not-self is not insuperable. Language provides a window on to the movements of mind. What words are used and how they are put together reflect the shape and character of the mental life of the speaker. Words can be used as objective indices of particular states of mind. In the following illustration, the absence of doubling is prominent among these indices.

The depiction of not-self through this illustration also has the value of giving a sense of the kind of consciousness that James called self that is complementary to his description outlined in Chapter 2. It is sometimes easier to describe what something is by showing what it is not.

A portrayal of someone who is almost without self is given by the Swedish actress Sofia Helin, who plays Saga Noren, a brilliant detective in a Scandinavian crime drama TV series. She gives us picture of a high functioning person who could be diagnosed as having Asperger's Syndrome, the cause of which is unknown. The accuracy of her portrayal and the empathy that she brings to the part, has led to her receiving thanks from people in the Asperger's Society in Sweden. They were pleased that she was made to be the hero of the series and not depicted from the point of view of disability.[24]

As the series opens, there appears to be nothing wrong with her. She is blonde and beautiful, with a slightly scarred face, stylishly dressed in leather trousers and long coat. She drives a Porsche. Nevertheless, she is idiosyncratic. She is blunt not only with suspects but also with colleagues, to the point of apparent rudeness and unfriendliness. Her responses are often monosyllabic, while sentences lack recursion and qualifying clauses. Her face is impassive, showing few expressions of emotion. She never laughs or smiles. This demeanour creates some problems with her staff. She seems unaware of the finer feelings involved in personal relations. Her speech is devoid of reference to feelings. It is impersonal, at times resembling a textbook.

As the characterization develops, she shows awareness that her difficulty in making relationships is a deficiency. She knows that people see her as lacking an emotional life but, also, they do not realize she can be hurt. Although she seems to have no access to the 'little emotions', the fluxes of feeling making up the peculiarly human consciousness and that are currency of much ordinary conversation, she does have affects.

In an unobtrusive way evidence emerges of her failure to achieve the dual consciousness that is the marker of self. She understands neither irony nor figurative language, reprimanding a junior officer for not using words in their literal sense. She cannot lie, a behaviour that, in the child, is early indication of double consciousness. It shows that 'I know some things that you don't know'. If asked a question on a factual matter she feels compelled to answer, in an almost reflexive way, with what she knows to be the truth.

Saga also shows one of Hughlings Jackson's cardinal indices of the failure to develop the consciousness characteristic of humanity. She is without what he called 'mental diplopia'. She lacks a sense of humour. Jokes puzzle her. Jackson took humour seriously, even what he considered the simplest form of humour, punning. 'I seriously mean that the analysis of puns is a simple way of beginning the methodical analysis of the process of normal and abnormal mentation.'[25] He considered that all mentation depends upon a match-mismatch process. 'The process of all thought is tracing relations of resemblance and difference, from the simplest perception – to say what a thing is, is to say what it resembles and differs from – up to most complex reasoning.'[26] 'Humour, being the "play" of the mind, is having deep, fanciful resemblances in things known to be very different.'[27]

Saga cannot play. Nor does she seem able to experience pleasure. Even sex is merely a necessary gratification of a physiological urge, like hunger.

Saga's deficiencies in social skills, shown linguistically in difficulties with figurative language, are likely to have their basis, at least in part in the failure to achieve a concept of two co-ordinated zones of personal existing, the personal/private and the communal/public. The difference is enshrined in most languages in what has been called the T and V distinction in pronominal usage resembling the *tu* and *vous* in French.[28] T is spoken in the personal, friendly or intimate zone while V is for more formal and public speech.

Because the awareness that living involves a traffic between two co-ordinated zones of reality, public and private, which a child achieves at about 4, is not given to her, Saga behaves in a public space, her workplace, as if it were private, bemusing her colleagues. For example, she changes her shirt in front of them and, having gathered from self-help groups that chit-chat is a good way to make contact with people, she tells the group at morning tea that she has started her period. Intimacy, involving that which is inner, is beyond her. She cannot manage expressions of feeling, either her own or others. When she receives spontaneous hugs, she freezes. She does however, have one part of psychic life that is hidden. It involves a set of traumatic memories, which are hedged about by fear and loathing, not experienced as 'inner' but separate.

A further difficulty is related to her failure to play, which involves the paradoxical co-existence of the real and unreal. For her the actual/imaginary polarity seems not to exist. She has no imagination, the achievement of which Sartre believed is the hallmark of human consciousness.[29] For her the only reality she inhabits and senses is actual and immediate. Since the future is not actual and only to be imagined, she never thinks about it. Her lack of imagination contributes to her alarming lack of empathy. She relentlessly interviews recently bereaved witnesses to a crime as if she has no understanding of how they might feel. She is protected from making errors that are too grave by the help of her professional partner, a senior Danish detective, Martin, who is the opposite to her, all too human, but with the capacity to understand her.

Saga does not operate in this way. She works with facts. If she were an actual person, and not a fiction, observers would judge her to be a success. She has achieved a high rank in the police force. She strides through a crime scene straight-backed with an almost military air of authority, giving orders that are crisp, succinct and promptly made. She has a prodigious memory, a remarkable eye for detail and the capacity quickly to make logical connections. Yet, as Sofia Helin allows us to see, and to feel, beneath all this, and created by a fundamental lack, is a sadness, the melancholia of an isolate, living alone in the world.

The story of Saga illustrates one of the many paradoxes of selfhood. What we experience and conceive as entirely individual may have evolved as a result of its functions in making interpersonal bonds and in contributing to the formation of a social group and its culture. Self not only grows in a social environment, its main function may be the furtherment of that environment.

Notes

1 Fraiberg, S. (1979, p. 90).
2 Fraiberg, S. (1979, p. 282).
3 Fraiberg, S. (1979, p. 97).
4 Fraiberg, S. (1979, p. 112).
5 Fraiberg, S. (1979, p. 94).
6 Fraiberg, S. (1979, p. 95).
7 Fraiberg, S. (1979, p. 101).
8 Fraiberg, S. (1979, p. 112).
9 Hobson, R. P. (2004, p. 193).
10 Hobson, R. P. (2004, p. 195).
11 Fraiberg, S. (1979, p. 147).
12 Fraiberg, S. (1979, p. 148).
13 Fraiberg, S. (1979, p. 250).
14 Fraiberg, S. (1979, p. 256).
15 Fraiberg, S. (1979, p. 261).
16 Petitto and Marentette (1991).
17 Petitto *et al.* (2004).

18 Woolfe *et al.* (2002).
19 Peterson and Siegal (1999).
20 Chess, S. (1971).
21 Spencer and Meadow-Orlans (1996).
22 Meadow-Orlans, K. (2004).
23 Sacks, O. (1991, p. 40).
24 Helin, S. (2012).
25 Jackson, J. H. (1874, p. 359).
26 Jackson, J. H. (1874, p. 362).
27 Jackson, J. H. (1874, p. 360).
28 Brown and Gilman (1960).
29 Sartre, J. P. (1966).

13

THE SHAPE OF CULTURE AND SELF

Like self and language, the structure of myth is made by the combination of two modes of thought. Myth is not, as the psychoanalyst Karl Abraham supposed, 'a fragment of the superseded infantile psychic life of the race'. Jung cited this remark in order to contradict it. 'Myths', he said, are 'the most mature product of that young humanity . . . myth-making and myth-inhabiting man was a grown reality and not a 4-year-old child.'[1]

In myth, the analogical thought of symbolic play is co-ordinated with the linear and logical mode of succession and facts, creating a system of tribal memory. For example, Lévi-Strauss cites the report of Donald Thomson who worked among the people of the Archer River area in Cape York, North Queensland. He observed that:

> The natives are acutely aware of the characteristic trees, underscrub and grasses of each distinct 'association area' using this term in its ecological sense. They are able to list in detail and without any hesitation, the characteristic trees in each, and also to record the string, resin, grasses and other products used in material culture, which they obtain from each association, as well as the mammals and birds characteristic of each habitat. Indeed, so detailed and so accurate is their knowledge of these areas that they note the gradual changes in marginal areas. . . . My informants were able to relate without hesitation the changes in fauna and in food supply in each association in relation to the seasonal changes.[2]

This system of knowledge is organized in a distinctive taxonomy leading Thomson, who later became Professor of Anthropology at the University of Melbourne, to say 'that the arrangement of animals and plants, and the foods or technological materials derived from them, bears some resemblance to a simple Linnaean classification'.[3]

Such facts, necessary to adaption to the environment, are stored and remembered in a vast collection of interconnected stories in which the imagined is interwoven with the real. Malinowski made the point that the imaginary and magical elements of the mythic construct deal with mysteries, such as the creation of the world and its constituents, which ordinary examination by the senses cannot penetrate. He noted that: 'The most essential point about magic and religious ritual is that it steps up only where knowledge fails.'[4]

Lévi-Strauss had found, as had other anthropologists, that the organization of culture in hunter-gatherer societies shows remarkable similarities between them despite large separations of distance. The patternings of the culture of the Australian aboriginal, built around the central motif of the Dreaming, shows similarities with those of other hunter-gatherers in Africa, the Americas and the Pacific Islands. These similarities lead to the view that the minds of men, wherever they are in the world, operate in ways that are essentially alike. The likeness is strikingly apparent in the customs and rules governing kinship and marriage. Jung drew on the work of John Layard in describing this pattern.

Layard (1891–1974), as a young anthropologist, accompanied an expedition to the New Hebrides (now Vanuatu). The expedition stopped at the small island of Malekula. The natives were unfriendly so the expedition moved on. Layard, however, remained for about a year, during which time he immersed himself in the native culture and recorded its language, myths and social structure.

Jung summarized Layard's observations.[5]

> [The] tribe falls into two halves or 'moieties' [which] show themselves in the layout of the settlements as well as in many strange customs. At ceremonies, for instance the two moieties are strictly segregated and neither may trespass on the other's territory. Even when going out on a hunt, they at once divide into two halves as soon as they set up camp, and the two camps are so arranged that there is a natural obstacle between them, e.g. the bed of a stream. On the other hand the two halves are connected by what Hocart calls 'the ritual interdependence of the two sides'.[6]

This division suggested to Jung, as it did to Lévi-Strauss, a process of 'endopsychic antithesis' fundamental to the organization both of the mind and the way in which that mind arranges the world around it, that is, in binary opposites such as east and west, high and low, day and night, male and female, water and land, left and right, and so forth.

A second division Jung noted is imposed upon the primary division:

> The social split by origin is a matrilineal division into two, but in reality it represents a division of the tribe and settlement into four. The quartering comes about through the crossing of the matrilineal by a patrilineal line of division.[7]

From these and other observations Jung was led to his notion of 'the quarternity, as an organizing schema par excellence, something like the crossed threads in a telescope. It is a system of co-ordinates that is used almost instinctively for dividing up and arranging a chaotic multiplicity'.[8]

The shape Jung describes is that of the mandala, a form that fascinated Jung and one that he believed symbolized self and its synthesis. He called it 'the psychological expression of the totality of the self'.[9] The basic motif of a mandala series 'is the premonition of a centre of personality, a kind of central point within the psyche, to which everything is related, by which everything is arranged, and which itself is a source of energy'.[10]

In a curious resonance with Jung, Lévi-Strauss described villages that have the form of mandala although he did not use the word. An example is the structure of a Bororo village in South America.[11] The structure of 'inner', the mental events that Jung explored, are mirrored in this instance, by those of the outer world, as if they are both the product of a common organizing property of mind. This idea leads to the notion that cultural organization, where it has been allowed to establish itself over a long period of time, is an analogue of mind. Anthropology, then, might be implicitly a study of mind. This was so for Lévi-Strauss. 'His ultimate concern', Edmund Leach believed, was 'to establish facts which are true about "the human mind".'[12]

In pursuit of his goal, Lévi-Strauss was influenced by, or at least chose to align himself with, a highly influential school of American anthropology, led by Franz Boas, which developed between the wars. Lévi-Strauss contacted Boas as soon as he arrived in America, in 1941. An association developed with Boas and his group. Their final meeting, at a ceremonial luncheon in 1942, was dramatic: 'Boas was very jovial,' remembered Lévi-Strauss.

> In the middle of a conversation, he shoved himself violently away from the table and fell backwards. I was seated next to him and bent down to lift him up. Rivet, who had started his career as a military doctor tried in vain to revive him. Boas was dead.[13]

A central figure in the brilliant group of students who surrounded Boas was Ruth Benedict. Boas was her mentor; Margaret Mead was her student, lover and great friend; Edward Sapir was also a friend. Cultures, wrote Benedict 'are individual psychology thrown large upon the screen, given gigantic proportions and a long time span'.[14] She was making quite explicit the view that there is a relationship between society and culture that is analogous to that between body and mind.

Benedict developed this idea in her famous and influential book, *Patterns of Culture*, in which she stated: 'A culture, like an individual, is a more or less consistent pattern of thought and action.'[15] She treated cultures like personalities. For example, Dobuan culture was conceived as paranoid.

Benedict's proposal was echoed, although in muted form, by Alfred Kroeber, Boas' first student whose later eminence caused him to be regarded as the dean of American anthropology. He suggested that a society without a culture would resemble a human without a self. 'If there were no cultures, humanity would be merely another species of brute animals.'[16] He contemplated the possibility of mindless societies.

Although sympathetic to the Boasian school, Lévi-Strauss wanted to go beyond them. Where Benedict was concerned with the peculiar qualities of particular cultures, Lévi-Strauss wanted to discover what all cultures share in order to identify the laws determining their fundamental 'shape'. His only field work was conducted in 1938–1939, in South America, in which he 'briefly surveyed'[17] half a dozen indigenous cultures, including that of the Bororo people. Their social organization was very like that observed by Layard.[18] Similar organizations, far removed from South America and the New Hebrides, are found in Australia. In describing the social division governing the lives of the Yolngu people of northern Australia, Howard and Frances Morphy make clear that these divisions are part of, and woven into, the larger pattern that comprises the life of the Yolngu people and their relationship with the world.

> The society is divided into two moieties, the Dhuwa moiety and the Yirritja moiety, each of which comprise a number of separate clans, which are the primary level of land ownership. The moieties (and clans) are patrilineal and exogamous: Dhuwa people marry Yirritja and the children belong to the moiety of their father. Not only are people and land divided on the basis of moiety but so too is the whole universe with plants, animals, fish and birds belonging to one moiety or the other. Each moiety has its own spiritual identity with discrete sets of ancestral beings. The ancestral beings created features of the clan's territories and are integral to the spiritual identity of its members. Networks of intermarriage link clans to each other. . . . From a Yolngu perspective land is a determining component of their lives . . . 'We marry that way because that is the relationship between our foundational places'. Relationships in land and water are not simply signs of relationships between humans, rather both are manifestations of the same established ancestral pattern in that sense both are thought to be living embodiments of the ancestors with a capacity to act. The land itself may be in some senses ontologically closer to the creative forces of the ancestral beings than people, since it is both created by the ancestral beings and the place to which the human spirits return.[19]

The Morphys, who speak the Yolgnu language, conclude their article with the observation that the coherence of whole cultural system depends, to a large extent, upon metaphorical correspondences. They write: 'Yolngu cosmology and society involve analogous processes of generalization and individuation. These processes articulate with one another and metaphor becomes a primary mode of expressing articulations.'[20] Lévi-Strauss had made similar observations in speaking of the Hopi people of Arizona who 'classify living creatures and natural phenomena by means of a vast system of correspondences'.[21]

Lévi-Strauss was struck by the similarities in the structures of social life and myth across cultures. Such a realization leads to the view that the human mind has a characteristic way of functioning in which form is discovered in what Jung had called 'chaotic multiplicity'. The world that humans create for themselves is continually shaped by a system of arrangements of which the shapers are unaware. The particular originality of Lèvi-Strauss was to propose that the language that was necessary to the creation of cultural products had the same structure as that which it produced. He took Saussure's distinction between the diachronic and synchronic, which had been developed by Jakobson, as basic not only to language but also to the structures of myth and the shapes of culture.

Culture then, as displayed in hunter-gatherer societies, connects individual humans to the worlds in which they live by a system 'defined with reference to two axes, one horizontal and one vertical, which correspond up to a point with Saussure's distinction between syntagmatic and paradigmatic relations'.[22] Beginning in this way, Lèvi-Strauss composed what he called a totemic operator, a hypothetical crystalloid and which is slung between the individual at one pole and a species at the other.[23] The connections between the two are made by layers of connectedness, based on metonym or analogy. The first correspondence between the human and the world so organized is by the body, each part of which has an analogical resemblance to the features of the world. Included in this system of organization of the world is a 'very extensive inventory of their zoological and botanical environment'.[24]

The image of the 'totemic operator' is very like Jung's archetypal 'regulator'. He also described a crystal-like structure. Like Lévi-Strauss, he derived his concept from cross-cultural studies and, like Lévi-Strauss, he thought of archetypal forms as conceptually similar to botanical families. Thus, in his system, 'archetypal forms refer to analogous patterns of imagery resulting from the selection, arrangement, and organization of the data of experience'.[25] They arise through man's innate potentialities for organising experience in a particular way. Hobson, in clarifying the concept of archetype, shows that it is close to that of the Lévi-Straussean structure. Hobson quotes Jung's description of the archetype as

> an unconscious 'regulator' which controls the activity of archetypal themes (motifs) from the raw materials of sensations of perception. . . . The archetypal form is conceived as a structural element analogous to the axial system of a crystal which, having no material existence, determines the stereometric but not the concrete form of the crystal.[26]

The similarity of the 'totemic operator' and the 'archetypal regulator' has fundamental implications. First, since the Jungian system derives from 'inner' experience such as 'individual psychological material . . . myths, religious imagery, and occult speculations', and the totemic system is an ordering of the external world, 'inner' and 'outer' seem to be joined by a common organising mechanism of mind. Thus, since myth, ritual, dream and social structure all seem to derive from the same process, the psyche and its world are interrelated, constantly nourishing and recreating each other.[27]

Mind and culture are as if analogues of each other.

Symbolic play as precursor of myth

Like Piaget, I see the child's symbolic play as the precursor of mythical thought. They are not precisely the same kind of mental function since mythical thought shows a greater co-ordination between the logical and analogical thought than does the state of mind underpinning symbolic play. Nevertheless, they share the same fundamental features. In this section similarities between these features are explored in order to support the Piagetian notion.

A main feature of symbolic play, which is not often discussed by investigators of this behaviour, is the relationship the child has with its world and with others while the playing is going on. It involves a paradoxical state of mind. The child is as if in an 'inner' world, yet someone else, who is 'outer', is part of this world. Piaget, who was not given to romanticism, called it 'a life of union'. The other, in this relationship, has a partly illusory presence in an embryonic inner world. The same other can metamorphose in milliseconds to someone who is truly other and part of the outer world. This happens when the relationship between the child and the other, often the mother, is altered by responses that are not 'within' the child's immediate experience. It is necessary that the child have both of these experiences of the other.

The experience the child has with the other during symbolic play is not fusion. There is a loss of the subject-object distinction but at the same time there is not. It is this curious quality of relationship that Ernst Cassirer found to be characteristic of mythological thought. I shall take a few pages to discuss Cassirer's ideas not simply because, as Kirk remarks, he has 'devoted more time and thought to the philosophy of myth than anyone else',[28] but because he entered into the experience of myth in a manner that differed from other writers on myth who 'were not concerned with how the cosmos presented itself to the individual and how it was integral to conceptions of self'.[29] Cassirer approached the subject empathically and, by this means, arrived at an understanding of mythological thought that, in one important way, goes beyond the conceptions of Lévi-Strauss and Jung. It involves the particular feeling central to this state of mind. A third motivation for giving some time to Cassirer is the sense that he has been treated unfairly by Kirk, who rejects Cassirer's 'vision' on the grounds that it is 'purely conjectural and rather improbable at that'.[30]

Through his immersion in the experience of myth, Cassirer realized that pre-literate 'man does not look at nature with the eyes of a naturalist who wishes to classify things in order to satisfy an intellectual curiosity. . . . His view of nature is neither merely theoretical nor merely practical; it is sympathetic'.[31] He goes on to say that 'the consanguinity of all forms of life seems to be a general presupposition of mythical thought'.[32] This leads to a 'firm belief in the unity of life.'[33]

Cassirer's use of the word 'sympathy' suggests that he was trying to describe a state of mind that resembles what Piaget observed during play. One of the meanings of 'sympathy', as given by the *Oxford English Dictionary*, is 'community of feeling', resembling Piaget's expressions, 'life of union' and 'an atmosphere of communion or syntonization'. The similarity of these descriptions is consistent with the view that symbolic play is a precursor to mythological thought. It is proto-mythological.

Like Jung, Bleuler, Piaget and others, Cassirer distinguished between two modes of thought. What others had called 'directed thought' he called 'verbal'; what Jung called 'fantasy-thinking' he labelled 'mythical'. Had he been aware of neurological evidence suggesting that these forms of thought reflect the activity of different sides of the brain he might have said the left brain was 'verbal' and the right 'mythical'. To speak, however, in such a way is to simplify a complex matter for communication purposes. The brain is always operating as a total system, with all parts of the brain involved at once. The right brain and left brain, act in co-ordination, in different ways. Despite this caveat I shall use terms like 'right hemisphere language' as a shorthand.

Although he did not know the neurology, Cassirer realized that the two thought forms 'are interwoven in every way'.[34]

A reading of such accounts as that of Spencer and Gillen helped Cassirer to gain an insight into living myth. Gillen had become friendly with the indigenous people in Central Australia and had learnt to communicate with them in their own language. In introducing the concept of the 'Dreamtime', Spencer and Gillen[35] helped to change a view of a culture that was seen as inferior, i.e. 'primitive', into an understanding that it was different rather than primitive, with its own particular structure. Although the term 'Dreamtime' is inadequate, since, as aborigines point out, it is not a dream but real, it has been useful and, it has been argued, continues to be so.[36]

Cassirer came to understand that Lévy Bruhl's concept of the 'pre-logical' nature of preliterate thought was wrong. Rather, it is a separate kind of thought, which Cassirer might have called analogical since the definition of 'sympathy' emphasizes the significance of 'correspondence'.[37]

In exploring the difference between this kind of thought and that which is logical, verbal and directed, Cassirer arrived at a most interesting conclusion. It was, he believed, a matter of perception. Mythological thought, he considered, 'depends upon a definite mode of perception'.[38] He was saying, in effect, that a way of seeing is a way of being. It is a way of seeing that resembles a poet's in which one thing can also be another thing. Adoption of this 'symbolical attitude' leads one to see, for example, a tree as a woman, as the Minna people of Western Australia see a certain group of Casuarina trees as representing the ancestral women, the Kana-Kurlangu women, dancing their way eastwards, dancing all the way from the west.[39]

Cassirer remarked upon the likeness between mythological thought and poetic thought: 'What first strikes us,' he wrote, 'is its close kinship to poetry.'[40] He quoted F. C. Prescott who had said: 'The myth maker's mind is the prototype; and the mind of the poet . . . is still essentially mythopoetic.'[41]

Poetry arises out of feeling, T. S. Eliot told us. So also, in the view of Cassirer, does the mythological experience. 'The real substratum of myth is not substratum of thought but of feeling.'[42]

Cassirer was writing before the concept of diachronic and synchronic cultures had become current. Nevertheless, he discerned that in mythological thought and the life of synchronic culture, time does not seem to pass as a succession of moments as it does in the diachronic world of the industrialized West. Rather, time presents itself as a state in which 'present, past and future blend into one another'.[43]

Time in the synchronic zone not only tends to be all time, it is also reversible. The notion of reversibility is illustrated in one of the Aboriginal myths about the origin of the kangaroo.

The kangaroo is the largest and fastest Australian animal. He goes like the wind. Through his speed he creates a wind, a slipstream moving behind him. In the myth, the wind creates the animal, blowing towards him violently, so that he cannot gain a toe-hold, even though he grows large hind-legs in order to do so. He is brought into the country by a huge wind he cannot resist.[44]

Synchronicity arises in the context of a reciprocal influence between the members of a culture and the culture itself. Howard Morphy puts it this way in writing on time in Australian Aboriginal Culture:

> Aboriginal people's experience of time is influenced by the existence of an encompassing cosmological schema – or theory about the world – that is generally referred to in English as the 'Dreaming' or 'Dreamtime'. The effect of the Dreamtime is to displace events in time so that things that happened in the past often have an immediacy that makes them part of the present. The Dreamtime is lived.[45]
>
> Whereas Western conceptualizations of time are heavily influenced by ideas of progression and development, Aboriginal concepts of time are essentially atelic (purposeless). Or, rather, purpose lies in the Dreaming, which is in many respects infinite and timeless.[46]

Perhaps Morphy might have used, rather than 'atelic', the term 'autotelic', which is the characteristic of symbolic play.

A final feature of symbolic play, which is replicated in mythological thought was identified by Vygotsky. He observed that the language of 'inner speech' was a language of predicates. The subjects of sentences tended to be removed. In the same way, those who live the life of the hunter-gatherer world as exemplified by the Aboriginal Aborigines, tend to remove themselves, as subjects, from the discourse. For example, in describing relations in space, Westernized people tend to refer to their own bodies. Things are placed at, or seen as, to the right or left. In contrast speakers in Pormpuraawan languages of north Queensland orient themselves in relation to the cosmos with which their lives are interwoven: 'Speakers of these languages rely on absolute direction terms' (e.g. 'north', 'south', 'east' and 'west'). Even such small events as table setting are indicated by the position of the sun rather than one individual's right or left which differs from another's.[47] The demotion of the subject from the centre of reality is implied in Cassirer's description of mythological thought: 'Man is not endowed with outstanding rank in this society . . . He does not ascribe to himself a unique and privileged place in the scale of nature.'[48] It is very hard, in talking with aborigines, to have them describe themselves as individuals. The somewhat egocentric Western sense of personal identity is diminished in these people who sense themselves as part of something larger. Self, on the other hand, is experienced in the same way as Westerners, suggesting that it is universal rather than culture bound.[49]

Concluding remarks

As suggested in the opening remarks to this section, its purpose has been to show that the proposal is plausible which suggests that symbolic play is the precursor not only of self but also of culture. The basic unit of culture, in its original form, is seen as myth. This idea leads on to the evolutionary hypothesis outlined in the following chapter.

Using Cassirer as an informed guide, a picture emerges of the 'shape' and main features of mythological thought, which resembles that of symbolic play. These ideas, are consistent with the main theme and argument of this book, which is that self emerges in a kind of conversation, involving analogical connectedness that is first seen in the proto-conversation and is then partly internalized by the stage of symbolic play before becoming a more fully inner activity and experience when the Jamesian duplex self appears. At this point, the characteristic story told by the child has progressed beyond a tale of limited spatial organization and lacking the dimension of time to one that more truly resembles a narrative.

Narratives, however, are of different types, some dominated by a 'pointing' kind of discourse and others by 'depiction'. Among the latter are myths, the bases of culture. It is proposed then, that the evolutionary purpose of self, if we can speak in such a way of a process that has no purpose except survival, is not for the individual, who values it so highly, but for the purposes of the group, of mankind as a system of co-operative endeavour, united by feeling.

Notes

1 Jung, C. G. (vol. 5, 1967, p. 24).
2 Thomson, D. F. (1946, pp. 165–167; cited by Lévi-Strauss, 1966, p. 45).
3 Lévi-Strauss, C. (1966, p. 45).
4 Malinowski, B. (1936, p. 34).
5 Layard, J. (1942, 1945).
6 Jung, C. G. (1954, vol. 16, p. 225).
7 Jung, C. G. (1954, vol. 16, p. 226).
8 Jung, C. G. (1959, vol. 9ii, p. 242).
9 Jung, C. G. (1959, vol. 9i, p. 304).
10 Jung, C. G. (1959, vol. 9i, p. 357).
11 Lévi-Strauss, C. (1968, p. 141).
12 Leach, E. (1970, p. 7).
13 Wilcken, P. (2010, p. 134).
14 Benedict, R. (1932, p. 24).
15 Benedict, R. (1934, p. 46).

16 Kroeber, A. (1948, p. 267).
17 Wilcken, P. (2010, p. 2).
18 Lévi-Strauss, C. (1968, p. 142).
19 Morphy and Morphy (2006, pp. 68–69).
20 Morphy and Morphy (2006, p. 82).
21 Lévi -Strauss, C. (1966, p. 40).
22 Lévi-Strauss C. (1966, p. 149).
23 Lévi-Strauss, C. (1966, p. 153).
24 Lévi-Strauss, C. (1966, p. 153).
25 Hobson, R. (1961).
26 Meares, R. (1977, p. 27).
27 Kirk, G. S. (1970, p. 265).
28 Morphy, H. (1996, p. 181).
29 Kirk, G. S. (1970, p. 265).
30 Cassirer, E. (1962, p. 82).
31 Cassirer, E. (1962, p. 82).
32 Cassirer, E. (1962, p. 82).
33 Cassirer, E. (1962, p. 83).
34 Cassirer, E. (1946, p. 83).
35 Spencer and Gillen (1899).
36 Morphy, H. (1996).
37 *Oxford English Dictionary* (1971).
38 Cassirer, E. (1962, p. 76).
39 Nungarrayi (2003, p. 7).
40 Cassirer, E. (1962, p. 75).
41 Prescott, F. C. (1927, p. 10).
42 Cassirer, E. (1962, p. 81).
43 Cassirer, E. (1962, p. 83).
44 Mountford, C. (1973, p. 128).
45 Morphy, H. (1999, p. 265).
46 Morphy, H. (1999, p. 267).
47 Boroditsky and Gaby (2010, p. 1635).
48 Cassirer, E. (1962, pp. 82–83).
49 Petchovsky, L. (2001).

14

AN EVOLUTIONARY HYPOTHESIS

As far as I am aware, none of those who have made proposals about the evolution of the human mind, or self, have based these proposals on observations of the development of this kind of consciousness in an individual life. The reasons for this are likely to be several. First, self is a controversial subject. Different definitions of self, lead to different ideas of development. There is no firm background against which to work.

A second impediment is Ernst Haeckel who, in 1866, loudly announced what he called 'the biogenetic law'. This states that development recapitulates evolution. Darwin gave only half-hearted support to his disciple, speculating that the 'law' might have value when comparisons are made embryonically: 'Thus the embryo comes to be left as a sort of picture, preserved by nature, of the ancient and less modified condition of each animal.'[1] Haeckel's literal and dogmatic espousement of his law, and his use of fraudulent diagrams to support it, has led to a near universal discreditation of his account. Nevertheless, those who have contributed to this discreditation, including Stephen Jay Gould,[2] concede that there is something in the idea. It would seem implausible, at least to me, that there is no resemblance between the way in which self evolves and the way it develops. Such resemblance is not recapitulation, just as the process of therapy is not a recapitulation of child development. Rather, resemblances are found between general principles, which guide very different processes. The general principle is what Wolf Singer called the 'iteration between self-similar operations'.

When I first came to consider the mystery of the evolution of human consciousness, I was led to the classic work by Frederic Wood Jones[3] on the anatomy of the hand since a traditional idea of human evolution focused on man's dexterity and early hominids' use of tools. It was supposed that evolution of the capacity for prehension, or manual grasping, was the forerunner of states of comprehension, or mental grasping. *Homo sapiens* was alternatively titled *Homo faber*, 'man the maker'. Wood Jones poured cold water on the idea. It is not the human hand that is remarkable.[4] Rather, it is the brain that has the capacity of creating what he called 'action patterns',[5] which govern the production of movement. Philip Lieberman has a similar idea about language. A particular vocal tract cannot alone produce language. A brain that determines the sequencing of articulatory musculature is required.[6]

Wood Jones, as a comparative anatomist, was interested in evolution. He saw particular significance in human altricality, that is, the fact that human babies are born immature, helpless and unable to move around relative to other primates. Chimpanzee babies, for example, can crawl at 1 month while human babies begin to crawl at about 7 months. The human baby requires extra parental care in order for it to survive.

Wood Jones believed that the prolonged period of 'infantile helplessness' in human babies was the origin of the human family since the father must be involved in care to a far greater extent than in chimpanzees.[7] Also, 'the display of maternal care becomes much more marked' in the higher primates.[8] He considered, like Savage-Rumbaugh and Fields,[9] that 'the importance of the Primate ability to carry and nurse a baby cannot be over-estimated'.[10] Modern observations allow Wood Jones evolutionary, idea to be developed further. My focus is on maternal care.

Human altricality is the outcome of the rapid growth during evolution of the human brain. The brain size of hominids increased during the process of evolution from australopithecus, whose brain capacity of about 450 cc did not greatly differ from chimpanzees, to 1100 cc in the more recent African specimens of *Homo erectus*, a capacity approaching the 1250 cc of modern humans. It had been supposed, in the past, that the growth in brain size came about through our ancestors use of tools. It is now seen that such a view is implausible. The tools made by proto-humans did not develop greatly in complexity during the nearly two million years preceding the appearance of *Homo sapiens*. Moreover, chimpanzees are capable of making tools. The traditional speculation has been replaced, at least by a number of evolutionary theorists, by a new hypothesis, which is social. The big brain of mankind arose, according to this theory, as a consequence of the demands of an increasing complexity in the relationships between the members making up a social group.[11] *Australopithecus* lived, perhaps, in a society resembling the simple dominance-submission society of non-human-primates while late *Homo erectus* may have been part of a larger, more complex social organization more nearly resembling the intricate tribal patterns of the first modern humans, the hunter-gatherers.

The big brain gave an evolutionary advantage but also brought disadvantage, in survival terms. The evolution of a pelvis suitable for birth of a child with a larger head had not kept pace with the evolution of the brain. As a result, those babies who were able to traverse the birth canal were born premature relative to non-human primates.[12]

The mother needed to make a larger personal investment in keeping the baby alive. Certain biologically given imperatives may cause her to make this investment.

The first, and most obvious of these, is the attachment system, which as Bowlby[13] pointed out, seems to have the evolutionary 'purpose' of protecting the infant from predators. This system is highly developed in non-human primates. A main affect driving this system is anxiety, displayed by both partners.[14] In rhesus monkeys, for example, the mother will chase after her baby if it wanders away.

Maintenance of contact between mother and child during the first few weeks of life depends upon the mother's anxiety. By about 2 or 3 months, however, it is the infant who seeks to maintain contact when the mother walks away. Maestripieri observes that after this time, mothers increasingly 'encourage their infants' independence by breaking contact with them frequently and physically rejecting their infants' attempts to make contact and gain access to the nipples'. This rejection process peaks at about 6 months 'when the mating season begins and the mother returns to estrus'.[15] However, as Goodall points out, chimpanzee infants continue to suckle and sleep with their mothers until 4 years of age.[16]

The attachment system is not sufficient motivation for the mother to continue care for the extended period necessary to the infant's survival in the case of both humans and chimpanzees. Some additional imperative must be involved for mothers to continue their care of babies.

This additional motivation is provided by the pleasure of play. Jane Goodall describes the pleasure some chimpanzee mothers display in frolicking with their babies, tickling and chasing around trees and so forth. The fun of this activity gives it value, which adheres to the baby.

Not all chimpanzees, however, display the additional motivation. Goodall described how one of the chimpanzee mothers she observed in the Gombe National Park, who she called Passion, showed no additional motivation. Contact between her and her infant seemed to be entirely driven by her infant's separation anxiety. Passion seemed oblivious to the infant's cries of distress, when for example, her baby tried to totter after her though barely able to walk. The infant's obvious separation anxiety persisted at least into its second year of life.[17]

Goodall knew that Passion had already lost one infant and surmised that she must have lost more, judging by her indifference towards her infant. In order for the child to survive, a behavioural imperative is necessary beyond the negative affect of anxiety that drives attachment. The additional motivational force is the reinforcement created by positive affect, by the pleasure of a certain kind play.

Human infants cannot frolic. They are relatively immobile. Play, if it is to develop, must go on in a different way, with a stationary child. The game that evolves is unique to the human primate. This is the proto-conversation. Peter Hobson notes that chimpanzees do not 'spend time gazing into each other's eyes, or engaging in the kinds of intense face-to-face interpersonal communication we see in human infants'.[18] Such face-to-face gazing is likely to be highly reinforcing, as suggested by the evidence presented by Edmund Rolls that was mentioned earlier.[19] In this face-to-face gazing, the eyes are particularly important.[20] In autism this kind of gazing is lacking.

There is a body of evidence suggesting that the behaviour of both partners in the proto-conversation\is a universal phenomenon, not merely a product of culture.[21] This idea implies that the behaviours of mothers and babies during this game are an aspect of our evolutionary heritage. This is not to say that the behaviours are instinctive. Rather, the phylogenetically determined behaviours are propensities to behave in a particular way. Culture, as Ochs and Schieffelin have argued, using evidence gained from studies of Samoan and Papuan cultures, influences the manifestation of mother-baby interplay.[22]

The tendency towards formation of the proto-conversation must have forerunner in an evolutionary past. One of these is the capacity for tenderness, which Wood Jones had noted as in increasing tendency from monkeys to the higher primates.[23] Tenderness is often bundled together with attachment but, since the two can be differentiated as positive and negative modes, it is better to conceive them as distinct although related developmental themes.

A further propensity towards an interplay between faces and voices of the mother-infant pair is suggested by an apparently innate attraction that female primates have towards babies. Maestripieri[24] notes that:

> In rhesus macaques, females of all ages are highly attracted to infants and show visible signs of arousal as their presence. They approach other females' infants, use particular facial expressions and vocalizations to get their attention, and engage in various types of social interactions with them.[25]

The visual stimulus of the baby's face is not sufficient in itself to trigger a response. Rather, the baby emits signals that have an effect on the caregiver, evoking the response. This 'effect of the infant on the caregiver'[26] is crucial. The gaze and smile are particularly powerful. In the pre-history of mankind the survival of a baby whose genes did not contain the repertoire for these behaviours would have been under threat. The mother would find it difficult to bring forth some means of contributing to the first form of the proto-conversation, which would have given her pleasure. The result might be indifference to the child, leaving it at risk from predators or in adequate nutrition. In the modern era mothers of children born blind have a similar difficulty (see Chapter 12).

The same risk for the baby's survival arises where the mother, or other caregiver, lacks the capacity to respond to the baby's signals. An evolutionary scenario now emerges in which those babies and women who can between them create pleasure through an interplay between faces and voices, have a tendency to survive relative to those who do not. Through a process of natural selection, the brains of human babies and mothers have evolved as if peculiarly designed for the proto-conversational game. The stage is now set, so some authorities believe, for the development of syntax and the emergence of narrative. They suggest that the rhythms and harmony of the proto-conversational game resemble not only music and dance but also narration.[27]

The emergence of syntax and the capacity for narration

Trevarthen and his colleagues suggest that within the apparently simple, but actually quite complex, behaviour of proto-conversational play are the seeds of the patterning necessary to the creation of stories. With Maya Gratier, he writes:

> Because verbal narrative invariably involves some form of action, or happening, it can be seen as being based on a sequencing of nonverbal acts. And this touches upon a first way in which narratives can be meaningful without words. Repeated chains of gesture, body movement and facial expression can stimulate shared narrative imagination – a sympathy for purposeful agency.[28]

Put another way, the to-and-fro movements of the proto-conversation, the interweaving of faces, voices, gestures and bodies are not merely a series of random reactions. Rather, they are co-ordinated in time, creating a temporal structure analogous to the temporal envelope of narrative, which must be told by the structuring of syntax.

Trevarthen is not alone in his belief. He is given authoritative support by the eminent developmentalist, Jerome Bruner, who considered that: 'One of the most ubiquitous and powerful discourse forms in human communication is narrative. Narrative structure is even inherent in the praxis of social interaction before it achieves linguistic expression.'[29] Bruner saw the proto-conversation as a little narrative.

These ideas suggest that the dynamic temporal structure of the proto-conversation has within it an embryonic syntax, the arrangement of words that makes narrative possible. In Chapter 10, it is proposed that syntactical language came into being through the appropriation of existing circuitry in the brain, in the manner of neuronal plasticity. 'Action patterns', to use Wood Jones' term for the sequencing of muscular movements of the hand and in the head and neck, which are involved in the proto-conversation, may be the basis and original form of verbal syntax.[30] Narrative, however, does not consist only of syntactically arranged words. It also involves words used symbolically. At any one moment in the temporal structuring of the proto-conversation it has, as remarked in previous chapters, a representing function, which is the first form of symbolic activity. The proto-conversation, then, has within it the primordia of the two main kinds of thought and language, variously called diachronic and synchronic, logical and analogical and so forth.

The question arises: if the proto-conversation holds the potential to develop into a proto-narrative, what caused this potential to be realized? The answer may lie, once again, on the demands created by the complexity of communal life presumably lived by the late hominids, such as *Homo erectus*. Society, it seems, was becoming more organized. New behaviours emerged that no other primates had performed. A prime example is the use of fire, first evident about 400,000 years ago,[31] that is, during the period that Tattersall[32] believes the human vocal tract was evolving its distinctive features. Cooking probably began about 250,000 years ago.[33] What appear to be hearths have been found in a cave in France, which are dated to 200,000 years before the present.[34]

In order to maintain the evolutionary advantages of new knowledge, the tribal group needed a means of sharing, storing and transmitting this knowledge, which would concern not only information necessary to direct survival, such as sources of food and water, but also the ways in which people should conduct their relations with others in order to preserve and nourish the fruitful cohesion and function of the group. A story of a particular kind would fulfil this function. A tribal group who developed this means of storing information would have gained an increased chance of survival relative to a group that lacked this capacity. The main implication of these ideas is that the evolutionary trajectory of *Homo sapiens* was towards the ability to construct a story, the prologue to which is necessarily a proto-language that involves the use of symbols.

The crucial narrative, however, which *Homo sapiens* evolved, and that gave it an evolutionary advantage, was not any kind of story. It had the structure of myth, depending upon the co-ordination of two forms of language and modes of thought, which have different developmental pathways and neurological bases. One concerns syntactical development, the other, symbolic. Cassirer distinguished the two themes as 'verbal' and 'mythical'. The latter is 'fragile' relative to the former. In the final chapter, a return is made to the therapeutic situation. The myth-like story emerges in an interplay between a presentational reality and what the physicist Wolfgang Pauli called a 'second meaning' – a symbolic re-representation. The story of Wolfgang Pauli's story of a transformational experience gives a description, from a different viewpoint, of a central hypothesis developed in this book.

Notes

1 Darwin, C. (1859, p. 338).
2 Gould, S. S. (1977).
3 Wood Jones, F. (1920).
4 Tallis, R. (2003, p. 24).
5 Wood Jones, F. (1926, p. 240).
6 Lieberman, P. (2007).
7 Wood Jones, F. (1926, p. 187).
8 Wood Jones, F. (1926, p. 186).
9 Savage-Rumbaugh, Shanker and Taylor (1998).
10 Wood Jones, F. (1926, p. 148).
11 Dunbar, R. (1996).
12 An alternative has been proposed for the cause of human altriciality. Its basis, the theory suggests, is metabolic rather than anatomical. The big brain of the foetus has energy demands, which at the point of gestational term, have become beyond what the mother can supply (Dunsworth *et al.* 2012). In either case, however, the outcome is the same. The infant is born requiring long-term nurture.
13 Bowlby, J. (1969).
14 Maestripieri, D. (2011, p. 517).
15 Maestripieri, D. (2011, p. 517).
16 Goodall, J. (1971, p. 141).
17 Goodall, J. (1971, pp. 140–141).
18 Hobson, R. P. (2004, p. 270).
19 Rolls, E. (2002).
20 Spitz, R. (1965).

21 Gogate *et al.* (2015).
22 Schieffelin (1998); Ochs and Schieffelin (1994).
23 Wood Jones, F. (1926, p. 185).
24 Maestripieri, D. (1994).
25 Maestripieri, D. (1994).
26 Lewis and Rosenbaum (1974).
27 Trevarthen *et al.* (2009).
28 Gratier and Trevarthen 2008, p. 125).
29 Bruner, J. (1990, p. 77).
30 This proposal can be seen as a contribution to the puzzle posed by Chomsky's notion of a Universal Grammar (e.g. Chomsky, 1973), which seems to have arisen in *Homo sapiens* without evolutionary precedent. Chomsky remarks that: 'Human language appears to be a unique phenomenon, without significant analogue in the animal world' (Chomsky, 1973, p. 62).
31 James (1989).
32 Tattersall, I. (2006, p. 73, excerpted from Tattersall, 2002).
33 Pennisi, E. (1999).
34 James, W. (1989).

15

AUTOMORPHOSIS

The dreams of Wolfgang Pauli

Wolfgang Pauli (1900–1958) was a brilliant theoretical physicist who won the Nobel prize in 1945 for his contributions to quantum theory. He seemed to arrive at original conclusions by a means that not only involved mathematical logic but also intuition. In his Nobel speech, for example, he said that he was 'unable to give a logical reason for the exclusion principle' for which he won the prize.[1]

One of his intuitive discoveries concerns the 'making of mind'. It emerges, he suggested, in a process he called 'automorphosis', that is, self-shaping. This idea anticipates the main theme of this book. That it should be proposed by one of the most extraordinary theoretical talents of the twentieth century gives authoritative support to a theory concerning the generative potential of 'analogical connectedness'.

The story of Pauli's arrival at the notion of 'automorphosis', in which Carl Gustav Jung is a main figure, is one of great interest.

Pauli was born in Vienna to a father who was an eminent scientist and a mother who was a politically active feminist and pacifist. Pauli was recognized in adolescence as being remarkably gifted. He was thought, even at that age, likely to become another Gauss or Boltzmann. At university, his professor very quickly discovered that he could teach him nothing more and so asked him to prepare an encyclopaedia article on relativity. This article was praised by Einstein, who in later years nominated Pauli as his successor. The following year, at the age of 22, he made his first original contribution.

At the age of 24, Pauli realized that the theory of three quantum numbers necessary to the description of the behaviour of subatomic particles, based on the work of Niels Bohr, was incomplete. It was not able to deal with a system larger than one electron. Pauli proposed that a fourth number was required. This number involved the concept of the electron's 'spin' or angular momentum, which could have the values + ½ or –+ ½ compared with the 'orbital' value of Bohr's postulate, which was a whole number. At the age of 25, further developments in his thought about the behaviour of electrons, and other subatomic particles, included the notion of shells of subatomic particles made up of a group of these particles, which resemble each other in terms of energy and spatial organization. Pauli showed that there was a limit to the number of electrons a shell could accommodate and formulated the principle underlying this limitation. This was the exclusion principle, which states that every particle in the shell has a behaviour that can be described by the four quantum numbers, but no two particles in the shell can have in common the same profile of quantum numbers. This proposal depended on observations of the patterns of light given off by atoms.

Perhaps the most famous of Pauli's achievements was the hypothesis of the existence of the neutrino. This arose out of the puzzle presented by the continuous energy spectrum of beta rays emitted during radioactive disintegration, which did not properly obey the law of conservation of energy. Niels Bohr approached the matter statistically, suggesting that the law of conservation of energy may not be applicable to all situations. Pauli could not agree. He considered the law of conservation of energy inviolable. Accordingly, he proposed 'the desperate remedy' that during beta decay not only was an electron emitted, but also an electrically neutral, practically massless particle the emission of which did not upset the law of conservation of energy. This idea was outlined in an open letter to a conference in Tübingen on 4 December 1930. His hypothesis was confirmed by experiment in 1956.

The elements of these theories – the number four, the concept of spin, the significance of the spectrum of colours, and the law of conservation of energy – are recurring themes in a large series of dreams recorded by Pauli following his encounter with Jung. Neither Jung nor Pauli seemed to recognize the relationship between Pauli's work and his dreams, at least during the first few hundred dreams, which will be discussed later.

In 1928, at the age of 28, Pauli was appointed professor of theoretical physics in Zurich. Despite his success in the world of physics, Pauli's life was a mess. Before he came to Zurich he was a lecturer in Hamburg. His nights were spent hanging out and drinking in the bars, cabarets and whorehouses of the notorious red-light district of Sankt Pauli. As he drank, he became more aggressive, sometimes getting beaten up in a brawl.[2] He habitually arrived at work late in the morning. By the age of 30, things had become worse. His 'open letter' regarding the neutrino was written 8 days after his divorce. His marriage, to a cabaret dancer, had lasted less than a year. The deterioration in his mental state was exacerbated by the suicide of his mother three years earlier and the rapid remarriage of his father. His relationships with his peers were often disagreeable and quarrelsome. He started to treat people as enemies.[3] Looking back at this time many years later, Pauli wrote: 'In the day calming works, in the night social entertainment in the underworld – without feeling, without love, indeed without humanity'.[4]

In January 1932, at the urging of his father, Pauli contacted Jung. Jung chose not to treat him, but instead referred him to a young trainee in his system, Erna Rosenbaum. In his introductory letter to Doctor Rosenbaum, Pauli wrote:

> [I contacted] Mr Jung because of certain neurotic phenomena which are connected with the fact that it is easier for me to achieve academic success than success with women. Since with Mr Jung rather the contrary is the case, he appeared to me to be quite the appropriate man to treat me medically.[5]

Rosenbaum was a physician, pretty, always laughing and, it seems, likely to be engaging. Jung instructed her to work with Pauli's dreams, 'to play a "positive role" and do no more than provide encouragement and indicate points that Pauli should work out more clearly'.[6] Doctor Rosenbaum wondered if her patient was 'crazy', She told Jung that Pauli 'told her stories with "such emotion that he rolled around on the floor" '.[7]

Pauli was a prolific dreamer, recording about 400 dreams during the time he saw Rosenbaum and then, following that, when he had some contact with Jung. Pauli saw Rosenbaum for the first five months of 1932 after which he continued to work on his dreams alone for some months, despite feeling lonely without her.[8] It was during this period 355 of the 400 dreams were produced. Jung took over from Rosenbaum in October 1932.[9] Ten letters were exchanged between Pauli and Jung during that time and the termination in October 1934. The letters between the pair continued for many years.

In April 1934, Pauli had remarried. It was a successful partnership. Pauli was remarkably changed. Jung wrote: 'He did not drink anymore, he became completely adapted and in every respect completely normal.'[10] His relationships with others took on a different character, as his obituary in *The Times* suggests:

> Pauli was one of the great theoretical physicists of his generation. As an originator of simple yet penetrating ideas he was perhaps the greatest. He was also a man of great charm, known personally to most of his colleagues, and held in affection by very many more – young as well as old.

What had begun with an attempt by Jung to remove his influence upon therapeutic process in order to observe archetypal imagery in 'unadulterated' form had turned into a highly effective therapy. What had happened? Jung made clear that interpretations were not involved. 'Only the last 45 (dreams) occurred under my observation. No interpretations were then attempted because the dreamer, owing to his excellent scientific training and ability did not require any assistance.'[11]

The dreams

Despite Jung's attempt to make the relationship between therapist and patient simply observational – which, Pauli was later to explain to him, is impossible[12] – it is clear that Pauli experienced his time with Erna Rosenbaum as more important than Jung had planned. So also was Pauli's relationship with Jung, which was maintained by correspondence and periodic meetings until the year before Pauli's death in 1958. The records of his dreams became the currency of these relationships.

In his account of the 400 dreams, Jung selected a series that he called 'the mandala dreams'.[13] In what follows, the dreams are numbered as in Jung's *The Symbolism of the Mandala* with the page numbers in brackets.

Throughout this intriguing series of dreams there appears imagery that seems to reflect Pauli's theoretical preoccupations. For example, an early dream 9(100) is related to the neutrino problem. The dream is of a 'pendulum clock that goes forever without the weights running down'. In real life, of course, such a machine is not possible. It disobeys the law of conservation of energy.

Pauli's dreams, however, were not all about physics but displayed an interweaving of a number of themes including those of the therapeutic relationship. For example, dream 10(101):

> The dreamer is in the Peterhofstatt in Zurich with the doctor, the man with the pointed beard, and the 'doll woman'. The last is an unknown woman who neither speaks nor is spoken to. Question: To which of the three does the woman belong?

The Peterhofstatt is an enclosed space, a precinct of the church of St Peter's, the tower of which has a clock with a strikingly large face. It is divided into four quarters. There are also four characters in the dream. The significance of the numeral four for Pauli is found not only in Pauli's proposal regarding the fourth quantum number but also in his concept of 2×2 matrices as a basis of spin operators. The theme of four is repeated in many of the dreams, often visually, as a square. Moreover, the unknown woman, presumably representing the therapist, is also a recurring image.

Pauli's dreams resonated with Jung's fascination with the imagery of the mandala, which has both a quadripartite and circular structure. Jung considered this image to 'signify nothing less than the psychic centre of the personality',[14] that is, the self.

Although a number of the dreams involve only the number four (e.g. 11(108), 15(118), 55(188)) many of them combine the square and the circle. Sometimes the circle is still, for example 38(178): 'A circular table with four chairs round it'. Jung remarked of this dream: 'The mandala is not in use'. In many cases, however, the circle is made by movement – a re-representation of Pauli's formulation about the spin of the electron. Examples of this dream structure include the following:

> [P]eople all walking to the left around a square.
>
> 18(137): [A] square space with complicated ceremonies going on in it, the purpose is to transform animals into men. Two snakes, moving in opposite directions, have to be got ridden of at once. Some animals are there, e.g. foxes and dogs. The people walk around the square and must let themselves be bitten in the calf by three animals at each of the four corners. . . . A voice proclaims 'These are attempts at being'.
>
> 16(119)

> The dreamer is in a square enclosure where he must keep still. It is a prison for Lilliputians (or children?). A wicked woman is in charge of

them. The children start moving and begin to circulate around the periphery. The dreamer would like to run away but may not do so. One of the children turns into an animal and bites him on the calf.

44(180)

A starry figure rotating. At the cardinal points of the circle there are pictures representing the four seasons.

49(189)

Four children are carrying a large dark ring. They move in a circle. The dark unknown woman appears and says she will come again, for it is the festival of the solstice. [See book cover]

56(190)

Some of the dreams include not only the square and rotation but also a motif of right compared with left rotation. In Pauli's formulation of spin, the electrons could go either left or right. Spin was, then, positive or negative. A further association between left and right in Pauli's theoretical speculations involved the neutrino. Many years after he dreamt these dreams, he put forward the idea that there existed two forms, a right-handed and a left-handed neutrino. Here is a dream in which left and right is a prominent theme. Jung gave an extended description of this dream because it seemed particularly interesting, having a cosmic character.

It is night, with stars in the sky. A voice says, 'Now it will begin'. The dreamer asks, 'What will begin?' Whereupon the voice answers, 'The circling can begin'. Then a shooting star falls in a curious leftward curve. The scene changes and the dreamer is in a rather squalid place of entertainment. The proprietor, who appears to be an unscrupulous crook, is there with some bedraggled-looking girls. A quarrel starts about left and right. The dreamer then leaves and drives round the perimeter of a square in a taxi. Then he is in the bar again. The proprietor says, 'What they said about left and right did not satisfy my feelings. Is there really such a thing as a left and right side of human society?' The dreamer answers, 'The existence of the left does not contradict that of the right. They both exist in everyone. The left is the mirror-image of the right. Whenever I feel like that, as a mirror-image, I am at one with myself. There is no right and no left side to human society, but there are symmetrical and lopsided people. The lopsided are those who can only fulfill one side of themselves either left or right. They are still in the childhood state'. The proprietor says meditatively, 'Now that's much better', and goes about his business.

26(164)

In this dream, we see an integration of a number of themes related to Pauli's ongoing theoretical preoccupations and also his life – the bars, the night and the women.

A further theme, which was apparent in earlier dreams, is that of four primary colours. This is likely to be connected to the significance of spectral lines in the evolution of quantum theory. Pauli wrote, at the age of 25, i.e. in 1925, 'I proposed to use the assumption of a nuclear spin to interpret the hyperfine structure of spectral lines.'[15] He saw spectroscopic data as a means of testing his theory.[16] Here is a dream in the four prime colours, which make up the main theme of the dream.

> The dreamer is falling into the abyss. At the bottom there is a bear whose eyes gleam alternately in four colours: red, yellow, green, and blue. Actually it has four eyes that change into four lights. The bear disappears and the dreamer goes through a long dark tunnel. Light is shimmering at the far end. A treasure is there, and on top of it the ring with the diamond. It is said that this ring will lead him on a long journey to the east.
>
> 39(178)

The diamond may be connected to Pauli's interest in the refractive properties of crystals. The structure of the diamond crystal also has echoes with the fourfold theme. Each carbon atom is linked to four equidistant neighbours so that a tetrahedral linkage occurs throughout the crystal.

The theme of the four colours is interwoven in an earlier dream, 23(157), involving the unknown woman who Jung interprets as Pauli's anima, the archetype of the female principle. In this dream, the dreamer is seated opposite the unknown woman whose portrait he is supposed to be drawing. However, what he draws is not a face but three-leaved clovers or distorted crosses in four different colours: red, yellow, green and blue. The number three and its relationship with four was another of Pauli's pre-occupations. In connection with this dream, Pauli spontaneously drew a wheel, with spokes and the four quarters painted in the above colours. In the middle is a blue four-petalled flower.

The culmination of these dreams, in which there seems to be a movement towards the integration of a number of themes, is a dream Pauli called 'The Great Vision'. Here it is:

The Great Vision

> There is a vertical and a horizontal circle, having a common centre. This is the world clock. It is supported by the black bird.
>
> The vertical circle is a blue disc with a white border divided into $4 \times 8 = 32$ partitions. A pointer rotates upon it.
>
> The horizontal circle consists of four colours. On it stand four little men with pendulums, and round about it is laid the ring that was once dark and is now golden (formerly carried by the children).
>
> The 'clock' has three rhythms or pulses:

1 *The small pulse*: the pointer on the blue vertical disc advances by 1/32
2 *The middle pulse*: one complete revolution of the pointer. At the same time the horizontal circle advances by 1/32.
3 *The great pulse*: 32 middle pulses are equal to one revolution of the golden ring.

59(194)

This dream, 59(194), made a remarkable impression on Pauli. It was accompanied by 'a feeling of most sublime harmony',[17]suggesting a sense of personal unification. It came toward the end of the first third of the dream material.

Jung was puzzled by the image. He wrote: 'We can only venture the hypothesis that disparate and incongruous elements have combined here in the most fortunate way, simultaneously producing an image which realized the "intentions" of the unconscious in the highest degree'.[18] He suggested that it was a three-dimensional mandala.[19] It is really four-dimensional – it involves time.

If the vertical disk of blue and white were the sky and the horizontal was the earth, the image might reflect a sense that the structure of the atom resembles or is an analogue of, the shape of the earth or the solar system. The most striking feature of the dream is the unification of many of the elements of the dream, which are analogues of the components of quantum theory. They include the numbers three and four, the pendulum, the four colours and the notion of spin, which may be complete or fractional. The number 32 is new. It also comes from Pauli's theory. According to his principle, the electron shells fill up as groups of 2, 8, 18 and 32.

This whole system of the atom and the world is borne aloft by the black bird. Jung tells us, in another volume, that a blackbird may be an emblem of the self.[20]

Pauli's quest

Pauli knew that something important had happened to him as a result of his conversations with Erna Rosenbaum and Jung. After ending his sessions with Jung, a decision probably urged upon him by his wife who disapproved of Jung, Pauli acted as if he had a quest to understand what had occurred in his relatively brief therapy, which was the basis of the change that he experienced.

As time went on in his exploration, his objective became larger. He came to realize that although quantum theory provides a good model for the inanimate world, it could not explain the world of the living. As he wrote toward the end of his intellectual journey: 'As a result of the development . . . of quantum theory since 1910 physics has gradually been compelled to abandon its proud claim that it can, in principle, understand the whole universe.'[21]

Something else was needed in order to describe a universe that includes not only life but also mental life. In the end, he was seeking a model of reality that encompasses the 'whole world' and includes the mind. He aspired towards a 'scientific theory of nature'.[22] The search began in a small way, as he described it to a friend:

> After having reached a fairly low point in the winter of 1931/2, it then slowly went upward again. Thereby I also became acquainted with psychic matters that I did not know before and which I want to summarize under the name *proper activity of the soul.* That there are things which are spontaneous products of growth and may be called symbols, an object-psychic theory that cannot and should not be explained from material causes, is beyond doubt for me.[23]

It seemed that in his encounter with Jung, Pauli entered an entirely unfamiliar world. Although Jung made no interpretations, Jung was certainly not silent. He spoke of the symbolism of the dreams, using a vast literature made up of alchemical, religious and mythological sources, including references to Eastern symbolism and Christian, Hermetic and Gnostic thought. Speaking to an audience at the Tavistock Clinic in 1935, he said of Pauli: 'The man got into order again because he accepted the symbolic data.'[24] The matter, however, was not as simple as Jung made it seem.

In further exploring what had happened between 1932 and 1934, Pauli continued to record his dreams, telling them in the morning to his wife over breakfast.[25] The value he sensed in such a project had a background. Earlier in his career he had been fascinated by Johannes Kepler and the way he thought. He identified, to some extent, with the seventeenth-century astronomer, whose *Harmonices Mundi* (*Harmonies of the World*) Pauli may have been reading as he was working towards the exclusion principle.[26] Like Pauli himself, Kepler came to his conclusion about the elliptical movements of the planets about the sun on the basis not only of scientifically gathered data but also through a type of thinking that was quite different to the scientific and logical.

Pauli began to study Kepler in depth. His researches led, in 1952, to a publication entitled *The Influence of Archetypal Ideas on the Scientific Theories of Kepler*. In immersing himself in the intellectual world of Kepler, Pauli found that Kepler was truly a creature of the seventeenth century.

The seventeenth century in Europe was a time of transition between the cultural acceptance of magic and superstition and the scientific world view of the 'enlightenment', that long century between the English and French revolutions. The great figures of the seventeenth century encompassed both modes of thought. The prime example was Isaac Newton, who was the idol of Voltaire, the chief proponent of the enlightenment. Voltaire was horrified to learn of Newton's absorption in alchemical thought, considering it a blemish on the great scientist's reputation. Pauli realized, as he wrote, that Kepler's 'ideas represent a remarkable intermediary stage between the earlier, magical-symbolic and the modern, quantitative mathematical description of nature'.[27] It became clear to Pauli that both modes of thinking were necessary to Kepler's scientific creativity. A sense of spirituality pervaded Kepler's mathematics. He could feel the mind of God in the shapes of the world, identified by geometry. The fundamental shape, the elemental ordering system was, in his view, governed by the number three. Pauli quoted Kepler who described 'The image of the triune God is in the spherical surface, that is to say, the Father's in the centre, the son's in the outer surface and the Holy Ghost's in the equality relation between points of circumference.'[28]

This spherical organization of the deity led, again in Pauli's view, to a passionate adherence to the Copernican theory of planetary motion. There is a 'correspondence', as Pauli put it, an analogical relationship 'between the sun and its surrounding planets and his abstract spherical picture of the Trinity'.[29] Pauli concluded that

> because he looks at the sun and the planets with this archetypal image in the background he believes with religious fervour in the heliocentric system – by no means the other way around, as a rationalistic view might cause one erroneously to assume.[30]

Kepler's planetary laws emerged not purely as a consequence of data, logic and rationality but in an interplay with another system of thinking, which was not rational but symbolic. The puzzle presented by this reciprocal activity and its creative outcome seems to have preoccupied Pauli. His wife Franca said he never talked to her about physics but about philosophy. His main concern was the 'unification of rational and irrational'.[31]

As Pauli delved deeper into Kepler's way of thinking, he 'hit upon this strange fellow R. Fludd', as he later told Jung.[32] Fludd was an English physician and Rosicrucian whose view of the world differed fundamentally from that of Kepler in that he believed that the key to the universe was the number four. They argued in print. The difference between these two men in the way that they saw the universe interested Pauli because his own thought resonated, at least in part, with both of them.

Writing to a friend, Pauli said:

> Once (in Hamburg) my path to the Exclusion Principle had to do precisely with the difficult transition from three to four, namely, to attribute to the electron a fourth degree of freedom (soon to be explained as 'spin') beyond the three translations. . . . That was really the *main work*.[33]

Since he came across the ordering significance of the numbers three and four, Pauli concluded that 'there is an important psychological and, perhaps, natural philosophical problem connected with these numbers'.[34]

In following the dissonance between the 'trinitarian' view of Kepler and the 'quaternary of Fludd', Pauli began to study Middle Ages philosophy, he found two different trends, 'the platonic' and the 'alchemistic',[35] the former being trinitarian and the latter quaternary.

During this period of study, Pauli was in correspondence with Jung, whose preoccupation was the quaternary. At the same time Pauli was making a systematic study of physical terms as archetypal symbols. He had realized, perhaps a year or two after his initial break from Jung that his dreams often represented conceptions of physics that had been 'transposed' into the symbolic order.[36]

It seemed as if his own creativity arose through a 'conversation' between two systems of reality, one of which was the world of physics (that was rational) and the other, which was symbolic, found in his dreams (and irrational). In this way, he resembled Kepler. For Pauli, however, the conversation was not only between his dreams and his waking life but also in the outer world between his dreams and his therapist's responses.

Pauli wrote: 'I *dream* of physics the same way Herr Jung (and other non-physicists *think* about physics'.[37] He was not disparaging Jung. He was saying, in another way, that in their conversations, he, Pauli, represented the rational, logical pole while Jung spoke of the dream, giving forth analogical representations of the material that Pauli presented to them. Later, this 'conversation' became internal.

The culmination of his quest came, it seems, in 1951, with a 'sudden illumination'. Writing to Jung in 1952 he said:

> In the spring of 1951 the word 'Automorphism' (taken from mathematics) came flying towards me. This is a word for the picturing of a system on itself, a reflection of the system into itself, for a process, that is, in which the inner symmetry, the connexial richness (relations) of a system reveals itself. In abstract algebra there also are elements engendering the automorphism . . . and to those, very likely, correspond in the analogy the 'archetypes' as arranging factors, as you have defined and conceived them.[38]

Self-organization and the origin of mind

Pauli had solved his puzzle. Self, he was saying, is a system in which growth occurs by a representation, a 'picturing', of self to itself. This view resembles that developed more recently by Humberto Maturana and his younger colleague, Francisco Varela, who put forward a model of growth, and of life, derived from studies of neural networks. What they called 'the organization of living' is circular. 'In a living system,' they write, 'the product of its operation is its own organization.'[39] The circularity they spoke of was similar to a 'reflection of the system into itself'. Maturana and Varela were pioneers of the concept of self-organization as the origin of life. They called this process 'autopoiesis' – self making.

Another major figure in the history of this concept is Benoit Mandelbrot, who created fractal geometry – a language, as he said, 'to speak of clouds'. It is a mathematics that might reflect the non-linear shapes of the natural world, and that the linearity of traditional geometry cannot do. He was able to demonstrate amazingly complex shapes emerging from a simple iteration.[40]

The central feature of fractal geometry is 'self-similarity'. Within the larger pattern that emerges from the reverberations of the Mandelbrot set there remains always, at a miniature level, the original pattern. Mandelbrot's example is a cauliflower. A small piece of it resembles the cauliflower itself.

In previous works, I have suggested that the Mandelbrot set provides a metaphor for the self-organization that might occur in the therapeutic situation,[41] in which beneficial change is the outcome of 'a reverberations between two poles of representation'.[42]

The essential elements of a self-organizing system are coupling, amplification, and representation.[43] These elements are reflected in the Mandelbrot set, which is a series of complex numbers for which the sequence does not approach infinity, as in the following, where z is a complex number and c a constant.

$$z \rightarrow z^2 + c$$
$$z^2 + c \rightarrow (z^2 + c)^2 + c$$
$$(z^2 + c \rightarrow ((z^2 + c:)^2 + c)^2 + c \text{ and so on}$$

In the first line of the iteration, an emblem of a certain reality, the z, is represented in amplified form as squared. This representation, however, is not a copy of the original since a constant is added to it. It is self-similar. In the second line, this representation is re-represented, again with the addition of a constant. The fundamental shape of the original proposition is retained. In the third line of this reverberating interplay there is a re-re-representation. This progression is an interesting echo of Hughlings Jackson's theory, who conceived the emergence of mind or self as one that starts with a single representing unit that is re-represented and then re-re-represented.

The pattern of interplay in the Mandelbrot set provides an image of essential elements of the proto-conversation. The baby's immediate expression is represented on the right side of the equation and the mother's amplified response is on the left. It always contains something that is her own and so is not merely an enlarged copy. The same kind of iteration is found in the structuring of a certain kind of generative therapeutic conversation.[44]

Although studies of neural networks and the mathematics of complexity can provide preliminary models for conceiving the origin of human consciousness, they are limited. They are not derived from human reality and so are created in divorce from the world of feelings and imaginings, which are essential to that reality. Pauli's 'Automorphosis', on the other hand, begins with no prior theoretical basis. It is a hypothesis, empirically derived and based on actual experience.

The term 'automorphosis' may be better that 'autopoiesis'. 'Self-shaping' is more a precise description of the human process than 'self-making'. On the other hand, 'poiesis' signifies that the maker is like a poet. Partridge notes that 'in erudite English, poiesis is occasionally used for creative power or the creative act'.[45] Paulian automorphosis resembles poetry in that it entails analogical representation of a personal reality.

Pauli realized that what he thought about during the day was turned into a different 'language' during the night. He wrote in 1948:

> I understand the occurrence of quantitative outcomes and conceptions of physics in spontaneous fantasies in a qualitative, transposed, hence symbolic sense. The existence of this phenomenon is known to me for about 12 to 13 years from personal dreams which evolve completely uninfluenced by other persons.[46]

In these dreams, notions such as 'wave, electric dipole, thermo-electricity, magnetism, atom, electron shells, atomic nucleus, radioactivity'[47] appear as symbols. This realisation was, at first, shocking to Pauli's scientific sensibility.

Pauli told Jung that: 'I gradually came to acknowledge that such fantasies or dreams are neither meaningless nor purely arbitrary but rather convey a sort of "second meaning" of the terms applied.'[48] He was suggesting that the mind-brain system creates two descriptions of a particular reality. These descriptions are complementary. Both are necessary to a complete description of that reality. He compared this kind of complementarity to the complementarity principle of Niels Bohr in which light and energy can be conceived as made of either particles or waves dependent upon the manner of observation. Bohr proposed that wave and particle theories, rather than being contradictory, were 'complementary pictures' of the same phenomenon. Pauli wrote to Jung, in commenting on a Jungian manuscript: 'The epistemological situation with regard to the concepts "conscious" and "unconscious" seems to offer a pretty close analogy to the under mentioned complementary situation in physics.'[49]

In this passage, Pauli is using the term 'unconscious' to conform with Jungian language in which the 'unconscious' refers to the world of dreams. Jung tended to speak of the 'unconscious' as a place while Pauli, I believe, would have conceived it as a process. Pauli's own terms for the two complementary descriptions was 'symbolic' and 'quantitative' (natural sciences).[50] The 'symbolic' aspect is emotional, imprecise, and concerned with both mental and physical. The 'quantitative' description is measurable. It is that part of reality that is verifiable and which positivists, or at least some positivists, wanted to make the only reality. It was to this latter philosophy that Pauli adhered in his early life, under the influence of his famous godfather, Ernst Mach. 'I was baptized', Pauli wrote later 'as "Antimetaphysical".'[51]

Pauli's formulation of the complementary nature of the 'quantitative' and 'symbolic' was congenial to Jung, who was fascinated by the theory of correspondentia 'propounded by the natural philosophers of the Middle Ages and particularly the classical idea of *the sympathy of all things*'.[52] Pauli had drawn Jung's attention

> to the fact the Niels Bohr used correspondence as a mediating term between the discontinuation (particle) and the continuum (wave). Originally (1913–1918) he called it the 'principle of correspondence' but later (1927) it was formulated as the 'argument of correspondence'.[53]

The two descriptions of reality given by Pauli resonate with distinctions made between logical and analogical modes of thought; diachronic and synchronic forms of language; interpersonal and intrapersonal kinds of relatedness; and the different functions of left and right hemispheres. Although, in discussing these matters with Jung, Pauli spoke of the symbolic description, or 'second meaning' of reality, as 'unconscious', he did not confine this description to the realm of self. It is also part of waking life.[54] In talking with Jung, Pauli extended his symbolic/quantitative dichotomy to include the notion of time, in this way linking it to the synchronic/diachronic dimension. He suggested to Jung that his mandala imagery and concept of quaternity might be represented in terms of physical processes. Accordingly, he created the following diagram.[55]

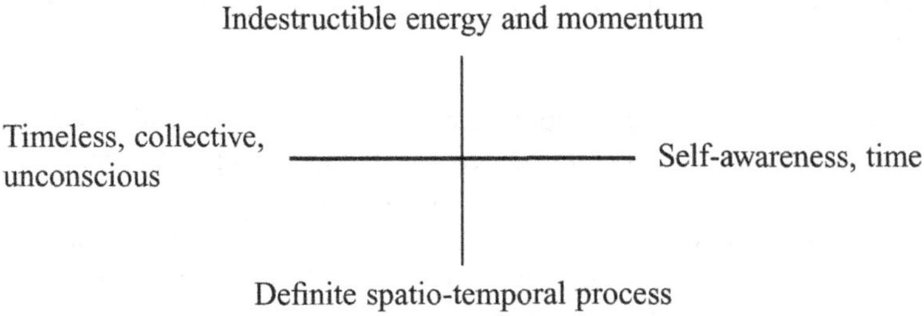

His view, however, of synchronicity more nearly resembles that of the linguists than that of Jung. In commenting on Pauli's distinction between chronological and achronological reality, Primas suggests that: 'It is rewarding to replace the Cartesian dualism of thinking and extended substances by an epistemic duality of *tensed* and *tenseless* descriptions.'[56]

Pauli was proposing a duality, like the various dualisms that are the heart of self, which is not Cartesian and that does not distinguish mind and matter by reducing the former to the latter. Speaking at the symposium honouring the 200th anniversary of Columbia University, Pauli has this to say:

> Matter has always been and will always be one of the main objects of physics . . . even light has become matter now, due to Einstein's discoveries. It has mass and also weight; it is not different from ordinary matter, it too having both energy and momentum.
>
> Taking the existence of all these transmutations into account what remains of the old ideas of matter and substance? The answer is *energy*. This is the true substance, that which is conserved; only the form in which it appears is changing.[57]

Two years earlier, in approaching the same problem, he said this: 'The general problem of the relation between psyche and physis, between inside and outside, can hardly be regarded as solved by the term "psychophysical parallelism" advanced in the last century.'[58]

Between inside and outside

In concluding that the symbolic and the quantitative are different descriptions of the same phenomenon, Pauli was in accord with the thought of E. R. Dodds, working in an entirely different field at the same time. Dodds was an Irish scholar of Greek culture and language who delivered a course of lectures at Berkeley in 1949, which became the basis of his classic work *The Greeks and the Irrational*. Dodds wrote:

> Man shares with a few others of the higher mammals the curious privilege of citizenship of two worlds. He enjoys in daily alternation two distinct kinds of experience – each of which has its own logic and limitations; and he has no obvious reason for thinking one of them more significant than the other.[59]

Dodds was working at a time before the evidence emerged that all mammals, but not reptiles, exhibit rapid eye movement sleep suggesting that other mammals may have a dream experience resembling that of humans. The very large difference between humans and other creatures is that they tell their dreams. Dodds gives a detailed account of the descriptions of dreams by Homeric poets, in which the dreams were treated as 'objective facts'.[60]

The huge jump between the worlds created by other primates and those created by humans can be explained by the use of language, which enables us to conduct a traffic between the two zones Pauli called symbolic and quantitative and that I am calling analogical and logical. The proposal put forward here is that this traffic, as Pauli implies, which is essentially 'between inner and outer', brings forth the type of consciousness that is peculiar to the human primate, the Jamesian self.

At each turn of the interplay, 'the reflection of the system into itself' creates a change. Pauli remarked that: 'The mere apprehension of the dream has already, so to speak, altered the state of the unconscious, and thereby, in analogy with a measurement in quantum physics, created a new phenomenon.'[61] I am taking Pauli's use of the term 'unconscious', in which he was following Jung, to refer not only to dreams but also to that part of waking life which has its own line of development beginning with the proto-conversational game between mother and child and going on to include symbolic play. Pauli's 'conversations', which involved dreams were first within himself, with an 'apprehension' of dreams. This was followed by a secondary 'telling' to Rosenbaum, Jung and his wife.

The depictions that go on during the 'picturing of a system in itself' have a curious but important aspect. The picturing must be made within the system and not externally as if by an observer. In both the proto-conversation and in symbolic play, the depictions are made within the subjective space of the child. The same is so in the therapeutic situation.

To think about what is happening in 'automorphosis' is to feel that one is within the impossible reality of M. C. Escher, a circularity exemplified in his famous 'Waterfall' in which water going down the waterfall ends up at the top.

The 'conversation' between the two zones of personal reality is between one that can speak, and one that cannot. That which can speak, the syntactical and logical reality, must use its words in a different way of seeing. The language is reshaped according to the rules of the analogical system. This 'doubling' is also illustrated by M. C. Escher. His 'Up and Down' shows two perspectives on an aspect of reality unified by a single view.

Pauli saw such a conversation going on within the brain-mind system. In a paper given to the Psychological Club in Zurich in 1948 he suggested that perceptions, which are quantitative, and aspects of the logical and linear system of thought, are re-processed by the symbolic, analogical system, which was for Jung, the archetypal. The reprocessed material emerges as an idea. Perhaps we might call it, following James, 'the experience'. Pauli saw Jung's archetypal function 'as the long sought for bridge between the sense perceptions and the ideas and are, accordingly, a necessary presupposition even for evolving a scientific theory of nature'.[62]

A reverberating system, very like what Pauli describes, has its first form in the outer world, between the experience of the child and its analogical representation by the other.

Becoming

A relationship in which one partner is able analogically to depict the feeling-toned state of the other contributes to the development of self in three main ways. First, it makes this experience 'real', giving it 'meaning'. Second, where this depiction creates the sense of connection, or 'fit', it potentiates coherence. Third, in its 'picturing of a system, on itself, a reflection of the system into itself', it participates in a process of self-organization leading to a state of personal emergence, or 'becoming', which is a main feature of the Jamesian self.

In his letter to Jung in which he presented his automorphism thesis, Pauli also spoke of the centrality of 'becoming', causing him to prefer the philosophy of Heraclitus to those philosophers whose focus was on 'being', which was for Pauli a static concept.[63] Heraclitus' famous remark that: 'People step into the same river, and different waters flow on to them'[64] was a metaphor of the view that all reality, human and cosmic, is characterized by change.

Notes

1 Enz, C. P. (2002, p. 125).
2 Miller, A. (2009, p. 55).
3 Jung, C. G. (1977, p. 174).
4 Miller, A. (2009, p. 231).
5 Cited by Miller, A. (2009, p. 128).
6 Cited by Miller, A. (2009, p. 128).
7 Miller, A. (2009, p. 129).
8 Enz, C. P. (2002, p. 241).
9 Enz, C. P. (2002, p. 247).
10 Jung, C. G. (1977, vol. 18, p. 175).

11 Jung, C. G. (1953, vol. 12, p. 42).
12 Jung, C. G. (1960, vol. 8, p. 229).
13 Jung, C.G. (1953, vol. 12, pp. 91–213).
14 Jung, C. G. (1953, vol. 12, p. 94).
15 Enz, C. P. (2002, p. 118).
16 Enz, C. P. (2002, p. 123).
17 Jung, C. G. (1953, vol. 12, p. 194).
18 Jung, C. G. (1953, vol. 12, p. 195).
19 Jung, C. G. (1968, vol. 12, p. 226).
20 Jung, C. G. (1953, vol. 12, p. 194).
21 Cited by Seager, W. (2009, p. 92).
22 Cited by Miller, A. (2009, p. 179).
23 Enz, C. P. (2002, p. 240).
24 Jung, C. G. (1977, vol. 18, p. 285).
25 Enz, C. P. (2002, p. 249).
26 Miller, A. (2009, p. 65).
27 Cited by Enz, C. P. (2002, p. 418).
28 Enz, C. P. (2002, p. 417).
29 Enz, C. P. (2002, pp. 417–418).
30 Enz, C. P. (2002, pp. 417–418).
31 Enz, C. P. (2002, p. 288).
32 Enz, C. P. (2002, p. 418).
33 Pauli to Fierz (1951). Cited by Miller, A. (2009, p. 66).
34 Pauli to Fierz (1951). Cited by Miller, A. (2009, p. 66).
35 Enz, C. P. (2002, p. 420).
36 Enz, C. P. (2002, p. 422).
37 Enz, C. P. (2002, p. 422).
38 Letter to Jung, 27/2/1952. Cited by Enz, C. P. (2002, p. 503).
39 Maturana and Varela (1980, p. 82).
40 Mandelbrot, B. (1983).
41 Meares, R. (2000, pp. 127–128).
42 Meares, R. (2000, p. 127).
43 Capra, F. 1996.
44 Meares, R. (2005, pp. 202–210).
45 Partridge, E. (1983).
46 Enz, C. P. (2002, p. 422).
47 Enz, C. P. (2002, p. 422).
48 Letter to Jung 16/6/1949.
49 Jung, C. G. (1960, vol. 8, p. 229n).
50 von Meyenn, K. (2009, p. 23).
51 Cited by Miller, A. (2009, p. 20).
52 Jung, C. G. (1960, vol. 8, p. 489).
53 Jung, C. G. (1960, vol. 8, p. 489n).
54 Enz, C. P. (2002, p. 248).
55 Miller, A. (2009, p. 185).
56 Primas, H. (2009, p. 176).
57 Pauli, W. (1954).
58 Cited by Primas, H. (2009, p. 171).
59 Dodds, E. R. (1951, p. 102).
60 Dodds, E. R. (1951, p. 109).
61 Cited by Seager, W. (2009, p. 90).
62 Cited by Miller, A. (2009, p. 179).
63 Meier, C. A. (2001, pp. 78, 80–81).
64 Hussey, E. L. (2005, p. 378).

16

A PERSONAL MYTH

The 'becoming' of which Pauli spoke involves, in both the development of self and the evolution of culture, a trajectory towards the telling of a story having the feature of myth, as outlined in Chapter 14. Trevarthen has written of: 'a new idea of the human mind as motivated for the "poetry" or creative stories of culture'.[1]

We expect, then, that in the late stages of psychotherapy a story having a mythical or poetical structure might begin to be told, particularly in those cases in which the primary disorder is a disruption of the development of self. This final chapter addresses the possibility that, as life goes on, for most people, a dynamically evolving personal myth is created that in most cases is unconscious. In the therapeutic situation, it typically appears out of an initial state of low complexity and the conversational style of a chronicle, which is merely a catalogue of events, a state of stimulus entrapment.[2]

In the late phases of therapy, an increased complexity can be identified by linguistic analyses.[3] This emergent state of mind is made of a number of 'layerings'. One of these, figuratively below conscious mental life, may have the embryonic form of poetry or myth. It corresponds to Jackson's second 'half' of language, mentioned in Chapter 9, which is made of images and underlies the process of 'verbalizing'. This kind of story is not spoken of, and can only be inferred by 'pictures' evoked by what could seem, to superficial observation, merely digressive, wandering, inconsequential chatter. The coherence of this state of mind is implicit, a half-sensed narrative, symbolically told. This condition is illustrated later in the chapter.

Jung and the notion of a personal myth

Following his break with Freud, finalized in 1914,[4] Jung felt himself isolated, on the verge of breakdown[5] and without a clear direction to his life. He wrote:

> After the parting of the ways with Freud, a period of uncertainty began for me. It would be no exaggeration to call it a state of disorientation. I felt totally suspended in mid-air, for I had not yet found my own footing.[6]

During this time, he began to immerse himself in a study of myth, the nature of which led to his book *Symbols of Transformation*. 'The whole thing, 'he said, 'came upon me like a landslide.'[7]

In attempting to find a way out of his state of chaos and derealization, Jung asked himself:

> 'What is the myth you are living'. I found no answer to this question, and had to admit that I was not living a myth, or even in a myth . . . So, in the most natural way, I took it upon myself to get to know 'my' myth and I regarded this as the task of tasks.[8]

He implied that from henceforth it would be his aim to participate in his patient's discovery of their personal myths. This would be the basis of an approach to therapy her termed 'amplification'. Its significance is discussed by Robert Hobson.[9]

Myth as analogue and 'form of feeling'

Jung was searching for a myth that would have the effect of an analogical representation. He wanted to discover a 'picture' of the reality, which he felt to be most truly his own. This discovery, he felt would make 'real' a state of mind in which a sense of 'reality' was lacking. In finding in the outer world a shape that resonated with something central in his personal experience, his isolation would be ended. He would be 'in contact' with the outer world. He wrote:

> It was clear to me from the start that I would find contact with the outer world and with people only if I succeeded in showing – and this would demand the utmost intensive effort – that *the contents of psychic experience are real*, and real not only as my own personal experiences, but as collective experiences which others also have.[10]

Jung is articulating here the effect postulated to follow the mother's re-presentation of the baby's presentational state during the proto-conversation, when it creates a feeling of analogical 'fit'. It contributes to a sense not only of the real but also of connectedness with the other. A myth may function as a large form of such a re-presentation. Hobson called it a 'form of feeling'.[11] It can amplify a personal experience, showing it in larger, more coherent form, but also containing something else, beyond the presentational expression. Jung's younger colleague, Jolande Jacobi, described the procedure of amplification as, 'a process by which the dream content is broadened and enriched with the help of analogous images'.[12] Jung wrote:

> The *amplification* is always appropriate when dealing with some obscure experience which is so vaguely adumbrated that it must be enlarged and expanded by being set in a psychological context in order to be understood

> by all. That is why, in analytical psychology, we resort to amplification in the interpretation of dreams, for a dream is too slender a hint to be understood until it is enriched by the stuff of association and analogy and thus amplified to the point of intelligibility.[13]

Jacobi notes that 'analogues are selected . . . because their nucleus of meaning is identical with, or similar to, that of the dream content under investigation.[14]

Of this process, Hobson noted that it 'can be of utmost value for some patients. For others it can be disastrous – indeed, fatal.'[15] He was implying that the analogy offered may have persecutory effect of certain interpretations directed towards imparting 'insight'.[16] A main contribution to such persecutory effect is that the so-called interpretation is experienced as coming from 'outside' the individual's feeling of personal reality. It is made as if by an observer of, rather than a participant, in this reality. The analogue must give a sense of 'fit'.

An illustrative session

The personal myth is a story, which has never been told before, created in a certain kind of conversation. Its form is not fixed but changes as the conversation evolves. It is not told in the specific words of the conversation but in images that underlie these words. An example is provided by a session occurring toward the end of a successful therapy. Extracts of the session taken from an audiotape are presented here with the patient's permission. The following discussion elaborates briefer presentation of this material in other places.[17] The patient, 'Julia', was a middle-aged and divorced woman who had been referred by physicians who found her to be depressed. They had been investigating her for a skin condition believed, at first, to be a manifestation of collagen disease. The biochemistry, however, was unconvincing. The skin condition involved recurrent episodes of formication, that is, a sensation of ants crawling over her skin, particularly in the lower abdominal and pubic areas.

Julia's symptoms arose in the context of estrangement from her older son and conflicting feelings of intimidation and attraction in relation to various male acquaintances, which culminated in her being physically assaulted in the stairwell of the apartment block in which she resided. This assault consisted of an obese male neighbor thrusting his large abdomen into her abdomen in an intimidating way, as if he were trying to bump her out of the way. Julia was extremely distressed by this and it was shortly after this that the formication and pruritis developed. Her background was traumatic. She described a childhood characterized by neglect, ridicule and emotional and physical abuse. Her mother would 'excoriate' her with criticism. There was a vague story of a termination of pregnancy. Her younger son had committed suicide 10 years previously. She had left a deeply unsatisfying marriage to a man she discovered had had incestuous relationships in his family of origin.

The therapist was a trainee. This was her second case. She developed a remarkable facility for making contributions to the therapeutic conversation that had the form of analogical representation and the effect of 'fit'. They were made naturally and as if within the subjective space of her patient.

The skin symptoms remitted early in this relatively brief therapy. Towards its end, a transformation had been achieved in the patient's mood and in the sense of herself and the world in which she lived.

The session, although 'just a conversation', has a curious 'intensity', a quality that the art historian, Terry Smith,[18] has identified as characteristic of an art work of significance in which an implicit coherence is achieved, reminiscent of Coleridge's 'more than usual state of emotion with more than usual order'.[19]

The session begins with Julia talking of an article on good design in architecture, which she had read in a newspaper:

> *Julia*: There's more to a living environment than utility . . . I mean, here we are in a huge land not all of it can be used, but we're cramped . . . into little boxes.

What Julia says is the product of the two interwoven styles of thought and language discussed in earlier chapters. Within the theme regarding outer events is another, which comes from the inner zone, which is personal and that Pauli had characterized as symbolic. In ordinary day-to-day conversing the former theme is likely to be taken up, leading perhaps, to a discussion of urban planning. The therapist, however develops what is implicitly symbolic. Her reply is complex although seemingly simple: 'Not to have that freedom to sort of soar up and out'.

She speaks with a quiet enthusiasm, as if transforming the energy of Julia's criticism into a positive force. Her response has an antinomial structure, resembling the poetic. She creates an analogue of what is presented to her by picturing its opposite. In the words of the poet W. S. Merwin, she has 'caught sight of the other side of darkness'.[20] Freedom is the other half of a system of meaning involving personal restriction.

The language used in this brief reply is of a particular kind resembling Vygotsky's 'inner speech',in which the child 'tends to leave out the subject and all words connected with it, condensing his speech more and more until only predicates are left'.[21] The words 'you do' are omitted from the therapist's response. She is using the language of the right hemisphere,[22] which, relative to syntactical left hemisphere language, is likely to promote the sense of inner life and the potentiation of symbolic expression.

The structure of a spoken expression reflects not only the 'shape' of a state of mind but also the form of the relationships in which it is spoken.[23] A strictly syntactical, propositional form of expression, designed for communication with the 'outer' world, for traffic between self and other, exhibits a subject-object distinction. The language of 'inner speech, on the other hand, implies a state in which this distinction is relatively lost. The other is experienced not as entirely 'outer' but as an element of subjective space. This state of mind, and relationship, was beautifully described by Piaget. As he watched a 3-year-old boy playing by himself, he noted that:

> What he says does not seem to him to be addressed to himself but is enveloped with the feeling of a presence, so that to speak of himself or to speak to his mother appears to him to be one and the same thing.[24]

The therapeutic use of 'inner speech' is likely to promote such an experience, or at least some adult equivalent of it, and to promote what Piaget called 'an atmosphere of communion',[25] a feeling of connection.

The difference between these two conditions can be represented pictorially by the disposition of faces. In the subject-object state, the faces confront each other, as when, for example, one asks a question of the other. In the second state the conversants sit metaphorically side by side, gazing together at a third thing, which I have likened to an 'empathic screen',[26] a concept resembling Thomas Ogden's 'analytic third'.[27]

Julia's response shows a remarkable change in state. She says: 'Oh yes. It's lovely to be in a spacious place.' Her voice conveys a sense of pleasure, an effect of presumably, of a sense of 'fit' between the personal, or, inner element of her opening remark and the representing analogue. Her pleasure is conveyed not only by the rising inflection of her voice but also in her imagery.

When she speaks of a 'spacious place', her expression, like her opening remark, is double. She refers both to an actual place and a personal one. The actual space is where she sits with her therapist, in a high ceilinged room in an old and graceful building. The other spaciousness is felt not only as psychic but in the totality of experience, including the body. Personal accounts suggest that a state of connection between self and other evokes an expanding sense of self and a feeling of wellbeing associated with enhanced rhythmicity.[28]

The therapist has caused a shift in her patient's state, occurring within seconds, in a way that resembles a self-organizing system operating over a longer period of time. The therapist's language has the structure, the theory of self-organization would predict, of promoting a state of 'becoming'. The essential features of a self-organizing system are coupling, amplification and representation.[29] All are displayed, as if in miniature, in a dozen words. First, the therapist's response is 'coupled' to what is essential in Julia's image of 'little boxes'. Second, she amplifies this image. This involves more than a 'matching' with or 'mirroring' of the state of being 'cramped', in which 'translations' of this word might be used. These are cognitive operations. Instead, the therapist uses another faculty, that of imagination. Hers is a creative act, akin to a poet's: 'Imagination and amplification in psychotherapy', the title of Hobson's paper on amplification, announces the primary role of imagination in its creation.

Finally the therapist's creation is a representation. It is a 'picturing' of a state, related in an antinomial way, of a bird in the box, who now flies free. She provides an analogue for a 'little emotion'.

Following the 'spacious place', Julia switches to another scene, which is brought to her mind by resemblance. She is reminded of another room, in a university building that, like the one she is in now, was old and spacious. Julia's state of self, implicit in the doubleness of her opening remark, is now overtly apparent in the exhibition of autobiographical memory. This kind of memory is a manifestation of what Singer called 'the inner-eye function'.[30]

This is followed by a series of resemblances each of which is a container, each container smaller than the last, like recursions in a sentence, in the manner of Russian dolls. These scenes successively are the pathology department in the university building; the specimen museum in that department; fetuses in bottles in a room in that museum. Here she stumbles. The conversation goes as follows:

Julia:	I wondered as I came through school and we had all of this hard religious instruction, what then happens to the soul of the aborted foetus or the, um, or one who hasn't made it?
Therapist:	Mmm.
Julia:	There would have been a soul.
Therapist:	Mmm, there would have been.
Julia:	Yeah. Anyway, well that's a big one.
Therapist:	Yeah.
Julia:	Yes so all of this, the windows, the curtains, it's very much the . . . very similar.

'Anyway' is a filler word, often used to indicate a change of topic. It signifies an altered state. The subject of 'the soul of the aborted foetus' is apparently an area of distress and anxiety about which Julia hesitates to speak. Perhaps the stumbling also involves embarrassment. Accordingly, she shifts attention to the room where she sits, to 'the windows, the curtains'. Once again, the therapist's response is structurally fashioned so as to be within Julia's subjective space. The word 'you' is omitted in her response to the complex state – another 'little emotion', which has blocked the progress of Julia's thought.

Therapist:	It's kind of unnerving isn't it to wonder what happened to those babies' souls I guess 'cause they're so helpless aren't they?
Julia:	Yeah, so it would not be of their making. Um, there must be, um, I'd imagine they'd be . . . Oh then but if I'm right about the, um, everything, the whole concept being thought out way beyond where we're at . . . Remember when I said about the planets kind of spilling out of the . . . and it's all in, in, ah, [pause] it's all been planned? So that, that would have been planned for too wouldn't it? The soul of the . . . ah . . .

The words 'unnerving' and 'helpless' seem to resonate with Julia's wondering and her distress. She shifts back to a larger state of mind in which the imagery, of 'the planets kind of spilling out', is a product of imagination. She now ponders the mystery of the planets and then the notion of the spirit. This leads her to wonder whether she might be led into an experience of spiritual life with the help of a guru who lives and works in a tower near where she lives.

Emergence of a personal myth

The linking between successive scenes of this conversation depends, although not entirely, on analogical representing. Much that is analogical is created through contours of the voice, in brief vocalizations. The successive scenes are as follows:

1 Personal space – general
(The cramped environment)
↓
2 Personal space
(The clinic building)
↓
3 A particular space
(University building)
↓
4 A room in that space
(Pathology)
↓
5 Spaces in this room
(Display cases)
↓
6 Spaces in these spaces
(Foetuses in bottles)
↓
7 Abstract spaces
(Where do their souls go?)
↓
8 Larger abstract spaces
(The mystery of the planets)
↓
9 Vaster space
(The notion of the spirit)
↓
10 Embodiment of this space
(The guru in the tower)
↓
11 A personal space
(The pursuit of the spirit)
↓
12 The therapeutic space
(Music)

This session is unusual. Absent from it are complaints about symptoms, fears, rages, descriptions of current events, interpersonal difficulties and so forth. Importantly, trauma is not consciously addressed. Yet it is there, in the foetuses in the bottles.

The wandering course of Julia's memories and imaginings has the form of the stream of consciousness. Yet it is a conversation. The stream of consciousness can be conceived as an inner conversation, between self and self, the embryonic form of which is displayed by Piaget's 3-year-old subject at play. The therapist is experienced in this session as analogous to a second self, an outcome that is the product of a consistent approach, both disciplined and creative, dependent upon a particular conversational style involving analogical representation and the use of 'right 'hemispheric' language.

The session is the culmination of the therapy. The appearance of self in the world, as manifest linguistically, is the goal towards which therapy is directed. It is not 'cure', since the word implies stasis. 'Healing' and 'growth' are better terms. The stream of consciousness is both a manifestation of healing and growth and also their agent.

The kind of consciousness in which the stream effect is experienced can be conceived, as remarked in Chapter 1, as multi-tiered. This figurative concept sees conscious life and verbal expression near the top of the hierarchy. Lower down, and so, earlier in evolution, are the images that are the other half of language. Once again, Piaget's 3-year-old at play gives us a glimpse of the developmental forerunner of this complex state of mind. This scene provides a 'metaphor' for conceiving and understanding the kind of consciousness peculiar to the human being.[31]

The images, though implicit, are fundamental and the core of the experience. They can be inferred from the words that attempt to depict them as a series of scenes or pictures. Techniques of linguistics can reveal such 'incipient, yet to be fully realized and recognized patterns of meaning'.[32] In this session, the patterns, or images, make up a coherent structure, like a story of a mythical kind. In this case, it resembles the myth of the hero.

As Jung describes it, this myth, although having multiple forms, characteristically begins with a descent into an underworld, or zone of darkness.

> The purpose of the descent as universally exemplified in the myth of the hero is to show that only in the region of danger (watery abyss, cavern, forest, island, castle, etc.) can one find the 'treasure hard to attain' (jewel, virgin, life-potion, victory over death).[33]

'Dread and resistance' are associated with this 'delving'.

There is a notional descent in scenes 2 to 6. She starts in the actual world. Each step on the way takes her lower. Here she encounters the 'dread and resistance'. The hero faces a trial, a struggle, a period of crisis. The treasure that it is necessary to find and grasp is guarded by some kind of monster, which can be seen as a replication of traumatic memory. 'The combination of snake or dragon with treasure and cave represents an ordeal in the life of the hero.'[34]

The encounter with the monster, and its being overcome, leads to recovery of the treasure and its consequent 'boon'.[35] The hero is changed and enhanced. He begins his ascent to the world he has left, following the pattern of descent and return epitomized in the imagery of the 'night sea journey'.[36]

Following her encounter in memory with dead foetuses, which may have evoked echoes of a terminated pregnancy, traumatic sexuality, and a dead son, Julia's conversation changes in a subtle way, to what can be understood as a form of consciousness higher than autobiographical memory. The following scenes are made by imagination, created in illusory spaces, a more complete release from the narrowness of presented time and space than afforded by the operation of memory displayed earlier in the telling of the 'myth'.[37] What has happened to Julia can be compared with the experience of Pauli in which a processing of experience had gone on in a way that was unconscious, in the manner of dream. Traumatic material, which is asymbolic, is transmuted into symbolic form so that it can be integrated into a personal story, which is not a mere chronicle but which resembles a myth, having a symbolic basis.

The music of what is happening[38]

In the final scene of Julia's metaphoric journey, she returns to the place where she began. However, the form of relatedness that she sets up in this scene has become more complex. It seems to involve a co-ordination of the subject-object mode with the other mode, in which the other is sensed as within subjective space. Such a co-ordination reflects a higher order consciousness, similar perhaps, to the 'doubleness' of Shakespeare. Julia speaks of the pleasure in listening to music with a companion who, like her, values the music. This is what she says, omitting the therapist's linkages:

Julia: I find if I'm with somebody at a concert, somebody whom I know is enjoying it as much as I am . . .

It is, 50 to 100 per cent more enjoyable, I'm sure . . .

Yeah. Well you look at the face of someone who's into it, and you pick up, you pick up, ah what do you pick up? [pause] You pick up their enjoyment, you pick up what they're experiencing. Yeah . . .

You can see the inspiration on the face and you know that they're getting out of it what you . . . different if you're with somebody whose come along just for company, forget it.

Julia speaks without mentioning the therapist or apparently being aware that she might be talking about the present relationship. Nevertheless, she is looking into the therapist's eyes as she speaks. Her words tell, unwittingly, of the transformational power of a relationship having the patternings of music.

Notes

1 Trevarthen, C. cited in Gratier and Trevarthen (2009, p. 150).
2 Meares, R. (1998, 1997, 1993, pp. 101–110; 2005, pp. 88–96).
3 Butt *et al.* (2010, pp. 263–293); Butt *et al.* (2014, pp. 310–315); Meares *et al.* (2005, p. 676).
4 McGuire, W. (1974, p. 540).
5 Hobson, R. F. (1961).
6 Jung, C. G. (1963, p. 170).
7 Jung, C. G. (1967, p. xxiii).
8 Jung, C. G. (1967, pp. xxiv–xxv).
9 Hobson, R. F. (1971).
10 Jung, C. G. (1963, pp. 194–195; cited by Hobson, R. F. 1971, p. 82).
11 Hobson, R. F. (1985).
12 Jacobi, J. (1968, p. 84).
13 Jung, C. G. (1953, p. 277).
14 Jacobi, J. (1968, pp. 85–86).
15 Hobson, R. F. (1971, p. 80).
16 Meares and Hobson (1977).
17 Meares and Jones (2009); Meares *et al.* (2012).
18 Smith, T. (1998).
19 Coleridge, S. T. (1977, p. 524).
20 Merwin, W. S. (2008, p. 67).
21 Vygotsky, L. S. (1962, p. 145).
22 Meares *et al.* (2012, pp. 39–41).
23 This idea comes from the M. A. K. Halliday (1975), the founder of Systemic Functional Linguistics.
24 Piaget, J. (1959, p. 243).
25 Piaget, J. (1959, p. 243).
26 Meares, R. (1983).
27 Ogden, T. H. (1994).
28 Meares, R. (1980); Meares, R. (1984).
29 Capra, F. (1996, p. 226).
30 Singer, W. (2001, p. 124).
31 Meares, R. (1993, 2005).
32 Butt *et al.* (2014, p. 316).
33 Jung, C. G. (1953, p. 322).
34 Jung, C. G. (1960, p. 292).
35 Campbell, J. (1968, p. 30).
36 Jung. C. G. (1967, p. 210).
37 Bartlett, 1932, p. 314. Bartlett places autobiographical memory at the same level as imagination. I believe, however, that certain feats of imaginative creativity, such as the Shakespearean, are beyond the capacity to bring to mind memories of actual events.
38 Heaney's line is changed in order to convey a sense of movement.

REFERENCES

Acheson, A. (1903). *Shakespeare and the Rival Poet*. London: AMS Press.

Alba, D. M., Moya-Sola, S. and Kohler, M. (2003). Morphological affinities of the Australopithecus afarensis hand on the basis of manual proportions and relative thumb length. *Journal Human Evolution*, *44*(2), 225–254.

Anisfeld, M. (1996). Only tongue protrusion modelling in matched neonates. *Developmental Review*, *16*, 149–161.

Aristotle (1941). De Poetica (I. Bywater, Trans.). In R. McKeon (ed.), *The Basic Works of Aristotle* (pp. 1455–1487). New York: Random House.

Armstrong, D. (1981). *The Nature of Mind*. New York: Cornell University Press.

Asfaw, B., White, T., Lovejoy, O., Latimer, B., Simpson, S. and Suwa, G. (1999). Australopithecus garhi: a new species of early hominid from Ethiopia. *Science*, *284*(5414), 629–635.

Auden, W. H. (1989). *The Dyer's Hand and Other Essays*. New York: Vintage International.

Auden, W. H. (2010). The creation of music and poetry. In E. Mendelson (ed.), *The Complete Works of W. H. Auden: Prose* (Vol. IV, pp. 190–197). Princeton, NJ: Princeton University Press.

Ayer, A. J. (1936). *Language, Truth and Logic*. London: Victor Gollancz.

Bak, T. H., O'Donovan, D. G., Xuereb, J. H., Boniface, S. and Hodges, J. R. (2001). Selective impairment of verb processing associated with pathological changes in Brodmann areas 44 and 45 in the motor neurone disease-dementia-aphasia syndrome. *Brain*, *124*(1), 103–120.

Balsters, J. H., Cussans, E., Diedrichsen, J., Phillips, K. A., Preuss, T. M., Rilling, J. K. and Ramnani, N. (2010). Evolution of the cerebellar cortex: the selective expansion of prefrontal-projecting cerebellar lobules. *Neuroimage*, *49*(3), 2045–2052.

Bard, K. A. and Vauclair, J. (1984). The communicative context of object manipulation in ape and human adult infant pairs. *Journal of Human Evolution*, *13*(2), 181–190.

Baron-Cohen, S. (1987). Autism and symbolic play. *Developmental Psychology*, *5*(2), 139–148.

Baron-Cohen, S., Leslie, A. M. and Frith, U. (1985). Does the autistic child have a 'theory of mind'? *Cognition*, *21*(1), 37–46.

Bartlett, F. (1932). *Remembering*. London: Cambridge University Press.

Bate, J. (1998). *The Genius of Shakespeare*. Oxford: Oxford University Press.

Bateson, M. C. (1979). The epigenesis of conversational interaction: A personal account of research development. In M. Bullowa (ed.), *Before Speech: The Beginning of Human Communication* (pp. 63–77). London: Cambridge University Press.

Beaton, A. and Marien, P. (2010). Language, cognition and the cerebellum: grappling with an enigma. *Cortex*, *46*(7), 811–820.

Beebe, B., Jaffe, J., Feldstein, S., Mays, K. and Alson, D. (1985). Interpersonal timing: the application of an adult dialogue model to mother-infant vocal and kinesic interactactions. In T. Field (ed.), *Infant Social Perception*. New York: Ablex.

Behrensmeyer, A. K. (2006). Atmosphere: climate change and human evolution. *Science*, *311*(5760), 476–478.

Bendedict, R. (1932). Configurations of culture in North America. *American Anthropologist*, *34*, 1–2.

Bendedict, R. (1934). *Patterns of Culture*. Boston, MA: Houghton & Mifflin.

Bender, R., Tobias, P. V. and Bender, N. (2012). The Savannah hypotheses: origin, reception and impact on paleoanthropology. *History and Philosophy of the Life Sciences*, *34*(1–2), 147–184.

Bergson, H. (1913). *Creative Evolution* (A. Mitchell, Trans.). New York: Henry Holt.

Bodner, E., Palgi, Y. and Kaveh, D. (2013). Does the relationship between affect complexity and self-esteem differ in young-old and old-old participants? *The Journals of Gerontology. Series B, Psychological Sciences and Social Sciences*, *68*(5), 665–673.

Bohr, N. (1958). *Atomic Physics and Human Knowledge*. New York: Wiley.

Bornstein, M. and Tamis Le Monda, C. (1997). Maternal responsiveness and infant mental abilities: specific predictive relations. *Infant Behaviour and Development*, *20*(3), 283–296.

Boroditsky, L. and Gaby, A. (2010). Remembrances of times East: absolute spatial representations of time in an Australian aboriginal community. *Psychological Science*, *21*(11), 1635–1639.

Bower, T. (1974). *Development in Infancy*. San Francisco, CA: Freeman.

Bowlby, J. (1969). *Attachment*. London: Hogarth.

Boym, S. (2001). *The Future of Nostalgia*. New York: Basic Books.

Bradley, A. C. (1923). Shakespeare's Antony and Cleopatra. In A. C. Bradley (ed.), *Oxford Lectures on Poetry* (pp. 279–310). London: Macmillan.

Broadfield, D. C., Holloway, R. L., Mowbray, K., Silvers, A., Yuan, M. S. and Marquez, S. (2001). Endocast of Sambungmacan 3 (Sm 3): a new *Homo erectus* from Indonesia. *The Anatomical Record*, *262*(4), 369–379.

Brown, R. and Gilman, A. (1960). The pronouns of power and solidarity. In T. A. Seboek (ed.), *Style in Language* (pp. 253–276). Cambridge, MA: MIT Press.

Brown, S. (2000). The music language of music evolution. In B. Merker and S. Brown (eds), *The Origins of Music* (pp. 271–301). Cambridge, MA: MIT Press.

Brown, S., Martinez, M. J. and Parsons, L. M. (2006). Music and language side by side in the brain: a PET study of the generation of melodies and sentences. *European Journal of Neuroscience*, *23*(10), 2791–2803.

Bruner, J. S. (1975). The ontogensis of speech acts. *Journal of Child Language*, *2*, 1–19.

Bruner, J. S. (1983). *Child's Talk: Learning to Use Language*. New York: Norton.

Bruner, J. S. (1990). *Acts of Meaning*. Cambridge, MA: Harvard University Press.

Bruner, J. S. and Sherwood, C. C. (1976). Early rule structure: the case of 'peekaboo'. In J. Bruner, A. Jolly and K. Sylva (eds), *Play: Its Role in Evolution and Development*. Harmondsworth, UK: Penguin.

Buber, M. (1937). *I and Thou*. Edinburgh, UK: T & T Clark.

Buchanan, T. W., Lutz, K., Mirzazade, S., Specht, K., Shah, N. J., Zilles, K. and Jancke, L. (2000). Recognition of emotional prosody and verbal components of spoken language: an fMRI study. *Cognitive Brain Research*, *9*(3), 227–238.

Buckner, R. L. and Carroll, D. C. (2007). Self-projection and the brain. *Trends in Cognitive Sciences*, *11*(2), 49–57.

Burton, R. (1893) [1621]. *The Anatomy of Melancholy* (Vol. III). London: John Nimmo.

Butt, D. G., Henderson-Brooks, C., Moore, A. and Eyal, R. (2014). Motivated selection in verbal art, 'verbal science' and psychotherapy. In Y. Fang and J. Webster (eds), *Developing Systemic Functional Linguistics: Theory and Application* (pp. 295–318). Sheffield, UK: Equinox.

Butt, D. G., Moore, A. R., Henderson-Brooks, C., Meares, R. and Haliburn, J. (2010). Dissociation, relatedness and 'cohesive harmony': a linguistic measure of degrees of 'fragmentation'? *Linguistics and Human Sciences*, *3.3*(2007), 263–293.

Byrne, R. W. and Whiten, A. (1988). *Machiavellian Intelligence*. Oxford: Oxford University Press.

Calvin, W. H. (2004). *A Brief History of the Mind: From Apes to Intellect and Beyond.* Oxford: Oxford University Press.

Calvin, W. H. (2006). The emergence of intelligence. *Scientific American*, *16*(2), 84–92.

Campbell, J. (1968). *The Hero with the Thousand Faces*. Princeton, NJ: Princeton University Press.

Cantalupo, C. and Hopkins, W. D. (2001). Asymmetric Broca's area in great apes. *Nature*, *414*(6863), 505.

Capra, F. (1996). *The Web of Life*. New York: Doubleday.

Carpenter, H. (1992). *W. H. Auden: A Biography*. Oxford: Oxford University Press.

Carpenter, M., Nagell, K. and Tomasello, M. (1998). Social cognition, joint attention and communicative competence from 9 to 15 months of age. *Monographs of the Society for Research in Child Development*, *63*(4), i–vi, 1–143.

Cassirer, E. (1944, 1953–1957). *An Essay on Man*. New Haven, CT: Yale University Press.

Cassirer, E. (1946). *Language and Myth* (S. K. Langer, Trans.). New York: Dover.

Cassirer, E. (1962). *An Essay on Man: An Introduction to a Philosophy of Culture*. New Haven, CT: Yale University Press.

Chekhov, A. P. (1998). *Uncle Vanya* (P. Negri and K. Casey, eds). North York, ON: General Publishing Company.

Cheney, D. and Seyfarth, R. (1990). *How Monkeys See the World: Inside the Mind of Another Species*. Chicago, IL: Chicago University Press.

Chess, S. (1971). Autism in children with congenital rubella. *Journal of Autism and Childhood Schizophrenia*, *1*(1), 33–47.

Chiron, C., Jambaque, I., Nabbout, R., Lounes, R., Syrota, A. and Dulac, O. (1997). The right brain hemisphere is dominant in human infants. *Brain*, *120*(6), 1057–1065.

Chomsky, N. (1972). *Language and Mind.* New York: Harcourt Brace.

Clark, W. E. L. G. (1955). Frederic Wood Jones 1879–1954: an appreciation. *Journal of Anatomy* *89*(2), 255–267.

Clarke, E., Reichard, U. H. and Zuberbuhler, K. (2006). The syntax and meaning of wild gibbon songs. *PLoS One*, *1*, e73.

Cohen, T. (1979). Metaphor and the cultivation of intimacy. In S. Sacks (ed.), *On Metaphor* (pp. 1–10). Chicago, IL: University of Chicago Press.

Coleridge, S. T. (1977) [1802]. *Dejection: An Ode*. Harmondsworth, UK: Penguin.

Coleridge, S. T. (1977). *From Biographia Litteraria* (I. A. Richards ed., Vol. XIV). Harmondsworth: Penguin.

Collis, G. (1981). *Social Interaction with Objects: A Perspective On Infancy* (K. Immelmann, G. Barlow, L. Petrinovitch and M. Main, eds). Cambridge: Cambridge University Press.

Compston, A. (2007). From the archive: quantitative management of contraction in lowest level co-ordination. Hughlings Jackson lecture (given January 29, 1931, by C. S. Sherrington). *Brain, 130*(54), 884–886.

Conrad, J. (1900). *Lord Jim. Collected Edition 1946*. London: Dent.

Cooper, M. and Johnson, A. (1984). *Poisonous Plants in Britain and Their Effect on Animals and Man*. London: Stationery Office.

Corballis, M. (2003). From hand to mouth: the gestural origins of language. In M. Christiansen and S. Kirby (eds), *Language Evolution* (pp. 201–218). Oxford: Oxford University Press.

Corballis, M. (2011). *The Recursive Mind: The Origins of Human Language, Thought and Cognition*. Princeton, NJ: Princeton University Press.

Cowan, J. (1992). *Mysteries of the Dreaming: The Spiritual Life of Australian Aborigines*. Bridport, UK: Prism.

Craig, W. J. (1922) *Histories and Poems of Shakespeare*. Oxford: Oxford University Press.

Crockenberg, S. and Litman, C. (1990). Autonomy as competence in 2-year-olds: maternal correlates of child defiance, compliance and self assertion. *Developmental Psychology, 26*(6), 961–971.

Damasio, A. R. (1996). *Descartes' Error*. London: Papermac, Macmillan.

Damasio, A. R. (1999). *The Feeling of What Happens: Body, Emotion and the Making of Consciousness*. New York: Harcourt-Brace.

Damasio, A. R. (2012). *Self Comes to Mind*. London: Vintage: Random House.

Darwin, C. (1996) [1859]. *The Origin of Species. Facsimile Edition*. New York: Gramercy books/Random House.

Darwin, C. (1871a). *The Descent of Man and Selection in Relation to Sex. Pt. III, Facsimile Edition*. London: John Murray.

Darwin, C. (1871b). *The Descent of Man in Relation to Sex (Volume. I)*. London: John Murray.

David, A. S. and Kopelman, M. D. (2009). Neuropsychology in relation to psychiatry. In A. S. David, S. Fleminger, M. D. Kopelman, S. Lovestone and J. D. C. Mellers (eds), *Lishman's Organic Psychiatry: a Textbook of Neuropsychiatry* (4th edn, pp. 29–102). Chichester, UK: Wiley-Blackwell.

Davidson, D. (1978). What metaphor means. In O. Sacks (ed.), *On Metaphor* (pp. 29–46). Chicago, IL: University of Chicago Press.

de Heinzelin, J., Clark, J. D., White, T., Hart, W., Renne, P., WoldeGabriel, G.mand Vrba, E. (1999). Environment and behaviour of 2.5-million-year-old Bouri hominids. *Science, 284*(5414), 625–629.

Deacon, T. (1997). *The Symbolic Species: The Co-evolution of Language and the Brain*. New York: Norton.

Decety, J. and Chaminade, T. (2003). When the self represents the other: a new cognitive neuroscience view on psychological identification. *Consciousness and Cognition, 12*(4), 577–596.

Dent, N. J. H. (2005). Logos. In T. Honderich (ed.), *Oxford Companion to Philosophy* (p. 545). Oxford: Oxford University Press.

Descartes, R. (1968) [1637–1641]. *Discourse on Method and the Meditations* (F. Sutcliffe, Trans.). Harmondsworth, UK: Penguin.

Dissanyake, E. (2000). Antecedents of the temportal arts in early mother infant interaction. In N. Wallin, B. Merker and S. Brown (eds), *The Origins of Music* (pp. 389–410). Cambridge, MA: MIT Press.

Dissanyake, E. (2009). Root, Leaf, blossom, or bole: concerning the origin and adaptive function of music. In S. Malloch and C. Trevarthen (eds), *Communicative Musicality: Exploring the Basis of Human Companionship*. Oxford: Oxford University Press.

Dodds, E. R. (1951). *The Greeks and the Irrational*. Berkeley, CA: University of California Press.

Doidge, N. (2007). *The Brain that Changes Itself*. New York: Penguin.

Dunbar, R. (1996). *Grooming, Gossip and the Evolution of Language*. London: Faber & Faber.

Dunbar, R. (1993). Co-evolution of language in humans. *Behavioral & Brain Sciences, 16*, 681–735.

Dunbar, R. (1992). Neocortex size as a constraint on group size in primates. *Journal of Human Evolution, 20*, 469–493.

Dunbar, R. I. and Shultz, S. (2007). Evolution in the social brain. *Science, 317*(5843), 1344–1347.

Dunsworth, H. M., Warrener, A. G., Deacon, T., Ellison, P. T. and Pontzer, H. (2012). Metabolic hypothesis for human altriciality. *Proceedings of the National Academy of Sciences, 109*(38), 15212–15216.

Eagleman, D. M. (2008). Human time perception and its illusions. *Current Opinion in Neurobiology, 18*(2), 131–136.

Edelman, G. (1992). *Bright Air, Brilliant Fire: On the Matter of the Mind*. New York: Basic Books.

Edelman, G. (2004). *Wider than the Sky*. London: Penguin.

Edelman, G. (2006). *Second Nature: Brain Science and Human Knowledge*. Yale, CT: Yale University Press.

Eimas, P. D., Siqueland, E. R., Jusczyk, P. and Vigorito, J. (1971). Speech perception in infants. *Science, 171*(3968), 303–306.

Eisenberger, N. I., Lieberman, M. D. and Williams, K. D. (2003). Does rejection hurt? An FMRI study of social exclusion. *Science, 302*(5643), 290–292.

Elder, J. and Pederson, D. (1978). Preschool children's use of objects in symbolic play. *Child Development, 49*, 500–504.

Eldredge, N. and Tattersall, I. (1992). *The Myths of Human Evolution*. New York: Columbia University Press.

Eliade, M. (1959). Methodological remarks in the study of religious symbolism. In J. Kitagawa and M. Eliade (eds), *The History of Religions: Essays on Methodology*. Chicago, IL: University of Chicago Press.

Eliot, T. S. (1942). The music of poetry. In T. S. Eliot (ed.), *On Poetry and Poets* (pp. 26–38). London: Faber & Faber.

Eliot, T. S. (1945). The social function of poetry. In T. S. Eliot (ed.), *On Poetry and Poets*. London: Faber & Faber.

Eliot, T. S. (1953). The three voices of poetry. In T. S. Eliot (ed.), *On Poetry and Poets* (pp. 89–102). London: Faber & Faber.

Eliot, T. S. (1957). *On Poetry and Poets*. London: Faber & Faber.

Empson, W. (1973). *Seven Types of Ambiguity*. Harmondsworth, UK: Penguin.

Enard, W., Przeworski, M., Fisher, S. E., Lai, C. S., Wiebe, V., Kitano, T. and Paabo, S. (2002). Molecular evolution of FOXP2: a gene involved in speech and language. *Nature, 418*(6900), 869–872.

Enz, C. P. (2002). *No Time To Be Brief: A Scientific Biography of Wolfgang Pauli*. Oxford: Oxford University Press.

Everett, B. (2008). *Shakespeare and the Elizabethan Sonnet*. London: Review of Books, 8 May 2008.

Fadiga, L., Craighero, L. and D'Ausilio, A. (2009). Broca's area in language, action and music. *Annals of the New York Academy of Sciences*, *1169*, 448–458.

Fazio, P., Cantagallo, A., Craighero, L., D'Ausilio, A., Roy, A. C., Pozzo, T. and Fadiga, L. (2009). Encoding of human action in Broca's area. *Brain*, *132*(7), 1980–1988.

Fellows, L. K. and Farah, M. J. (2005). Dissociable elements of human foresight: a role for the ventromedial frontal lobes in framing the future, but not in discounting future rewards. *Neuropsychologia*, *43*(8), 1214–1221.

Fernald, A. (1992). Human maternal vocalizations to infants as biologically relevant signals: an evolutionary perspective. In J. H. Barkow, L. Cosmides and J. Tooby (eds), *The Adapted Mind: Evolutionary Psychology and the Generation of Culture* (pp. 391–428). Oxford: Oxford University Press.

Fernald, A. and O'Neill, D. (1993). Peekaboo across cultures: how mothers and infants play with voices, faces and expectations. In K. MacDonald (ed.), *Parent-Child Play: Development and Implications* (pp. 259–285). Albany, NY: State University of New York.

Ferraro, J. V., Plummer, T. W., Pobiner, B. L., Oliver, J. S., Bishop, L. C., Braun, D. R. and Potts, R. (2013). Earliest archaeological evidence of persistent hominin carnivory. *PLoS One*, *8*(4), e62174.

Fisher, S. E. and Scharff, C. (2009). FOXP2 as a molecular window into speech and language. *Trends Genet*, *25*(4), 166–177.

Flavell, J. H., Green, F. L. and Flavell, E. R. (1993). Children's understanding of the stream of consciousness. *Child Development*, *64*(2), 387–398.

Focillon, H. (1942). *The Life of Forms in Art* (C. Beecher Hogan and G. Kubler, Trans.). New Haven, CT: Yale University Press.

Fraiberg, S. (1977). *Insights from the Blind*. New York: Meridian/New American Library.

Fraisse, P. (1963). *The Psychology of Time* (J. Leith, Trans.). New York: Harper Row.

Frazer, J. (1922). *The Golden Bough*. London: Macmillan.

Freud, S. (1950) [1932]. My contact with Josef Popper-Lynkeus. In J. Strackey (ed.), *Collected Papers* (Vol. V, pp. 295–301) London: Hogarth.

Friedman, W. J. (2000). The development of children's knowledge of the times of future events. *Child Development*, *71*(4), 913–932.

Frith, C. D. and Frith, U. (1999). Interacting minds-a biological basis. *Science*, *286*(5445), 1692–1695.

Frith, U. and Frith, C. D. (2003). Development and neurophysiology of mentalizing. *Philosophical Transactions of the Royal Society of London. Series B, Biological Sciences*, *358*(1431), 459–473.

Frost, R. (1955). *Robert Frost: Selected by Himself*. Harmondsworth, UK: Penguin.

Frye, N. (1971) [1957]. *The Anatomy of Criticism*. Princeton, NJ: Princeton University Press.

Gallagher, H. L. and Frith, C. D. (2003). Functional imaging of 'theory of mind'. *Trends in Cognitive Sciences*, *7*(2), 77–83.

Geary, J. (2012). *I Is an Other: The Secret Life of Metaphor and How It Shapes the Way We See the World*. New York: Harper Perennial.

Geertz, C. (1973). *The Interpretation of Cultures: Selected Essays*. New York: Basic Books.

Geissmann, T. and Orgeldinger, M. (2000). The relationship between duet songs and pair bonds in siamangs, Hylobates syndactylus. *Animal Behaviour*, *60*(6), 805–809.

Gentner, D. and Jeziorski, M. (1993). The shift from metaphor to analogy in Western science. In A. Ortony (ed.), *Metaphor and Thought* (2nd edn, pp. 447–449). Cambridge: Cambridge University Press.

Gentner, D. and Goldin-Meadow, S. (2003). *Language and Mind: Advances in the Study of Language and Thought* (D. Goldin-Meadow and S. Gentner, eds). Cambridge, MA: MIT Press.

Gergely, G., Bekkering, H. and Király, I. (2002). Developmental psychology: rational imitation in preverbal infants. *Nature*, *415*, 755.

Gibbons, A. (2000). Chinese stone tools reveal high-tech Homo erectus. *Science*, *287*(5458), 1566.

Gibson, K. and Ingold, T. (1993). *Tools, Language and Cognition in Human Evolution*. Cambridge: Cambridge University Press.

Giocomo, L. M., Moser, M. B. and Moser, E. I. (2011). Computational models of grid cells. *Neuron*, *71*(4), 589–603.

Gogate, L., Maganti, M. and Bahrick, L. E. (2015). Cross-cultural evidence for multimodal mothers: Asian Indian mothers' adaptive use of synchronous words and gestures. *Journal of Experimental Child Psychology*, *129*, 110–126.

Goldstein, R. (2005). *Incompleteness: The Proof and Paradox of Kurt Gödel*. New York: Atlas: W. W. Norton.

Goodall, J. (1971). *In the Shadow of Man*. London: Collins.

Gould, S. J. (1977). *Ontogeny and Phylogeny*. Cambridge, MA: Harvard University Press.

Gratier, M. and Trevarthen, C. (2008). Musical narrative and motives for culture in mother-infant vocal interaction. *Journal of Consciousness Studies*, *15*(10–11), 122–128.

Graves, R. (1955). *The White Goddess*. London: Faber & Faber.

Gregory, R. L. (2004). *The Oxford Companion to the Mind* (2nd edn). Oxford: Oxford University Press.

Groos, K. (1898). *The Play of Animals: A Study of Animal Life and Instinct* (E. L. Baldwin, Trans.). New York: Appleton.

Groos, K. (1976) [1901]. *The Play of Man* (E. Baldwin, Trans.). New York: Arno Press.

Gruber, H. and Vonèche, J. (1977). *The Essential Piaget*. New York: Basic Books.

Gunstad, J., Cohen, R. A., Paul, R. H., Luyster, F. S. and Gordon, E. (2006). Age effects in time estimation: relationship to frontal brain morphometry. *Journal of Integrative Neuroscience*, *5*(1), 75–87.

Gusnard, D. A., Akbudak, E., Shulman, G. L. and Raichle, M. E. (2001). Medial prefrontal cortex and self-referential mental activity: relation to a default mode of brain function. *Proceedings of the National Academy of Sciences of the United States of America*, *98*(7), 4259–4264.

Halliday, M. A. K. (1973a). *Explorations in the Functions of Language*. London: Arnold.

Halliday, M. A. K. (1973b). The syntax enunciates the theme. In M. Douglas (ed.), *Rules and Meanings* (pp. 279–294). Harmondsworth, UK: Penguin.

Halliday, M. A. K. (1975). *Learning How to Mean: Exploration in the Development of Language*. London: Edward Arnold.

Harciarek, M. and Heilman, K. M. (2009). The contribution of anterior and posterior regions of the right hemisphere to the recognition of emotional faces. *Journal of Clinical and Experimental Neuropsychology*, *31*(3), 322–330.

Harrington, D. L., Haaland, K. Y. and Hermanowicz, N. (1998). Temporal processing in the basal ganglia. *Neuropsychology*, *12*(1), 3–12.

Harrison, J. E. (1912). *Themis*. Cambridge: Cambridge University Press.

Hauk, O., Johnsrude, I. and Pulvermuller, F. (2004). Somatotopic representation of action words in human motor and premotor cortex. *Neuron*, *41*(2), 301–307.

Hauser, M. D., Chomsky, N. and Fitch, W. T. (2002). The faculty of language: what is it, who has it and how did it evolve? *Science*, *298*(5598), 1569–1579.

Hazlitt, W. (1991). *William Hazlitt: Selected Writings*. Oxford: Oxford University Press.

Heaney, S. (1999). *Beowulf*. London: Faber & Faber.

Helin, S. (2012) Move over Sarah Lund: the Bridge star Sofia Helin interviewed. Interview with *The Guardian*, H. Kahleeli. Available at www.theguardian.com/tv-and-radio/2012/may/12/bridge-sofia-helin-saga-interview. Accessed 19 November 2015.

Henshilwood, C. and d'Errico, F. (2013). *Homo Symbolicus: The Dawn Of Language, Imagination and Spirituality*. Amsterdam, The Netherlands: John Benjamins.

Henshilwood, C. S., d'Errico, F. and Watts, I. (2009). Engraved ochres from the Middle Stone Age levels at Blombos Cave, South Africa. *Journal of Human Evolution*, *57*(1), 27–47.

Hobson, R. F. (1961). Critical notice on C. G. Jung: the archetypes and the collective unconscious. *Journal of Analytical Psychology*, *6*, 161.

Hobson, R. F. (1971). Imagination and amplification in psychotherapy. *The Journal of Analytical Psychology*, *16*(1), 79–105.

Hobson, R. F. (1985). *Forms of Feeling: The Heart of Psychotherapy*. London: Tavistock.

Hobson, R. P. (1993). *Autism and the Development of Mind*. Hillsdale, NJ: Laurence Erlbaum.

Hobson, R. P. (2004). *The Cradle of Thought*. London: Pan Macmillan.

Hobson, R. P. and Lee, A. (1999). Imitation and identification in autism. *Journal of Child Psychology and Psychiatry*, *40*(4), 649–659.

Hofstadter, D. (2001). Epilogue: analogy as the core of cognition. In D. Gentner, K. Holyoak and B. Kokinov (eds), *The Analogical Mind: Perspectives from Cognitive Science* (pp. 499–538). Cambridge, MA: MIT Press.

Holub, M. (1967). In the Microscope. In M. Holub (ed.), *Selected Poems* (p. 25). Harmondsworth, UK: Penguin.

Huizinga, J. (1996). *Autumn of the Middle Ages*. Chicago, IL: University of Chicago Press.

Hume, D. (1739). *A Treatise of Human Nature*. London: John Noon.

Hussey, E. L. (2005). Heraclitus of Ephesus. In T. Henderich (ed.), *Oxford Companion to Philosophy* (p. 378). Oxford: Oxford University Press.

Iidaka, T., Terashima, S., Yamashita, K., Okada, T., Sadato, N. and Yonekura, Y. (2003). Dissociable neural responses in the hippocampus to the retrieval of facial identity and emotion: an event-related fMRI study. *Hippocampus*, *13*(4), 429–436.

Ione, A. and Tyler, C. (2003). Neurohistory and the arts: was Kandinsky a synesthete? *Journal of the History of the Neurosciences*, *12*(2), 223–226.

Iser, W. (1993). *The Fictive and The Imaginary*. Baltimore, MD: Johns Hopkins Press.

Izard, C. (1984). Emotion-cognition relationships and human development. In D. Izard, J. Kagan and R. B. Zajonc (eds), *Emotions, Cognitions and Behaviour*. Cambridge: Cambridge University Press.

Jackobson, R. (1971). Two types of language and two types of aphasic disturbances. In R. Jakobson (ed.), *Selected Writings* (Vol. 2, pp. 239–259). Cambridge, MA: MIT Press.

Jackson, J. H (1958) [1874]. The psychology of joking. In J. Taylor, G. Holmes and I. M. A. Walshe (eds), *Selected Writings of John Hughlings Jackson* (Vol. II, pp. 359–364). New York: Basic Books.

Jackson, J. H. (1958). *Selected Writings of John Hughlings Jackson* (Vols I and II). New York: Basic Books.

Jacobi, J. H. (1968). *The Psychology of C. G. Jung* (7th edn). London: Routledge.

Jakobson, R. (1960a). Closing statement: linguistics and poetics. In T. Sebeok (ed.), *Style in Language* (pp. 350–377). London: Wiley.

Jakobson, R. (1960b). *Linguistics and Poetics*. London: Wiley.

James, W. (1890). *Principles of Psychology* (Vol. 1). New York: Holt.

James, W. (1892). *Psychology: Briefer Course*. London: Macmillan.

James, W. (1895). The knowing of things together. In J. J. McDermott (ed.), *The Writings of William James* (pp. 152–168). Chicago, IL: Chicago University Press, 1977.

James, W. (1902). *Varieties of Religious Experience: A Study of Human Nature*. New York and London: Longmans, Green & Co. Facsimile cited here, Whitefish, MT: Kessinger.

James, W. (1909a). *A Pluralistic Universe*. New York: Longmans Green. Replicated 1996, Lincoln, NE: University of Nebraska Press. This edition cited here.

James, W. (1909b). *Meaning of Truth*. London: Longmans, Green.

Jameson, F. (1974). *The Prison-House of Language: A Critical Account of Structuralism and Russian Formulism*. Princeton, NJ: Princeton University Press.

Janzen, G. and van Turennout, M. (2004). Selective neural representation of objects relevant for navigation. *Nature Neuroscience*, *7*(6), 673–677.

Jerison, H. J. (1973). *Evolution of the Brain and Intelligence*. New York: Academic Press.

Johnson, D. (2000). The Pleiades in Australian Aboriginal and Torres Strait Islander astronomies. In S. Kleinert and M. Neale (eds), *Oxford Companion to Aboriginal Art and Culture* (pp. 24–28). Oxford: Oxford University Press.

Jung, C. G. (1953). The symbolism of the Mandala (R. F. C. Hull, Trans.) *C.G. Jung: The Collected Works* (Vol. 12, pp. 91–213). London: Routledge & Kegan Paul.

Jung, C. G. (1954). *The Collected Works: Practice of Psychotherapy* (Vol. 16) (R. F. C. Hull, Trans.). London: Routledge & Kegan Paul.

Jung, C. G. (1959). Archetypes and the collective unconscious (R. F. C. Hull and C. G. Jung, Trans.). In *The Collected Works* (Vol. 9i). London: Routledge & Kegan Paul.

Jung, C. G. (1960). On the nature of the psyche. In *C. G. Jung: The Collected Works* (Vol. 8, pp. 159–236). London: Routledge & Kegan Paul.

Jung, C. G. (1963). *Memories, Dreams and Reflections* (R. E. Winston, Trans.). Recorded and edited by Aniela Jaffè. New York: Pantheon/Random House.

Jung, C. G. (1967). Symbols of transformation (R. F. C. Hull, Trans.). In *C. G. Jung: The Collected Works* (2nd edn). London: Routlege & Kegan Paul.

Jung, C. G. (1968). The structure and dynamics of the self. In *C. G. Jung: The Collected Works* (Vol. 9ii, pp. 222–265). London: Routledge & Kegan Paul.

Jung, C. G. (1977). The Tavistock lectures, 1935. In *The Symbolic Life of C. G. Jung, Collected Works* (Vol. 18, pp. 5–184). London: Routledge.

Kagan, J. (1972). Do infants think? *Scientific American*, *226*(3), 74–82.

Kandinski, W. (1982) [1913]. Reminiscences (K. Lindsay and P. Vergo, Trans.). In K. Lindsay and P. Vergo (eds), *Kandinsky: Complete Writings On Art*. London: Faber & Faber.

Karl, F. (1979). *Joseph Conrad: The Three Lives*. London: Faber & Faber.

Kasari, C., Sigman, P., Baumgartner, P. and Stipek, D. (1993). Pride and mastery in children with autism. *Journal of Child Psychology and Psychiatry*, *34*, 353–362.

Kaye, K. (1982). *The Mental and Social Life of Babies*. Chicago, IL: Chicago University Press.

Kermode, F. (2000). *Shakespeare's Language*. London: Allen Lane/The Penguin Press.

Kermode, F. (2004). *Pleasure and Change: The Aesthetics of Canon* (R. Alter, ed.). Oxford: Oxford University Press.

Kierkegaard, S. (1992) [1843]. *The Journals of Søren Kierkegaard; 1.2 Either/Or*. London: Penguin.

Kim, J. J., Andreasen, N. C., O'Leary, D. S., Wiser, A. K., Ponto, L. L., Watkins, G. L. and Hichwa, R. D. (1999). Direct comparison of the neural substrates of recognition memory for words and faces. *Brain, 122(6)*, 1069–1083.

Kirk, G. S. (1973). *Myth: Its Meaning and Functions in Ancient and Other Cultures*. Berkeley, CA: Cambridge University Press.

Kohut, H. (1971). *The Analysis of the Self.* New York: International Universities Press.

Kohut, H. (1977). *The Restoration of the Self.* New York: International Universities Press.

Korner, A. (2000). Liveliness. *Australian and New Zealand Journal of Psychiatry*, *34*(5), 731–740.

Kroeber, A. L. (1917). The superorganic. *American Anthropologist*, *19*(2), 163–213.

Kroeber, A. L. (1948). *Anthropology: Revised Edition*. New York: Harcourt Brace.

Kroeber, A. L. and Kluckhohn, C. (1952). *Culture: A Critical Review of Concepts and Definitions* (Vol. 47). Harvard, MA: Harvard University, Papers of the Peabody Museum of American Archeology and Ethnology.

Lafitte, S. (1971). *Chekhov: 1860–1904* (M. Budberg and G. Latta, Trans.). Paris and London: Hachette, Arts Book Society.

Lai, C. S., Fisher, S. E., Hurst, J. A., Vargha-Khadem, F. and Monaco, A. P. (2001). A forkhead-domain gene is mutated in a severe speech and language disorder. *Nature*, *413*(6855), 519–523.

Lakoff, G. and Johnson, M. (1980). *Metaphors We Live By*. Chicago, IL: University of Chicago Press.

Laplanche, J. and Pontalis, J. B. (1973). Primary process/secondary process (D. Nicholson-Smith, Trans.). In J. Laplanche and J. B. Pontalis (eds), *The Language of Psycho-analysis* Hogarth Press.

Lashley, K. (1951). The problem of serial order in behaviour. In L. A. Jeffress (ed.), *Cerebral Mechanisms in Behaviour* (pp. 112–136). New York: Wiley.

Layard, J. (1942). *The Stone Men of Malekula*. London: Chatto & Windus.

Leach, E. (1970). *Lévi-Strauss*. London: Fontana Modern Masters.

Leakey, L. S., Tobias, P. V. and Napier, J. R. (1964). A new species of the genus Homo from Olduvai Gorge. *Nature*, *202*, 7–9.

Leakey, R. and Lewin, R. (1992). *Origins Reconsidered: In Search of What Makes Us Human*. London: Little Brown.

Lee, K. H., Egleston, P. N., Brown, W. H., Gregory, A. N., Barker, A. T. and Woodruff, P. W. (2007). The role of the cerebellum in subsecond time perception: evidence from repetitive transcranial magnetic stimulation. *Journal of Cognitive Neuroscience*, *19*(1), 147–157.

Lester, B. M., Hoffman, J. and Brazelton, T. B. (1985). The rhythmic structure of mother-infant interaction in term and preterm infants. *Child Development*, *56*(1), 15–27.

Lévi-Strauss, C. (1955). *Tristes Tropiques*. Paris: Plon.

Lévi-Strauss, C. (1966). *The Savage Mind* (anon, Trans.). London: Weidenfeld & Nicolson.

Lévi-Strauss, C. (1968a). *Structural Anthropology*. London: Allen Lane.

Lévi-Strauss, C. (1968b). The structural study of myth (C. Jacobson and B. G. Schoepp, Trans.) *Structural Anthropology* (pp. 206–241). London: Allen Lane Press.

Lewis, M. (1992). *Shame: The Exposed Self.* New York: Free Press.

Lewis, M. and Rosenblum, L. A. (eds) (1974). *The Effect of the Infant on the Caregiver*. New York: Wiley.

Lewis, M. and Gunn, J. (1978). Self knowledge and emotional development. In M. Lewis and L. A. Rosenblum (eds), *The Development of Affect* (pp. 205–226). New York: Plenum.

Lieberman, D. E. and Bramble, D. M. (2007). The evolution of marathon running: capabilities in humans. *Sports Medicine*, *37*(4–5), 288–290.

Lieberman, P. H. (2006). *Towards an Evolutionary Biology of Language*. Cambridge, MA: Harvard University Press.

Lieberman, P. H. (2007). The evolution of human speech: its anatomical and neural bases. *Current Anthropology*, *48*(1), 39–66.

Lieberman, P. H. and McCarthy, R. (2007). Tracking evolution of language and speech. *Expedition Magazine*, *49*, 15–20.

Lieberman, P. H., Klatt, D. H. and Wilson, W. H. (1969). Vocal tract limitations on the vowel repertoires of rhesus monkey and other nonhuman primates. *Science*, *164*(3884), 1185–1187.

Lieberman, P. H., Crelin, E. and Klatt, D. H. (1972). Phonetic ability and related anatomy to the newborn and adult human, neanderthal man and the chimpanzee. *American Anthropologist*, *74*(3), 287–307.

Livio, M. (2002). *The Golden Ratio*. London: Review/Headline Books.

Locke, J. (1959) [1690]. *An Essay Concerning Human Understanding* (A. L. Fraser ed., Vol. 1). London: Rivington.

Locke, J. and Pearson, D. M. (1990). Linguistic significance of babbling: evidence from a tracheostomized infant. *Journal of Child Language*, *17*(1), 1–16.

Lucas, M. (2013). *Poetic Memory: Exploring the Subjective Nature of Intimate Memory Through Writing*. Unpublished thesis for Bachelor of Arts (Honours). Sydney, Australia: University of Technology.

Luria, A. R. (1973). *The Working Brain*. Harmondsworth, UK: Penguin.

Luria, A. R. (1994). The problem of the cultural behaviour of the child. In R. Van der Veer and J. Valsiner (eds), *The Vygotsky Reader* (pp. 46–56). Oxford: Blackwell.

Luria, A. R. and Vygotsky, L. S. (1992). *Ape, Primitive Man and Child* (E. Rossiter, Trans.). New York: Harvester/Wheatsheaf.

Lyons, D. M., Afarian, H., Schatzberg, A. F., Sawyer-Glover, A. and Moseley, M. E. (2002). Experience-dependent asymmetric variation in primate prefrontal morphology. *Behavioural Brain Research*, *136*(1), 51–59.

McArthur, T. (1992). *The Oxford Companion to the English Language*. Oxford, New York: Oxford University Press.

McGrew, W. (1992). *Chimpanzee Material Culture*. Cambridge: Cambridge University Press.

McGuire, W. (1974). *The Freud/Jung Letters* (R. Manheim and R. F. C. Hull, Trans., W. McGuire, ed.). London: Routledge & Kegan Paul.

MacLean, P. D. (1990). *The Triune Brain in Evolution: Role in Paleocerebral Functions*. Toronto, ON: University of Toronto Press.

Maess, B., Koelsch, S., Gunter, T. C. and Friederici, A. D. (2001). Musical syntax is processed in Broca's area: an MEG study. *Nature Neuroscience*, *4*(5), 540–545.

Maestripieri, D. (2011). Emotions, stress and maternal motivation in primates. *American Journal of Primatology*, *73*(6), 516–529.

Maguire, E. A., Frackowiak, R. S. and Frith, C. D. (1997). Recalling routes around London: activation of the right hippocampus in taxi drivers. *Journal of Neuroscience*, *17*(18), 7103–7110.

Mâle, E. (1961). *The Gothic Image*. London: Collins/Fontana.

Malinowski, B. (1926). *Myth in Primitive Psychology*. New York: Norton.

Malinowski, B. (1936). *The Foundation of Faith and Morals*. Oxford: Oxford University Press.

Malloch, S. and Trevarthen, C. (2009). *Communicative Musicality: Exploring the Basis of Human Companionship* (S. Malloch and C. Trevarthen, eds). Oxford: Oxford University Press.

Malloch, S., Shoemark, H., Črnčec, R., Newnham, C., Campbell, P., Prior, M. and Burnham, D. (2012). Music therapy with hospitalized infants: the art and science of communicative musicality. *Infant Mental Health Journal*, *33*(4), 386–399.

Mandelbrot, B. (1983). *The Fractal Geometry of Nature*. New York: Freeman.

Marshall, J. T. Jr and Marshall, E. R. (1976). Gibbons and their territorial songs. *Science*, *193*(4249), 235–237.

Matthews, E. (1999). Bergson's concept of a person. In J. Mullarkey (ed.), *The New Bergson* (pp. 118–134). Manchester, UK: Manchester University Press.

Maturana, H. and Varela, F. (1980). *Autopoiesis and Cognition*. Dordrech, The Netherlands: Reidel.

Maxwell, J. C. (1890) [1870]. Address to the mathematical and physical sctions of the British Association Report. Reprinted in W. D. Niven (ed.). *Scientific Papers of J. C. Maxwell (Volume II.)* Cambridge: Cambridge University Press.

Meadow-Orlans, K. P. (1980). *Deafness and Child Development*. Los Angeles, CA: University of California Press.

Meadow-Orlans, K. P. (2004). *The World of Deaf Infants*. Oxford: Oxford University Press.

Meares, R. (1977). *The Pursuit of Intimacy: An Approach to Psychotherapy*. Melbourne, Australia: Nelson.

Meares, R. (1980). Body feeling in human relations: the possible examples of Brancusi and Giacometti. *Psychiatry*, *43*(2), 160–167.

Meares, R. (1983). Keats and the 'impersonal' therapist: a note on empathy and the therapeutic screen. *Psychiatry*, *46*(1), 73–82.

Meares, R. (1984). Inner space: its constriction in anxiety states and narcissistic personality. *Psychiatry*, *47*(2), 162–171.

Meares, R. (1986). On the ownership of thought: an approach to the origins of separation anxiety. *Psychiatry*, *49*(1), 80–91.

Meares, R. (1993). *The Metaphor of Play: Disruption and Restoration in the Borderline Experience*. Northvale, NJ: Jason Aronson.

Meares, R. (1997). Stimulus entrapment. *Psychoanalytic Inquiry*, *17*(2), 223–234.

Meares, R. (1998). The self in conversation: on narratives, chronicles and scripts. *Psychoanalytic Dialogues*, *8*, 875–891.

Meares, R. (1999). The contribution of Hughlings Jackson to an understanding of dissociation. *American Journal of Psychiatry*, *156*(12), 1850–1855.

Meares, R. (2000). *Intimacy and Alienation: Memory, Trauma and Personal Being*. London: Routledge.

Meares, R. (2001). What happens next? A developmental model of therapeutic spontaneity. *Psychoanalytic Dialogues*, *11*, 755–769.

Meares, R. (2004). A poetics of change. *Psychoanalytic Dialogues*, *15*(5), 661–680.

Meares, R. (2005). *The Metaphor of Play: Origin and Breakdown of Personal Being, Revised and Enlarged Edition*. London: Routledge.

Meares, R. (2012a). *A Dissociation Model of Borderline Personality Disorder*. New York and London: W. W. Norton.

Meares, R. (2012b). The sense of the spirit as a form of conversation. *Asian Journal of Psychiatry*, *5*, 190–192.

Meares, R. A. and Hobson, R. F. (1977). The persecutory therapist. *British Journal of Medical Psychology*, *50*(4), 349–359.

Meares, R. and Orlay, W. (1988). On self-boundary: a study of the development of the concept of secrecy. *British Journal of Medical Psychology, 61(4)*, 305–316.

Meares, R. and Lichtenberg, J. (1995). The form of play in the shape and unity of self. *Contemporary Psychoanalysis*, *31*(1), 47–64.

Meares, R. and Jones, S. (2009). Analogical relatedness in personal integration or coherence. *Contemporary Psychoanalysis*, *45*(4), 504–519.

Meares, R., Schore, A. and Melkonian, D. (2011). Is borderline personality a particularly right hemispheric disorder? A study of P3a using single trial analysis. *Australian and New Zealand Journal of Psychiatry*, *45*(2), 131–139.

Meares, R., Butt, D. G., Henderson-Brooks, C. and Samir, H. (2005). A poetics of change. *Psychoanalytic Dialogues*, *15*(5), 661–680.

Meares, R., Bendit, N., Haliburn, J., Korner, A., Mears, D. and Butt, D. (2012). *Borderline Personality Disorder and the Conversational Model: A Clinician's Manual* (D. J. Siegel and A. Schore, eds). New York and London: W. W. Norton.

Meier, C. A. (2001). *The Pauli-Jung Letters, 1932–1958*. New Jersey, NJ: Princeton University Press.

Meltzoff, A. N. and Moore, M. K. (1977). Imitation of facial and manual gestures by human neonates. *Science*, *198*(4312), 74–78.

Merker, B. (2009). Ritual foundations of human uniqueness. In S. Malloch and C. Trevarthen (eds), *Communicative Musicality* (pp. 45–60). Oxford: Oxford University Press.

Merwin, W. S. (1988). *Rain in the Trees*. New York: Alfred A. Knopf.

Merwin, W. S. (2008). *The Shadow of Sirius*. Washington, DC: Copper Canyon Press.

Miller, A. (2009). *Deciphering the Cosmic Number: The Strange Friendship of Wolfgang Pauli and Carl Jung*. New York: Norton.

Minagawa-Kawai, Y., Matsuoka, S., Dan, I., Naoi, N., Nakamura, K. and Kojima, S. (2009). Prefrontal activation associated with social attachment: facial-emotion recognition in mothers and infants. *Cerebral Cortex*, *19*(2), 284–292.

Mithen, S. (2005). *The Singing Neanderthals: The Origins of Music, Language, Mind and Body*. London: Widenfeld & Nicolson.

Montaigne, M. (1946) [1580]. *Essays of Michel de Montaigne* (G. Ives, Trans.). New York: The Heritage Press.

Morieson, J. (2008). The case study of the Borrong. In J. Vaiskunas (ed.), *Astronomy & Cosmology in Folk Traditions and Cultural Heritage* (Vol. 10, pp. 258–262). Klaipeda, Lithuania: Klaipeda University Press.

Moro, A. (2008). *The Boundaries of Babel. The Brain and the Enigma of Impossible Language*. Cambridge, MA: MIT Press.

Morphy, H. (1996). Empiricism to metaphysics. In T. Bonyhady and T. Griffiths (eds), *Prehistory to Politics: John Mulvaney, the Humanities and the Public Intellectual* (pp. 163–189). Melbourne: Melbourne University Press.

Morphy, H. (1999). Aboriginal concepts of time. In K. Lippincott (ed.), *The Story of Time* (pp. 264–268). London: Merrell Holberton.

Morphy, H. and Morphy, F. (2006). Testing the waters: discriminating identities on the waters of Mud Bay. *Journal of Material Culture*, *2*(1–2*)*, 67–85.

Mountford, C. (1973). *The Dreamtime Book*. Adelaide: Rigby.

Murray, M. (1949). *The Splendour That Was Egypt: A General Survey of Egyptian Culture and Civilization*. London: Sidgwick & Jackson.

Napier, J. R. (1980). *Hands*. New York: Pantheon.

Nelson, K. (1992). Emergence of autobiographical memory at four. *Human Development*, *35*, 172–177.

Nelson, K. and Fivush, R. (2000). Socialization of memory. In E. Tulving and F. I. M. Craik (eds), *The Handbook of Memory* (pp. 283–295). Oxford: Oxford University Press.

Nitschke, J. B., Nelson, E. E., Rusch, B. D., Fox, A. S., Oakes, T. R. and Davidson, R. J. (2004). Orbitofrontal cortex tracks positive mood in mothers viewing pictures of their newborn infants. *Neuroimage*, *21*(2), 583–592.

Noriuchi, M., Kikuchi, Y. and Senoo, A. (2008). The functional neuroanatomy of maternal love: mother's response to infant's attachment behaviours. *Biological Psychiatry*, *63*(4), 415–423.

Nungarrayi, P. (2003). Introduction to dancing up country: the art of Dorothy Napangardi. *Sydney Museum of Contemporary Art*, 6–8.

Ochs, E. and Schieffelin, B. (1994). Language acquisition and socialization: three developmental stories and their implications. In B. Blount (ed.), *Language, Culture, and Society: A Book of Readings* (2nd edn, pp. 470–512). Prospect Heights, IL: Wareland Press.

O'Doherty, J., Winston, J., Critchley, H., Perrett, D., Burt, D. M. and Dolan, R. J. (2003). Beauty in a smile: the role of medial orbitofrontal cortex in facial attractiveness. *Neuropsychologia*, *41*(2), 147–155.

Ogden, T. H. (1994). The analytic third: working with intersubjective clinical facts. *The International Journal of Psychoanalysis*, *75*(1), 3–19.

Ogden, T. H. (1998). A question of voice in poetry and psychoanalysis. *Psychoanalytic Quarterly*, *67*(3), 426–448.

O'Keefe, J. and Dostrovsky, J. (1971). The hippocampus as a spatial map: preliminary evidence from unit activity in the freely-moving rat. *Brain Research*, *34*(1), 171–175.

O'Keefe, J. and Nadel, L. (1978). *Hippocampus as a Cognitive Map*. Oxford: Clarendon Press.

Overton, W. F. and Jackson, J. P. (1973). The representation of imagined objects in action sequences: a developmental study. *Child Development*, *44*(2), 309–314.

Oxford English Dictionary: Compact Edition (1971). Oxford: Oxford University Press.

Panofsky, E. (1953). *Early Netherlandish Painting, Its Origins and Character (Volume I)*. Cambridge, MA: Harvard University Press.

Pauli, W. (1954). *Matter. In Man's Right to Knowledge*. New York: Columbia University Press.

Paz, O. (1979). *Octavio Paz: Selected Poems*. Harmondsworth, UK: Penguin.

Penman, R., Meares, R. and Milgrom-Friedman, J. (1981). The mother's role in the development of object competency. *Archives de Psychologie*, *49*, 247–265.

Pennisi, E. (1999). Human evolution: did cooked tubers spur the evolution of big brains. *Science*, *283*(5410), 2004–2005.

Peretz, I. and Hyde, K. L. (2003). What is specific to music processing? Insights from congenital amusia. *Trends in Cognitive Sciences*, *7*(8), 362–367.

Petchovsky, L. (2001). Stream of consciousness and ownership of thought in Indigenous peoples in central Australia. In H. Formaine (ed.), *Landmarks: Papers by Jungian Analysts from Australia and New Zealand* (pp. 53–78). Canberra, Australia: Australian and New Zealand Society of Jungian Analysts.

Peterson, C. and Siegal, M. (1999). Representing inner worlds: theory of mind in autistic, deaf and hearing normal children, *Psychological Science*, *10*(2), 126–129.

Petitto, L. A. and Marentette, P. F. (1991). Babbling in the manual mode: evidence for the ontogeny of language. *Science*, *251*(5000), 1493–1496.

Petitto, L. A., Holowka, S., Sergio, L., Levy, B. and Ostry, D. (2004). Baby hands that move to the rhythm of language: hearing babies acquiring sign language silently on the hands. *Cognition*, *93*, 43–73.

Piaget, J. (1951). *Play, Dreams and Imitation in Childhood.* London: Routledge & Kegan Paul.

Piaget, J. (1952). *The Origins of Intelligence in Children* (M. Cook, Trans.). New York: International Universities Press.

Piaget, J. (1954). *The Construction of Reality in the Child.* New York: Basic Books.

Piaget, J. (1959). *The Language and Thought of the Child* (3rd edn). London: Routledge & Kegan Paul.

Piaget, J. (1969). *The Child's Conception of Time.* London: Routledge & Kegan Paul.

Piaget, J. (1977) [1969]. The semiotic or symbolic function (H. Weaver, Trans.). In H. Gruber and J. J. Vonéche (eds), *The Essential Piaget* (pp. 483–507). New York: Basic Books. Originally published in French.

Pip, M. E. (1996). *Telling It Like It Is, Was, and Will Be: The Influence of Narrative on Children's Event Memory.* Paper presented at the Second International Conference on Memory, Albano, Italy.

Poizner, H., Bellugi, U. and Iragui, V. (1984). Apraxia and aphasia for visual-gestural language. *American Journal of Physiology*, *246*, R868-R883.

Pouthas, V., George, N., Poline, J. B., Pfeuty, M., Vandemoorteele, P. F., Hugueville, L., Ferrandez, A. M., Lehéricy, S., Lebihan, D. and Renault, B. (2005). Neural network involved in time perception: an fMRI study comparing long and short interval estimation. *Human Brain Mapping*, *25*(4), 433–441.

Povinelli, D. J., Landry, A. M., Theall, L. A., Clark, B. R. and Castille, C. M. (1999). Development of young children's understanding that the recent past is causally bound to the present. *Developmental Psychology*, *35*(6), 1426–1439.

Prescott, F. C. (1927). *Poetry and Myth.* New York: Macmillan.

Primas, H. (2009). Complementarity of mind and matter. In H. Atmanspeacher and H. Primas (eds), *Recasting Reality: Wolfgang Pauli's Philosophical Ideas and Contemporary Science* (pp. 171–210). Berlin: Springer.

Pruetz, J. D. and Bertolani, P. (2007). Savanna chimpanzees, Pan troglodytes verus, hunt with tools. *Current Biology*, *17*(5), 412–417.

Quine, W. V. (1979). A postscript in metaphor. In S. Sacks (ed.), *On Metaphor* (pp. 159–160). Chicago, IL: Chicago University Press.

Quine, W. V. (2004). Symbols. In R. L. Gregory (ed.), *The Oxford Companion to the Mind* (pp. 896–897). Oxford: Oxford University Press.

Ramachandran, V. and Gregory, R. L. (2004). Synaethesia. In R. Gregory (ed.) *The Oxford Companion to the Mind* (pp. 897–901). Oxford: Oxford University Press.

Rapp, P. and Bachevalier, J. (2008). Cognitive development and aging. In L. Squire, D. Berg, F. Bloom, S. Du Lac, A. Ghosh and N. Spitzer (eds), *Fundamental Neuroscience* (pp. 1039–1066). Amsterdam, The Netherlands: Elsevier.

Richards, I. A. (1976). *Complementarities: Uncollected Essays.* Manchester, UK: Carcanet Press.

Richardson, R. D. (2007). *William James: In the Maelstrom of American Modernism.* Boston, MA and New York: Mariner, Houghton Mifflin.

Riecker, A., Wildgruber, D., Dogil, G., Grodd, W. and Ackermann, H. (2002). Hemispheric lateralization effects of rhythm implementation during syllable repetitions: an fMRI study. *Neuroimage*, *16*(1), 169–176.

Rizzolatti, G. and Arbib, M. (1998). Language with our grasp. *TINS*, *21*, 188–194.
Robinson, J. (1976). Sampling autobiographical memory. *Cognitive Psychology*, *8*, 578–595.
Rodman, P. S. and McHenry, H. M. (1980). Bioenergetics and the origin of hominid bipedalism. *Physical Anthropology*, *52*(1), 103–106.
Rolls, E. (2002). The function of the orbital cortex. In D. T. Stuss and R. T. Knight (eds), *Principles of Frontal Lobe Function* (pp. 354–375). Oxford: Oxford University Press.
Rose, H. J. (1978). Narcissus. In N. Hammond and H. Scullard (eds), *The Oxford Classical Dictionary* (2nd edn). Oxford: Clarendon Press.
Ross, E. D. and Monnot, M. (2008). Neurology of affective prosody and its functional-anatomic organization in right hemisphere. *Brain and Language*, *104*(1), 51–74.
Routledge, C., Wildschut, T., Sedikides, C., Juhl, J. and Arndt, J. (2012). The power of the past: nostalgia as a meaning-making resource. *Memory*, *20*(5), 452–460.
Rowse, A. L. (1963). *William Shakespeare: A Biography*. London: Macmillan.
Russell, B. (1971). *The Autobiography of Bertrand Russell: 1872–1914* (Vol. I). London: Allen & Unwin.
Sacks, O. (1991). *Seeing Voices*. London: Picador.
Sacks, O. (2008). *Musicophilia*. London: Picador/Pan Macmillan.
Sagan, F. (1954). *Bonjour Tristesse*. Paris and London: Juillard, Murrary.
Sartre, J. P. (1966). *The Psychology of Imagination*. New York: Citadel Press.
Saussure, F. (1970) [1916]. On the nature of language (extract from: course in general linguistics, 1916). In M. Lane (ed.), *Introduction to Structuralism* (pp. 43–56). New York: Basic Books.
Savage-Rumbaugh, S., Shanker, S. and Taylor, T. (1998). *Apes, Language and the Human Mind*. New York: Oxford University Press.
Schachter, A. (1966). *Cults of Boeotia*. Oxford: Oxford University Press.
Schellenberg, E. and Trehub, S. (1996). Natural musical intervals: evidence from infant listeners. *Psychological Science*, *7*, 272–277.
Schenker, N. M., Hopkins, W. D., Spocter, M. A., Garrison, A. R., Stimpson, C. D., Erwin, J. M. and Sherwood, C. C. (2010). Broca's area homologue in chimpanzees (Pan troglodytes): probabilistic mapping, asymmetry and comparison to humans. *Cereb Cortex*, *20*(3), 730–742.
Schieffelin, B. (1998). *Language Ideologies*. Oxford: Oxford University Press.
Schiff, S. (2010). *Cleopatra: A Life*. London: Virgin/Random House.
Schore, A. N. (1994). *Affect Regulation and the Origin of Self*. Mahwah, NJ: Erlbaum.
Schore, A. N. (2003a). *Affect Dysregulation and Disorders of the Self*. New York: Norton.
Schore, A. N. (2003b). *Affect Dysregulation and the Repair of Self*. New York: Norton.
Schore, A. N. (2005). Back to basics: attachment, affect regulation and the developing right brain: linking developmental neuroscience to pediatrics. *Pediatrics in Review*, *26*(6), 204–217.
Shultz, S. and Maslin, M. (2013). Early human speciation, brain expansion and dispersal influenced by African climate pulses. *PLoS One*, *8*(10), e76750.
Schwartz, A., Campos, J. and Baisel, E. (1973). The visual cliff: cardiac and behavioural correlates of the deep and shallow sides at 5 and 9 months of age. *Journal of Experimental Child Psychology*, *15*, 86–99.
Seager, W. (2009). A new idea of reality: Pauli on the unity of mind and matter. In H. Atmanspeacher and H. Primas (eds), *Recasting Reality: Wolfgang Pauli's Philosophical Ideas and Contemporary Science* (pp. 83–98). Berlin: Springer.

Shakespeare, W. (1995) *Antony and Cleopatra* (Arden edn, series 3). (J. Wilders, ed.). London: Bloomsbury, Arden Shakespeare.

Shephard, R. and Jordan, D. (1984). Auditory illusions demonstrating that tones are assimilated to an internalized musical scale. *Science, 226*, 1333–13334.

Sherrington, C. S. (2007) [1931]. Quantitative management of contraction in lowest level co-ordination: Hughlings Jackson lecture. *Brain, 130*, 884–886. [First published 1931 *Brain*, 54, 1–28.]

Singer, W. (1999). Neuronal synchrony: a versatile code for the definition of relations? *Neuron, 24*, 49–65.

Singer, W. (2001). Consciousness and the binding problem. *Annals of the New York Academy of Sciences, 929*, 123–146.

Smith, T. (1998). Intensity: modernism's phallic aesthetics: introduction. In T. Smith (ed.), *Visible Touch: Modernism and Masculinity* (pp. 1–27). Chicago, IL: Chicago University Press.

Sorce, J., Emde, R., Campos, J. and Klinnet, M. (1985). Maternal emotional signaling: its effect on the visual cliff behaviour of 1-year-olds. *Developmental Psychology, 21*, 195–200.

Spencer, B. and Gillen, F. (1899). *The Native Tribes of Central Australia*. London: Macmillan.

Spencer, P. E. and Meadow-Orlans, K. P. (1996). Play, language and maternal responsiveness: a longitudinal study of deaf and hearing infants. *Child Development, 67*(6), 3176–3191.

Spitz, R. (1965). *The First Year of Life*. New York: International Universities Press.

Spurgeon, C. (1935). *Shakespeare's Imagery and What It Tells Us*. Cambridge: Cambridge University Press.

Stanner, W. E. H. (1979). *White Man Got No Dreaming: Essays 1938–1973*. Canberra, Australia: Australian National University Press.

Steiner, G. (1980). The distribution of discourse. In G. Steiner (ed.), *On Difficulty and other Essays* (pp. 61–94). Oxford: Oxford University Press.

Stern, D. (1985). *The Interpersonal World of the Infant*. New York: Basic Books.

Stern, D. (2001). Face-to-face play: its temporal structure as predictor of socio-affective development. In J. Jaffe, B. Beebfe, S. Feldstein, C. Crown and M. Jasnon (eds), *Monographs of the Society for Research in Child Development* (2001/06/29 edn. Vol. 66, pp. 144–149). Oxford and Boston, MA: Blackwell.

Stevens, W. (1954). *The Collected Poems of Wallace Stevens*. New York: Knopf.

Stewart, L., Walsh, V., Frith, U. and Rothwell, J. (2001). Transcranial magnetic stimulation produces speech arrest but not song arrest. *Annals of the New York Academy of Sciences, 930*, 433–435.

Sullivan, M. W. and Lewis, M. (2003). Contextual determinants of anger and other negative expressions in young infants. *Developmental Psychology, 39*(4), 693–705.

Tallis, R. (2003). *The Hand*. Edinburgh, UK: Edinburgh University Press.

Tamietto, M., Latini Corazzini, L., de Gelder, B. and Geminiani, G. (2006). Functional asymmetry and interhemispheric cooperation in the perception of emotions from facial expressions. *Experimental Brain Research, 171*(3), 389–404.

Tattersall, I. (2002). *The Monkey in the Mirror: Essays on the Science of What Makes us Human*. New York: Harcourt.

Tattersall, I. (2006). How we came to be human. *Scientific American, 16*(2), 66–73.

Tessler, M. and Nelson, K. (1994). Making memories: the influence of joint encoding on later recall by young children. *Consciousness and Cognition*, *3*, 307–326.

Thomson, D. F. (1946). Names and naming in the Wik Monhan tribes. *Journal of the Royal Anthropoligical Institute of Great Britain and Ireland*, *76*(2), 157–167.

Tillmann, B., Bharucha, J. J. and Bigand, E. (2000). Implicit learning of tonality: a self-organizing approach. *Psychology Review*, *107*(4), 885–913.

Tolkien, J. R. R. (1950). *Beowulf and the Finnesburg Fragment. A Translation Into Modern English Prose By John R. Clark Hall, With Prefatory Remarks by J. R. R. Tolkien* (revised edn). London: George Allen & Unwin.

Tomasello, M. (1999). *The Cultural Origins of Human Cognition*. Cambridge, MA: Harvard University Press.

Tomasello, M. (2000). *The Cultural Origins of Human Cognition*. Cambridge, MA: Harvard University Press, paperback edition.

Tomkins, S. (1962–1963). *Affect, Imagery, Consciousness (Volumes I and II)*. New York: Springer.

Toth, N. (1985). Archaeological evidence for preferential right-handedness in the lower and middle pleistocene, and its possible implications. *Journal Human Evolution*, *14*(6), 607–614.

Toynbee, A. (1972). *A Study of History: One Volume Edition*. Oxford: Oxford University Press, Thames and Hudson.

Trevarthen, C. (1974). Conversations with a two-month-old. *New Scientist*, *62*, 230–235.

Trevarthen, C. (2004). Infancy, mind in. In R. L. Gregory (ed.), *The Oxford Companion to the Mind* (pp. 455–464). Oxford: Oxford University Press.

Trevarthen, C., Delafield-Butt, J. T. and Schögler, B. (2009). Psychobiology of musical gesture: innate rhythm, harmony and melody in movements of narration. In A. Gritten and E. King (eds), *Music and Gesture 2* (pp. 11–43). Aldershot, UK: Ashgate.

Tulving, E. (1972). Episodic and semantic memory. In E. Tulving and W. Donaldson (eds), *Organization of Memory* (pp. 381–403). New York: Academic Press.

Tulving, E. (1983). *Elements of Episodic Memory*. Oxford: Oxford University Press.

Tulving, E. (1985). Memory and consciousness. *Canadian Psychology*, *26*, 1–12.

Tulving, E. (2002). Chronesthesia: conscious awareness of subjective time. In D. T. Stuss and R. T. Knight (eds), *Principles of Frontal Lobe Function* (pp. 311–325). Oxford: Oxford University Press.

Tylor, E. B. (1958) [1871]. *Primate Culture*. London: John Murray. Reprinted, New York: Harper.

Uzgiris, I. (1991). The social context of infant imitation. In M. Lewis and Feinman (eds), *Social Influences and Socialization in Infancy* (pp. 215–251). New York: Plenum.

van der Veer, R. and Valsiner, J. (1988). Lev Vygotsky and Pierre Janet: on the origins of the concept of sociogenesis. *Developmental Review*, *8*, 52–65.

van der Veer, R. and Valsiner, J. (1991). *Understanding Vygotsky: A Quest For Synthesis*. Oxford: Blackwell.

Vargha-Khadem, F., Watkins, K., Alcock, K., Fletcher, P. and Passingham, R. (1995). Praxic and nonverbal cognitive deficits in a large family with a genetically transmitted speech and language disorder. *Proceedings of the National Academy of Sciences of the United States of America*, *92*(3), 930–933.

Vargha-Khadem, F., Watkins, K. E., Price, C. J., Ashburner, J., Alcock, K. J., Connelly, A., Passingham, R. E. (1998). Neural basis of an inherited speech and language disorder. *Proceedings of the National Academy of Sciences of the United States of America*, *95*(21), 12695–12700.

Vaughn, B. E., Kopp, C. B. and Krakow, J. B. (1984). The emergence and consolidation of self-control from 18 to 30 months of age: normative trends and individual differences. *Child Development*, *55*(3), 990–1004.

Vendler, H. (1988). *The Music of What Happens: Poems, Poets, Critics*. Cambridge, MA: Harvard University Press.

Vico, G. (1968) [1744]. Scienza nuova (T. Bergin and M. Fisch, Trans.) *The New Science of Giambattista Vico*. Ithaca, NY: Cornell University Press.

von Meyenn, K. (2009). Wolfgang Pauli's philosophical ideas viewed from the perspective of his correspondence. In H. Atmanspeacher and H. Primas (eds), *Recasting Reality: Wolfgang Pauli's Philosophical Ideas and Contemporary Science* (pp. 11–32). Berlin: Springer.

Vrba, E. S. (2005). Paleo climate and evolution. In E. S. Vrba, G. H. Denton, T. C. Partridge and L. H. Burckle (eds), *Paleo Climate and Evolution with Emphasis on Human Origins* (pp. 24–45). New Haven, CT: Yale University: Yale University Press.

Vygotsky, L. S. (1962). *Thought and Language* (E. Hanfmann and G. Vakar, Trans. and eds). Cambridge, MA: MIT Press.

Vygotsky, L. S. (1978). *Mind in Society: The Development of Higher Psychological Processes*. Cambridge, MA: Harvard University Press.

Watkins, K. E., Dronkers, N. F. and Vargha-Khadem, F. (2002). Behavioural analysis of an inherited speech and language disorder: comparison with acquired aphasia. *Brain*, *125* (3), 452–464.

White, N. (1995). *Hopkins: A Literary Biography*. Oxford: Clarendon Press.

Wilcken, P. (2010). *Claude Lévi-Strauss: The Poet in the Laboratory*. London: Bloomsbury.

Williams, L. M., Brown, K. J., Palmer, D., Liddell, B. J., Kemp, A. H., Olivieri, G. and Gordon, E. (2006). The mellow years? Neural basis of improving emotional stability over age. *Journal of Neuroscience*, *26*(24), 6422–6430.

Wimmer, H. and Perner, J. (1983). Beliefs about beliefs: representation and constraining function of wrong beliefs in young children's understanding of deception. *Cognition*, *13*(1), 103–128.

Winnicott, D. W. (1974). *Playing and Reality*. Harmondsworth, UK: Penguin.

Wittgenstein, L. (1922). *Tractatus Logico-Philosophicus*. London: Kegan Paul.

Wolff, P. (1963). Observations on the early development of smiling In B. M. Foss (ed.), *Determinants and Infant Behaviour* (pp. 113–138). London: Methuen.

Wood, M. (2005). *In Search of Shakespeare*. London: BBC books.

Wood Jones, F. (1920). *The Principles of Anatomy as Seen in the Hand*. London: Churchill.

Wood Jones, F. (1926). *Arboreal Man*. London: Arnold.

Wood Jones, F. (1929). *Man's Place Among the Mammals*. London: Arnold.

Wood Jones, F. (1931). Of words and little emotions. In F. Wood Jones (ed.), *Unscientific Essays* (pp. 14–24). London: Arnold.

Wolff, P. (1963). Observations on the early development of smiling. In B. M. Foss (ed.), *Determinants and Infant Behaviour* (pp. 113–138). London: Methuen.

Woolf, V. (1925). *The Common Reader* (Vol. I). London: Hogarth.

Woolf, V. (1937). *The Years*. London: Hogarth.

Woolf, V. (1978). *Moments of Being*. London: Triad/Granada.

Woolf, V. (1982). *The Diary of Virginia Woolf (Volume III, 1925–1930)*. London: Penguin.

Woolfe, T., Want, S. C. and Siegal, M. (2002). Signposts to development: theory of mind in deaf children. *Child Development*, *73*(3), 768–778.

Wright, G. T. (1991). *Shakespeare's Metrical Art*. Berkeley, CA: University of California Press.

Yates, F. (1966). *The Art of Memory*. Chicago, IL: Chicago University Press.
Zanarini, M. C., Frankenburg, F. R., DeLuca, C. J., Hennen, J., Khera, G. S. and Gunderson, J. G. (1998). The pain of being borderline: dysphoric states specific to borderline personality disorder. *Harvard Review of Psychiatry*, *6*(4), 201–207.
Zimmerman, C. (1994). *The Pastoral Narcissus: A Study of the First Idyll of Theocritus*. Boston, MA: Rowman & Littlefield.

AUTHOR INDEX

SUBJECT INDEX